FRASER VALLEY REGIONAL LIBRARY

39083513806068

D0707250

Island Craft

Island Craft

Your Guide to the Breweries of Vancouver Island

Jon C. Stott

TOUCHWOOD

Copyright © 2019 by Jon C. Stott

All rights reserved. No part of this publication may be reproduced,
stored in a retrieval system, or transmitted in any form or by any means,
electronic, mechanical, photocopying, recording, or otherwise, without
the prior written permission of the publisher. For more information,
contact TouchWood Editions at touchwoodeditions.com.

The information in this book is true and complete to the best of
the author's knowledge. All recommendations are made without
guarantee on the part of the author or the publisher.

Edited by Meg Yamamoto
Design by Colin Parks
Front cover art by Dobell Designs
Maps by Leinberger Mapping

LIBRARY AND ARCHIVES CANADA CATALOGUING IN PUBLICATION

Title: Island craft : your guide to the breweries of Vancouver Island / Jon C. Stott.
Names: Stott, Jon C., author. Description: Includes index. Identifiers: Canadiana
(print) 20190052872 | Canadiana (ebook) 20190052880 | ISBN 9781771512923
(softcover) | ISBN 9781771512930 (PDF) Subjects: LCSH: Microbreweries, British
Columbia, Vancouver Island, Guidebooks. | LCSH: Breweries,British Columbia,
Vancouver Island, Guidebooks. | LCSH: Beer, British Columbia, Vancouver Island
Guidebooks. Classification: LCC TP573.C3 S763 2019 | DDC 663/.42097112,dc23

We gratefully acknowledge the financial support of the Government
of Canada through the Canada Book Fund and the Province of
British Columbia through the Book Publishing Tax Credit.

Canadä

PRINTED IN CANADA AT FRIESENS

23 22 21 20 19   1 2 3 4 5

For my sister Sheri and my extended Victoria family

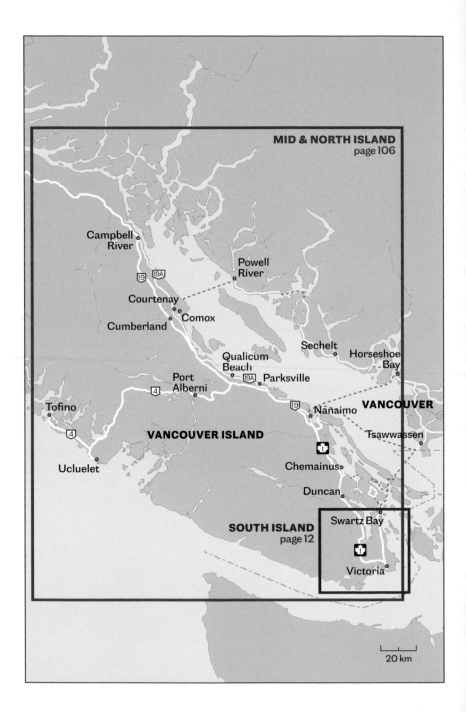

MID & NORTH ISLAND
page 106

Campbell River

Powell River

[19] [19A]

Courtenay

Comox

Cumberland

Sechelt

Horseshoe Bay

Qualicum Beach

[19A] Parksville

Port Alberni

[4]

Tofino

[4]

VANCOUVER ISLAND

[19] Nanaimo

VANCOUVER

Tsawwassen

Chemainus

Ucluelet

Duncan

SOUTH ISLAND
page 12

Swartz Bay

Victoria

20 km

CONTENTS

FOREWORD

I first met Jon Stott shortly after his first beer-related book, *Beer Quest West*, was published. Having obtained a review copy of the book for an article in the *Celebrator Beer News*, I was intrigued by Jon's writing style—his narrative was not a dry catalogue of Alberta and British Columbia breweries and their beers but rather an entertaining account of his travels in search of good beers and the people that brew them. Eventually I met Jon for lunch at Spinnakers, the first of seven years of noon meetings that we enjoy every time Jon is in Victoria. To this day we share a passion for beer and enthusiastically swap tales over ever-longer lunches.

His new book, *Island Craft*, is a fascinating description of his "journey of a thousand sips" over the length of Vancouver Island. Meandering from Victoria—Canada's beer capital—to Campbell River, Jon takes his readers to over thirty breweries and brewpubs, sampling their brews and spinning uplifting yarns about his travels and the people behind the beers. What's more, he digs deep and crafts intimate portraits of the folks he meets and their love of making beer.

Some of the brewers he introduces us to were homebrewers forever, making their switch to commercial brewing a natural choice. Others set out with different aspirations altogether—one was a literary scholar, another a stonemason, and another a research scientist, yet all succumbed to the magic of creating beer. Jon shares the stories of how they came to be where they are today and lets them tell their stories in their own words. He captures the brewers' passion, their trials and tribulations, and their success stories. One consistent theme is the almost-universal agreement that successful breweries flourish in small communities where there is a strong relationship between the brewery and the locals.

Island Craft is for anyone and everyone interested in the beers of Vancouver Island. You don't need to be a beer aficionado to get a lot out of this book because Jon has added several useful appendices that will appeal to novices and experts alike. Here you will find detailed information about each of the breweries as well as authoritative insight on everything from ingredients to brewing to equipment to packaging to how best to enjoy a beer.

Jon's love of all things beer is compelling, and I'm confident you'll be intoxicated with the same heady passion as you drink in the writing of *Island Craft*. To Jon—and to you, the reader—I raise a glass of Hermannator, with a hearty "Cheers!"

—John Rowling, Victoria BC, 2018

PREFACE

Two major trends have shaped the North American brewing industry as it exists today: the development of large national (and later international) breweries at the expense of regional breweries, and the growth of small, local breweries in what has become known as the craft beer movement or revolution. Starting in the middle of the 20th century, the total number of operating breweries decreased until the early 1980s as larger breweries set out to become national by purchasing smaller regional breweries and then absorbing or closing them.

As the size and influence of these megabrewers increased and the total number of operating breweries decreased (in 1980 there were only 92 in the United States and 40 in Canada), a countermovement began. In the late 1970s and into the 1980s, a few small local breweries opened, mainly along the west coast of the United States and Canada. Originally called microbreweries because of their size and often affectionately dubbed "cottage" or "boutique" breweries, these new operations offered products very different from the pale, bland, mass-produced lagers that dominated the North American market. They brewed a wide range of styles, most of which had not been seen in Canadian and American retail stores for several generations. The craft beer movement, as it is now known, developed slowly during the 1980s; the number of operating breweries rose fairly rapidly in the last decade of the 20th century and first decade of the 21st. Since 2010, there has been an explosion of new craft breweries and brewpubs. By 2018, there were more operating breweries in both the United States and Canada than there had been in well over a century. Many of these new breweries were located in metropolitan centres, and some of them had become so large that their products were available regionally and even nationally. But a growing number opened in small cities and even little villages, supplying limited amounts of beer to local patrons and tourists.

During this nearly 70-year period, brewing activity on Vancouver Island has been a microcosm of these trends. In 1950, two breweries operated in Victoria. Silver Spring Brewery, which had opened late in the 19th century, closed its operations in 1957. Victoria-Phoenix Brewing, which opened in 1858, was renamed Lucky Lager Brewing in 1954 in recognition of its major product, a pale American lager. It was acquired in 1958 by Labatt Brewing, which was quickly becoming a national brewery, and then was closed in 1981, as Labatt began a consolidation process. Victoria, along with the rest of Vancouver Island, found itself without a brewery for the first time since the Prohibition era of 1917–21.

The Island was without a brewery for less than two years: in 1983, the Prairie Inn and Cottage Brewery (which closed in 1996) opened in Saanichton; a year later, Spinnakers Gastro Brewpub began business in Victoria; and the next year, Island Pacific Brewing (now called Vancouver Island Brewing) opened a brewery in Saanichton. The latter two continue to operate. A glance at the lists of the various Vancouver Island breweries that have opened since that time reveals a steady increase in the number of craft breweries over the next two decades.

Island Craft: Your Guide to the Breweries of Vancouver Island is an examination of the craft breweries and brewpubs I visited during the winter and spring of 2018 and presents the backstories of the breweries, examines the relationships between the breweries and the communities in which they operate, profiles owners and brewers, and provides tasting notes about many of the beers each place offers. Part I is a narrative of my visits around Greater Victoria and southern Vancouver Island, beginning at Canada's oldest and longest continuously operating brewpub and concluding just outside the town of Sooke at a brewery that had opened only a few weeks before I stopped by. Part II describes the vibrant and rapidly growing craft beer scene from Duncan north.

Five appendices include information for visitors who might wish to stop at the breweries that dot a Vancouver Island beer map. Appendix 1, "Directory of Vancouver Island Breweries and Brewpubs," includes basic facts (addresses, phone numbers, websites, and names of owners and brewers), information about brewing operations (brewhouse sizes, regularly produced beers, and Canadian Brewing Awards won), information about food service and tours, policies about admitting children and dogs, and wheelchair accessibility. Appendix 2 is a glossary of beer and brewing terms. Appendix 3, "A Guide to Beer Styles," provides brief descriptions of many styles of craft beer, along with examples of each style from breweries I visited. Appendix 4 is an essay about basic ingredients, the brewing process, and the packaging and drinking of beer. Appendix 5 is an annotated list of books about beer and brewing.

Although the glossary and the appendix on beer styles are intended to provide readers with definitions of beer terms included in *Island Craft*, four are so frequently used that they should be defined here:

Lager: One of the two main categories of beer. Lagers use bottom-fermenting yeasts, take longer to brew, and are fermented at lower temperatures. They are generally lighter in colour and body than ales. Most of the beer drunk around the world is North American pale lager, a style best exemplified by Budweiser.

Ale: The other main category of beer. Ales use top-fermenting yeasts, take less time to brew, and are fermented at higher temperatures. Ales are generally darker in colour, fuller-bodied, and more robustly flavoured than lagers.

ABV: Alcohol by volume, expressed as a percentage, which ranges from around 4 percent to 10 percent. When it is known, the ABV of a specific beer is included in the text.

IBUs: International Bitterness Units, which indicate the bitterness, created by the hops, in a specific beer. The IBUs of lighter lagers may be around 15, while those of some India pale ales can reach and even exceed 100. When available, the IBUs in a specific beer are included in the text. (Sometimes the term International Bittering Units is used.)

One final note: literally and figuratively, brewing is a fluid industry. Breweries relocate or close, new breweries open, owners and brewers change, some styles are discontinued and others introduced, hours that breweries are open to the public change. If you are planning visits to any of the breweries discussed in *Island Craft*, be sure to check brewery websites or Facebook pages before you go.

A SENTIMENT-ALE STROLL

On a misty Sunday afternoon in November, I made a three-kilometre walk from the intersection of Douglas Street and Burnside Road, a few blocks north of downtown Victoria, British Columbia, south along Douglas and then Government Streets, west across the Johnson Street Bridge and along Esquimalt Road until I reached Catherine Street. There I turned south and walked 100 or so metres to my destination. The purpose of my peregrinations was to pass by several buildings and places that were important to both the brewing history of Victoria and my personal encounters with Victoria's beers. "Oh," my pun-loving friend replied when I later told him of my walk, "you've been on a sentiment-ale stroll. It was a historic-ale journey too!"

My departure point was in front of a building that now housed beneficiaries of governmental social services agencies. The nearly 60-year-old building had begun its life as the Ingraham Hotel, the "Ingy," as many locals affectionately dubbed it, and on its main floor was one of the largest beer parlours in Western Canada. Here, late in the afternoon of December 2, 1960, I had my first legal glass of beer.

Because one of the people who were helping me celebrate was a woman, the party entered the "Ladies and Escorts" side of the establishment, not the "Gentlemen" side. The room was enormous. A pall of cigarette smoke extended a few feet down from the ceiling, there were no windows, and the smell of stale, spilt beer permeated the air. Our server plunked down two 20-cent glasses of beer for each of us. In those days, patrons couldn't make a selection from a variety of styles from several breweries; they accepted whatever generic, bland, pale North American lager was being served. None of us ordered anything to eat, but had we been hungry, we could have ordered pepperoni sticks, pickled eggs from a large jar filled with murky-looking liquid, or a packet of potato chips. People who had real appetites would wait until six o'clock, when government regulations required beer parlours to close for an hour. Patrons could either head home or walk a few metres to the hotel's café. In addition to beer, other liquid refreshment was limited to tomato juice (which everyone called "red"), soda pop, and water. There were no games or music, and people didn't circulate from table to table socializing. (If you moved to a new table, you had to get the server to take your glass there.) You just sat there, talked to the people on either side of you, and drank your beer.

The beer parlour was a product of British Columbia liquor laws that were established in the 1920s after the end of the province's experiment with Prohibition. In order to reach a compromise with prohibitionists and those who yearned for a return to the almost Wild West–like saloon of earlier years, the provincial government took control of the sale and distribution of liquor. Packaged beer, wine, and spirits were available only at government liquor stores; beer was the only liquor that could be consumed publicly and then only by the glass. This consumption was permitted only at "beer parlours," the name an attempt to glamorize the gloomy rooms. In the 1950s, regulations were modified to allow light snacks to be served, and a couple of years after I celebrated my first legal beer, the division of seating areas by gender was done away with.

After standing for a few minutes in a drizzle that was threatening to become a shower, waxing poetic about my first legal beer, I began walking south, stopping next at the corner of Government and Discovery Streets. I stood in the entryway to one of the small businesses that occupied a building where the Lucky Lager Brewing Company once stood. Kitty-corner was the small parking lot and storefront-like entrance to Phillips Brewing and Malting Company, a 16-year-old craft brewery that is now one of the largest and most influential craft breweries in Western Canada.

Lucky Lager, which had begun brewing in 1858 as Victoria Brewery, had occupied the space at Government and Discovery since 1860 and operated under the names Victoria Brewing and then Victoria-Phoenix Brewing until 1954, when it took the name Lucky Lager Brewing Company. Labatt Brewing bought the plant in 1958. When the Ingraham Hotel beer parlour opened in 1960, it became the biggest by-the-glass seller of Labatt products in the province. So it is most likely that first legal beer I had was a Lucky Lager. In the late 1970s, Labatt decided to consolidate its British Columbia operations: in 1981, it closed the brewery on Government Street, moved operations to New Westminster, and soon after razed the Government Street building. Lucky is now brewed in the Labatt facilities in Creston, in the Interior of British Columbia, and in Edmonton, Alberta, although the advertising on the package proclaims the use of the "Original Vancouver Island Recipe." The ingredients aren't listed on the package or the cans, so we don't know what the recipe was. Nonetheless, this beer, now imported from far away, has a cult following in many places outside the Greater Victoria area and represents the stiffest competition faced by Vancouver Island's growing number of craft brewers.

Phillips Brewing and Malting, operating kitty-corner from the site of the old brewery, creates beers that are completely different from what Lucky Lager was and still is. It began operations in 2001 in a small warehouse space in Esquimalt, the creation of Matt Phillips, a Maritimer whose interest in the growing craft beer movement led him west. Working alone the first year, he created styles quite different from those offered by other local craft brewers and certainly different from Lucky Lager. Now Phillips employs close to 100 people to do the jobs he once had to perform by himself. His brewery, which moved to its present Government Street location in 2008, has become one of the largest wholly Canadian-owned, private breweries in Western Canada.

I crossed the Johnson Street Bridge, passed Vic West Park, where, nearly seven decades ago, my father had taken my sisters and me to see the Clyde Beatty Circus, and arrived at my destination, a structure that once had been a large, early 20th century–style house located a stone's throw from the waters of Victoria's Outer Harbour. Since 1984 it had been the home of Spinnakers, Canada's first and longest-running brewpub. I'd first visited it in the summer of 1988 and tasted my first British Columbia craft beer. "The food is good, the view is spectacular, and they make their own beer," a friend reported enthusiastically. The view *was* spectacular: there were windows that looked out over a trail, along which people jogged and walked dogs, onto the sparkling salt waters through which a Black Ball Ferry was moving on its way to Port Angeles, Washington. I remember having a "ploughman's lunch," a traditional English pub plate that my father and mother had always enjoyed on their visits to London. It tasted much better than pepperoni sticks and pickled eggs. I chose an ESB (extra special bitter) for my beer, another of my father's English favourites. It had been brewed in the tanks I had seen when we first came in. It tasted much different from my inaugural legal beer, downed at the Ingraham—in fact, it had taste.

My sentiment-ale stroll over, I walked back to my car, thinking about the places, past and present, in front of which I had stopped, and realized I'd been thinking about and remembering two very different time periods and beer cultures. Lucky Lager Brewing and the Ingraham had been examples of the type of beer manufactured and one of the ways it was consumed in the 1950s and 1960s. Beer was a generic commodity that people frequently drank in environments that emphasized drinking, often without enjoyment, in settings that were not conducive to pleasant social interrelationships. Drinking beer mass-produced in large production facilities like the Lucky Lager plant was basically the only permitted activity. Looking out windows at whitecaps, ferry boats, or passersby, tapping your feet to live music played by a local group, or walking across the room to invite a friend to a game of billiards or darts was not a possibility. On the other hand, Spinnakers produced a variety of flavourful beer styles, which could be enjoyed with good food and in the company of good friends. In the 1980s, a new beer culture had begun to evolve.

On my way back to my sister's house, where I was staying, I stopped at one of the many private liquor stores that had proliferated over the last two or three decades and purchased a bottle of Spinnakers Estate Sooke Bitter and a six-pack of Lucky Lager. I also picked up a copy of the latest issue of *The Growler: B.C. Craft Beer Guide*, a quarterly, *Reader's Digest*–sized magazine. That evening, after I'd told my sister about my sentiment-ale stroll—it turned out that, unbeknownst to me, she'd also been at the Ingraham that long-ago December day—I opened a can of Lucky. It warranted only one sip. "People on Vancouver Island are certainly lucky they have other beer choices," I muttered. Then I poured the Sooke Bitter into a glass and took a sip. It was delicious: hoppy, but not too hoppy, with a solid malt backbone. It had been brewed in the Spinnakers brewhouse and used hops recently harvested from owner Paul Hadfield's farm, located in Sooke just over an hour's drive from the brewpub. My sister and I finished the bottle—all 650 millilitres of it—and we both wished that I'd bought two.

As I sipped, I thumbed through the pages of *The Growler*, noticing with amazement not only the large number of craft breweries and brew-pubs open or soon to open on Vancouver Island but also the number of small towns and communities in which they operated and the variety of beer styles they were creating. *It would be fun and very interesting to visit all of these breweries*, I thought. In recent years I'd written books about my beer travels in New Mexico, along US Highway 101 in Washington and Oregon, and to towns and cities around Lake Superior. Why not return to Vancouver Island, where I'd lived the first 21 years of my life, and explore the beer culture that has expanded rapidly since

2010, when I'd researched 13 Island breweries for my first beer book, *Beer Quest West*? And so, in January and April 2018, I returned to Vancouver Island and set about visiting breweries, tasting many excellent and award-winning brews, and getting to know the people who created them.

PART I
SOUTH ISLAND

From Spinnakers to Sooke
CRAFT BREWERIES OF GREATER VICTORIA
AND SOUTHERN VANCOUVER ISLAND

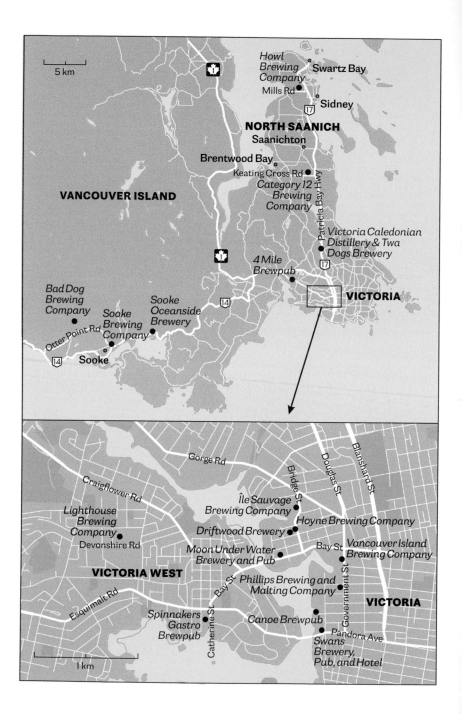

With a handful of exceptions, the brewing that took place on Vancouver Island before the beginning of the craft beer movement in 1984 occurred in Victoria. Between 1858, when Victoria Brewery began business, and 1981, when it closed as Labatt Brewing's Lucky Lager production facility, 21 breweries operated in what was first the capital of the Crown Colony of Vancouver Island and later the capital of the province of British Columbia. The most active brewing period took place in the 1880s, when 11 breweries were open. The number should not be surprising. In the last half of the 19th century, Victoria was probably the most important West Coast port north of San Francisco. Not only was it a capital city, but also it was the Hudson's Bay Company's most important trading post on the West Coast, the base of the Royal Navy's Pacific Fleet, and during the later 19th century, the point of arrival, the main supply location, and the point of departure for thousands of people seeking to strike it rich in the various gold rushes that took place on the British Columbia mainland.

The presence of those wealth seekers, along with personnel from the naval base, was a reason for the opening of a large number of saloons in Victoria, drinking establishments that were usually what could euphemistically be called "rough and rowdy." And the beer consumed was made by these pioneering breweries. Only two survived the Prohibition years of 1917–21, Victoria Brewery (renamed Victoria-Phoenix) and Silver Spring. Strict government restrictions on the brewing, selling, and public consumption of liquor, along with the growth of larger, more cost-efficient breweries in the Vancouver area, no doubt limited the number of Victoria-area breweries from the 1920s until the beginning of the 1980s.

Between 1983, when Prairie Inn Neighbourhood Pub and Cottage Brewery opened, and the end of 2017, 18 craft breweries or brewpubs have operated in Victoria or nearby southern Vancouver Island. Two, Prairie Inn and Cottage Brewery (which many do not consider a craft brewery because it used malt extract instead of malt) and Hugo's, have closed; the others still brew beer. Spinnakers, Canada's first self-contained brewpub, which opened in May 1984, is the eldest of the 16 that were brewing at the end of 2017; Bad Dog Brewing, a small production facility located a few kilometres southwest of Sooke, close to the southern tip of the Island, began selling beer in December 2017. Until the end of the first decade of the 21st century, most of the breweries/brewpubs were clustered near Victoria's Inner Harbour or along Government Street. Newer breweries set up first in an area north of Rock Bay, then in Saanich, and then in the communities/towns of View Royal, Langford, and Sooke. Six are brewpubs; 10 are production breweries that range in size from very small, with a few local accounts, to very large, distributing their products throughout British Columbia and into the provinces that lie east of the Rocky Mountains.

CHAPTER 1

VICTORIA'S PIONEER CRAFT BREWPUBS

Spinnakers Gastro Brewpub, Swans Brewery, Canoe Brewpub

I began what my punning friend called "a journey of a thousand sips" at **Spinnakers Gastro Brewpub**, Canada's first self-contained modern brewpub, an establishment that certainly deserved the overused adjective "iconic." The sun was not glinting off the water on this grey January 2018 morning, but there were still people strolling, jogging, and walking their dogs on the path by the water, just as there had been when I'd first visited nearly three decades earlier. I walked past the fermenting tanks standing at the edge of the parking lot and past the gift shop that featured malt vinegar made on site, bottled mineral water from a well beneath the property, local baked goods and chocolates, and souvenir glasses and apparel. Opposite the gift shop, a large plate-glass window gave a view of the eight-hectolitre brewing system—the original equipment—in the basement below.

I climbed the stairs to the second-storey pub area—a later addition to the building—and, as I made my way to a table facing the windows that wrapped around two sides of the large room, I noticed two pool tables, bags of brewing malt stacked against the

Kala Hadfield, a member of the Spinnakers brewing team, stands with her father, Paul Hadfield, Spinnakers owner and one of the co-founders of Canada's longest continuously running brewpub. ➜

north wall, three television sets, and a bar counter behind which were mounted 26 taps that dispensed Spinnakers' ales and lagers, along with a few ciders made in-house. When I sat down I was surprised to notice a well-bundled patron sitting on the balcony, shielded by plastic screens from the drizzle, sipping a beer. I hoped that the beer was a style called winter warmer.

I'd sat at the same table in January 2009, when I first met owner-publican Paul Hadfield, who, in recounting the founding and early days of the brewpub, had told an interesting story about the main-floor windows at Spinnakers. When one of the government inspectors had examined the plans for the new neighbourhood pub, he was alarmed to find that there would be large, nearly floor-to-ceiling plate-glass windows along the front wall of the building. In the late 1970s, topless waitresses and pole dancers had been popular features in some liquor-serving establishments. What if passersby, especially young boys, should look in the windows and see such people? Hadfield explained that the purpose of the windows was to enable people inside to enjoy the spectacular scenery outside and that topless servers or pole dancers were definitely not in the plans. The windows were allowed to remain.

This was just one of the hurdles that Hadfield and his partners, one of whom was John Mitchell, the founder of Horseshoe Bay Brewing, Canada's first craft brewery, had to overcome. Early in the 1980s, Mitchell was sharing some beers he'd brought back from England with friends when the discussion among the group, which included Paul Hadfield, turned to the idea of opening a pub in Victoria, not just a neighbourhood pub but one that made its own beer on premises. Hadfield set about looking for a suitable location and building and discovered an old heritage house in Vic West, which at the time was a not very fashionable area on the western shore of the harbour. "I knew that

waterfront restaurants did very well," he remembered. "And this house had great potential."

The first step involved holding a meeting with people in the neighbourhood to get their approval of and input on the creation of a local pub. "There wasn't much of a neighbourhood around, but people from the area showed up and were very supportive. In fact, after we opened, they were among our most loyal patrons," Hadfield remembered. Then came dealings with the federal and provincial governments over their radical proposal: to sell beer in the same building in which it was made. "At one point," Hadfield laughed, "we were afraid that we'd have to put our beer in kegs, load it on a truck, drive out of the parking lot, turn around, come back, and then take the kegs to the serving area."

The hurdles overcome, Spinnakers opened in May 1984, changing Victoria's drinking scene. John Mitchell produced three English-style beers: an ESB (extra special bitter), an English dark mild, and a light-bodied golden ale (which served as an entry-level beer for those who'd never ventured beyond mainstream pale North American lagers). His wife, Jenny, created English-style pub grub. Spinnakers quickly became popular not only with British expatriates (of which Victoria has always had more than its share) but also with other Victorians (who often brought out-of-town guests with them) and summer tourists. Within a few weeks of opening, the owners had already submitted expansion plans to government authorities. "We realized that, even though we were full every day and had to work hard to keep enough beer on tap, we couldn't survive financially with just a 65-seat place," Hadfield explained. Over the next few years, the ground-floor seating area was expanded, and a second-floor area, which became the pub, added.

When I'd chatted with Hadfield in 2009, we'd been joined by then head brewer Rob Monk. He has since moved on to become head brewer at Yukon Brewing in Whitehorse and is one of several brewers who started at Spinnakers before going on to either own or head operations at other breweries. Among these are Barry Ladell, one of the founders of Longwood Brew Pub in Nanaimo; Mike Tymchuk, formerly one of the owners of Calgary's Wild Rose Brewery and now head brewer of Cumberland Brewing on the northern part of the Island; and Matt Phillips, owner of Victoria's enormously successful Phillips Brewing and Malting.

"We don't have a head brewer now," Paul Hadfield's daughter Kala, one of Spinnakers' brewers, told me on my current visit. "There's a group of seven in the brewhouse. It's a very collaborative effort. We're able to make a great range of beers, because we can draw on many talents." Kala has been around craft beer all her life. "I remember going to parties when I was younger. Kids were bringing six-packs of cheap beer; I'd bring a growler from Spinnakers. Everyone wanted to try it." She was working at the brewpub's bar when her father encouraged her to fill a vacancy in the brewhouse. "I started working as a cellarman [someone who oversees the fermentation of beer] and learned brewing from the basement up."

Kala had spent some time exploring the lively, creative craft beer culture in Portland and had become familiar with the increasingly wide range of styles being brewed. "I'd developed a palate for hoppy Northwest IPA styles, and as I got more involved in the brewing, I suggested that we make more of these." In 2009, Spinnakers did have an IPA (India pale ale) and had produced a couple of Belgian-style beers, but its beer list still focused on the English styles that had been so popular from the beginning. From 2011 onward, the number and range of styles had increased dramatically. Thirty-two different types of beers had been produced, including such lesser-known styles as bière de garde, gose, and rauchbier. A barrel-aging program was introduced. Such additives as apples, coffee, tayberries, oysters, and quince had been included in recipes. Just two weeks after my January 2018 visit, two barrel-aged beers, both using local fruits, would be released: Prunus Plum Sour and Rubus Blackberry Sour.

Spinnakers now offers a great deal more than beers your grandfather drank back in England. No wonder there were 26 taps at the bar. That evening, I looked at the website and discovered that 11 IPAs and pale ales, several saisons, sour beers, and lagers, along with something called Choco-Chilli Porter, were currently available at the brewpub. Kala had told me the lagers were most popular at the brewpub; of the canned and bottled beers, Juice Monkey, a 6 percent IPA, was the best seller.

Paul Hadfield, after nearly three and a half decades at Spinnakers, the pioneering patriarch of Vancouver Island's craft beer movement, joined Kala and me just as she was discussing the incredible variety of beer styles dispensed from the taps just across the room. He referred to this variety as he discussed the great change in craft brewing since 1984. "We only had three beers then," he noted. "And they seemed new and different to most of our patrons. Now we've got a style for everyone.

"In the early 1980s, we walked into a landscape still dominated by the culture of the beer parlours. We wanted to change that, to move beyond that culture. That was why being a neighbourhood pub that brewed its own beer and served food was so important." He went on to note that there are now many brewpubs on the Island and that a fairly recent law enabling production breweries to serve their own beer on premises had created a new kind of pub, a community gathering place, with each having its own atmosphere. He didn't mention that most of them had windows and none of them had clouds of cigarette smoke obscuring the ceilings.

Hadfield went on to talk about a recent visit he'd made to Nelson, a town of just over 10,000 in BC's southern Interior. "There are three breweries there: one that's been around since the early 1990s and two that opened just a while ago. Each one is a different expression of craft beer. There are so many lively, adventurous brewers around now, and people have the opportunity to explore all of the craft beer landscape." He mentioned the small breweries that have popped up in so many small towns, each one unique. Spinnakers was no longer the only show in town in Victoria, and that fact made the craft brewing scene much richer and stronger.

Hadfield's use of the word "unique" jogged my memory of a unique event that I remembered having read about many years ago: Spinnakers had created a beer, one of the ingredients of which was a batch of hops that had travelled in space. He filled me in on the details. It turned out that, in 1992, Bill Readdy, one of the members of a mission of the shuttle *Discovery*, had smuggled aboard some Cascade hops he'd bought at a Houston, Texas, homebrew supply shop. Readdy was a friend of Dr. John Voyce, a University of British Columbia professor who also happened to be a great fan of Spinnakers, visiting the brewpub whenever he came to Victoria. When the *Discovery* landed, Voyce suggested to his friend that some of the hops be sent to Spinnakers, which they were. A few weeks later, when a group of astronauts, including Readdy, stopped in Victoria on a cross-Canada tour, they were guests, along with Voyce, at Spinnakers, where Readdy tapped a cask of Discovery Ale, an amber beer made with those hops. There is no record of whether anybody answered the question "How does it taste?" by saying "Out of this world!" Hadfield did say that it was advertised as a low-gravity beer, a pun combining the weightlessness in space with a brewing term relating to the alcoholic strength of a beer.

The idea of a brewpub as part of a community ran throughout our conversation and was never so evident as when I asked Hadfield to talk about an event that could have brought about the end of the Spinnakers era: a fire that broke out on the afternoon of November 23,

2016, severely damaging most of the second floor and causing water and smoke damage below. Neither the equipment in the brewhouse nor the beer was harmed.

"I was in Hawaii when Kala texted me: 'Phone right away,'" he remembered. It wasn't until he returned home that he realized the event wasn't just about the building. "I saw a farmer being interviewed on TV who remarked that he'd lost his spinach market. It made me realize that this place was part of a wider community, an interdependent one. We wanted our employees to survive, so we began cleanup and renovations right away. We were back in business in nine days. It was wonderful to see how everyone had a kind of ownership in the place. People appreciated that this was a community centre."

Kala nodded. I understood that for them, the people who had worked for them over the years, and the people from astronauts to folks living just a few blocks away who came to visit, Canada's longest-operating brewpub was much more than just a place that served really good food and beer and had a great view.

〜〜〜〜〜〜〜〜

Had I made my visits to Victoria's pioneering brewpubs a few weeks later, I could have made the trip to my next two destinations by water. Victoria Harbour Ferry, which has a fleet of very small, cartoon-like boats and runs a tour called the Pickle Pub Crawl, had a stop close to Spinnakers and another near Swans Brewery and Canoe Brewpub. But they weren't operating in the winter, so I took the path I'd seen from my window seat at Spinnakers and strolled past several luxury high-rises, which had replaced the fuel tanks and small industrial buildings that had dominated the area in the days of my youth. As I reached the eastern end of the Johnson Street Bridge, I noticed an old friend sitting on a park bench a hundred or so metres away. The "friend" was a statue of Michael Williams, another pioneer of Victoria's craft brewing movement. He was sitting looking over at **Swans Brewery**, a Victoria landmark he'd created in the late 1980s. Whenever I visited Swans, I'd always walk over to the bench and, as it were, pay homage to the man and his vision.

Williams had been a sheep rancher and dog breeder and trainer before he began buying and renovating old Victoria buildings. One of his purchases had been an untenanted building that was long ago the home of Buckerfield's Farm Supplies, where he'd bought feed for his sheep many years earlier. His vision was to turn the 1913 structure into a fancy apartment building that had boutique stores on the ground floor. He would, he told people, transform an ugly duckling into a swan. The apartments and stores suffered during an economic downturn during the later 1980s, and Williams began reimagining: he would replace the struggling businesses with a pub on the ground floor. However, he was informed that to obtain a pub licence, he'd need to turn the apartments into a hotel, which he did. The elegant rooms were decorated with valuable paintings from his private collection.

Williams contracted Frank Appleton (who had been instrumental in the formation of British Columbia's first craft brewery, Horseshoe Bay Brewing, in the early '80s) to set up the brewhouse, design the recipes, and hire the first full-time brewer, Sean Hoyne. Appleton created what seems like a fairly standard range of beers now, but at the time was even "wilder" than what Spinnakers had begun with. It included a pale ale, a bitter, a brown, a lager, and something called Arctic Ale, based on a relatively unknown German style: kolsch. The pub was named Swans, in recognition of Williams's vision; but the brewery originally had to be called Buckerfield's to avoid legal conflicts with another brewery of the same name. (It is now Swans Brewery.) Both the brewery and the pub opened in 1989. Early in the new century, Hoyne moved two blocks to set up the brewery at the Canoe Brewpub. Andrew Tessier, his replacement, won over three dozen Canadian Brewing Awards medals, including 22 gold, for styles ranging from an English bitter to a coconut brown. In 2016, he moved on to the newly opened Axe & Barrel Brewing Company in the nearby community of Langford.

I was soon to meet Swans' third brewer, Chris Lukie (pronounced lew-key, not lucky!). Nodding farewell to the statue of Michael Williams, I walked toward the old building whose new elegance had been enhanced by a glassed-in sun porch that wrapped around two sides of the building and reminded me of pictures I'd seen of teahouses along the English seashore. When I entered the building, which had been bequeathed to the

University of Victoria by Williams, who died in 2000, I was impressed, as I always was, by the magnificent and very large West Coast Indigenous ceremonial mask that hung from the ceiling and amused

Chris Lukie, who came to Victoria without a job in hand, worked at Lighthouse Brewing before becoming head brewer at Swans. ↑

by the portrait of one-time Canadian prime minister Pierre Elliott Trudeau, draped in an elegant cape and looking haughty.

I was glancing at the list of beers on the chalkboard—it included such interesting names as YYJ Pilsner (YYJ being the Victoria airport code) and Muy ("very" in Spanish) Hoppy IPA—when Chris Lukie came out from the brewery, located in the back of the building in a space that once stored feed grains and now holds sacks of brewing malts. For him, the road to Swans was a long and circuitous one. A native of Winnipeg, a city that until recently could have been called a craft beer desert, he had been a homebrewer and had discovered good beer when he browsed the international section of a local liquor store. After earning bachelor's and master's degrees in food sciences, he was hired in the quality-control department of Calgary's Big Rock Brewery and later at the enormous Labatt plant in Edmonton.

The bug had bitten Lukie; he knew he wanted a career as a professional brewer, and he made the initial difficult steps toward achieving his goal. First, he took out a second mortgage on his house and left his family to spend three months studying at the prestigious World Brewing Academy of the Siebel Institute in Chicago and Doemens Academy in Munich, Germany. Back in Manitoba, there were no brewing jobs available. So he took another drastic step. "We sold our house and most of our stuff, packed the kids and the cat in the old Volkswagen, and took off to the West Coast. We loved the ocean and the warmth, and British Columbia was definitely the centre of craft brewing in Canada." The car broke down as they were waiting for the ferry to Victoria, but they finally reached their destination. Lukie didn't have a job, only hope, determination, and the prospect of much warmer winters than the ones he'd left behind. He landed work as a cellarman at Lighthouse Brewing, and when that job ended, he got his lucky break. "Matt Phillips texted me that there was an opening at Swans," he remembered. "I applied and here I am."

Lukie inherited a well-established line of beers, many of them winners of Canadian Brewing Awards medals. "I kept the Scotch Ale, the Raspberry Blonde, and one of the IPAs, but I tweaked some recipes and added others to reflect some of the current trends." Because the brewhouse had so many tanks, several of them standing empty, he had the luxury of offering a wide variety of lagers, which take longer than ales to ferment and condition, and, for most small breweries, take up too much tank space. In addition to the YYJ Pilsner, the lagers included a helles, a multigrain lager, a red pilsner, a SMASH (single-malt, single-hop) pilsner, and the marvellously named Swans Pitch Black

Chamomile Black Pilsner. The helles and the black pilsner were an interesting study in contrasts. The former is a smooth, golden-coloured, slightly malt-forward beer; the latter is dark in colour, but light in body. It's hop-forward, although, as it warms, the malt flavours emerge. The chamomile flower petals create a hint of tea, while the hops add spicy notes.

Lukie has also created some different, unusual beers, including Flammenbeer, a German-style rauch (smoked) ale, and Bourbon Kelp (a seaweed) Scotch Ale. Just before I arrived, Swans had released a bière de garde, a traditional French style, the name of which means "beer to be kept." On the label appears the humorous note "I forgot about this beer," and the forgetting has certainly been worthwhile. Amber in colour and light to medium in body, the 7.6 percent beer is crisp and clean; its slight malt sweetness is moderated by the hop bitterness, and as it warms slightly, very subtle, complex flavours emerge.

My favourite beer was the amber ale, which, although not that unusual a style, had a special meaning to me. Thomas Uphill Amber Ale was named after a man who'd been a member of the British Columbia legislature from 1920 to 1960. At the beginning of his career, when Prohibition was still in effect, Thomas Uphill had championed the rights of the common man, the worker, to have beer to drink, claiming that it was like mother's milk to babies. "It's a rugged beer," Lukie explained, "not refined, but satisfying. Drinking this beer is like taking an autumn walk in the woods." The beer had been released in October 2016, and at the release party historian Wayne Norton, who had suggested that Lukie create the beer, and several descendants of Uphill were in attendance. As I sipped it several weeks later, I remembered how, when I was a little boy, "Uncle Tom," as we called him, often used to spend weekends at the place next door to our Shawnigan Lake cabin. One day, when he heard that I was frightened of snakes, he said that he'd give me 50 cents (an enormous amount of money in those days) if I'd catch a snake and bring it to him. I did, and he presented me with the big silver coin, making sure that there were several people around to witness my triumph.

As our conversation was winding down, Lukie said, "I love hops, but they weren't very big in the beers around Manitoba. Now I make a lot of different IPAs depending on what is available. I ask myself, 'What hops are coming out, and how can I use them to make a new IPA?' I want my IPAs to be a celebration of hops." I thought that a person who grew up in the beer desert of Manitoba has certainly found a home in Victoria, a beer oasis where the love of hops is great.

<hr />

Canoe Brewpub, Victoria's third-oldest brewpub, is a very short walk from Swans—one block north on Store Street and then west on Swift Street, past Swift House, which provides extended tenancy for the formerly homeless, and Mermaid Wharf condos, which provide luxury accommodations for the wealthy. At the base of the hill is the main terminus of the harbour ferries and, beside it, docks for large sailing craft. The building in which the brewpub is housed was built in 1894 as the power plant for downtown Victoria. During the 1990s, it underwent $6 million in renovations, and after it opened in 1998, it became a destination for beer-loving locals and tourists. Inside the brick building, the original fir posts and brick walls create a simple, rustic atmosphere. A canoe is suspended from the ceiling beams, as are large banners featuring images of the labels of some of the early beers that had been created in the brewery just behind the bar, above which glisten seven stainless steel serving tanks. Patrons enjoy pub grub at tables on the three levels of seating, which fill in what must have been a cavernous interior before the renovations.

In 1998, Sean Hoyne left Swans, enthusiastically accepting the opportunity to create a new brewery and develop a line of beers that would appeal to the people who would soon come to the building that, he told me, was the brewery's "greatest asset." The view of the Inner Harbour patrons enjoyed, especially in the warmer months, was also a great asset, as was the gourmet food and the regular entertainment, and especially the beers that were dispensed from the shining tanks above the bar. Because there were only five of these tanks at first, Hoyne was limited in the number of styles that were available at any one time. So he created recipes for four year-round beers—a Vienna lager, a pale ale, an English bitter, and a brown ale—and a rotating seasonal.

In 2011, Hoyne left Canoe to fulfill what is nearly every professional brewer's dream: ownership of his own brewery. Before he departed, he told Daniel Murphy, who'd worked for a few years at Lighthouse Brewing, one of the city's earlier production craft breweries, that the Canoe job would soon be open.

Murphy, after he had graduated from an Australian university with a degree in English literature and creative writing, had decided to take a long vagabonding journey, seeking short-term employment at some of the stops he made. When he arrived in Victoria, he began looking for a job and noticed an ad seeking people to work on a canning line. "I figured it was probably for some fish-packing plant, but it turned out to be for Lighthouse Brewing. I'd never been inside a brewery; I had no idea what it looked like. In fact, back home, I'd been more interested in wine than beer."

He was hired—and that ended the vagabonding. For the next six years, he worked in and learned the processes of making the beverage he hadn't been that interested in before. "I learned about brewing in a reverse way—I began by packaging the finished product, then I became a cellarman involved the fermentation process, and finally I became a brewer." He played a large role in developing Riptide, a hoppy pale ale that was the first new Lighthouse beer in a decade.

While he'd been in Victoria, the craft brewing scene in Australia, which was influenced by the hoppy styles popular along the West Coast of the United States, had developed rapidly. He returned home and became a brewer at the unusually named Moo Brew, located on the island of Tasmania. But he missed Victoria. "It was so dry in Australia compared to Vancouver Island, and I missed all the greenery." He also missed the many friends he'd made among Victoria's craft brewers, with

whom he'd kept in regular contact. So, in 2011, he returned to Victoria and, it could be said, paddled his way to Canoe.

Taking over a brewery that, for over a dozen years, had produced a strong line of core beer styles represented a challenge. "I inherited the beers, not Sean's recipes," Murphy explained. "I wanted to maintain the core brands in the house style, which emphasized balance and sessionability, but I also wanted to give them a little more intensity and complexity. I wanted beers that appealed to both knowledgeable and general beer drinkers, so I mixed tradition with a little bit of adventure." The approach worked. In 2012, Red Canoe Lager and Beaver Brown won Canadian Brewing Awards silver medals, while River Rock Bitter picked up a bronze. Two years later, the bock took a silver, and in 2015, the lager won another silver.

In 2017, after six years of using his brewer's paddle to steer the direction of Canoe's products, Daniel Murphy helped alter the brewpub's course. During that year, Canoe underwent a major rebranding and a revision of the core beer recipes. Gone were names like Winter Gale and Siren's Song. On the chalkboard above the bar and on the labels appeared

Daniel Murphy was on a post-university trip around the world when he answered an ad for someone to work on the canning line at Lighthouse Brewing. A decade later, he became the head brewer at Canoe Brewpub. ←

merely the word "Canoe" followed by the style. Gone were the colourful paintings on the labels, replaced by the word "Canoe" followed by the style name and decorated with a stylized depiction of a paddle. "We didn't want gimmicks on the logos or gimmicky names; our brand was Canoe and we wanted to emphasize that," Murphy explained.

"We also wanted new recipes; our beers would have a broad appeal and be sessionable. But there'd be new approaches that would reflect my experiences both as a person and as a brewer." He gave as an example the simply named Helles (4.8 percent ABV, 12 IBUs), a very popular German-style lager. "In the winter of 2017, I had a ski vacation in Austria. It was wonderful to come off the slopes, sit by a fire, and sip a wonderfully crafted, traditionally brewed helles. I wanted to create a helles that, whenever I drank it, would revive those great experiences. We use pilsner malt, Saaz hops, and a Munich yeast strain that gives it that *je ne sais quoi* flavour. It tingles on the tongue. I'm proud of it; I think we make a solid presentation of a style that's very difficult to brew."

His fascination with North American–style pale ales, which developed during his first stay in Victoria and found expression in the Riptide Pale Ale he helped develop at Lighthouse Brewing, is evident in the new West Coast Pale Ale. "We use Amarillo and Citra hops and we dry-hop it, which is a challenge in the brewing system we have. We use a secret blend of North American and European malts along with Canadian pale malt. We want hop flavours and bitterness, but we want them tempered by the malts.

"I wanted our core list to embody styles from a variety of areas, such as the West Coast of Canada and the United States for the pale ale, and Germany for the helles," Murphy said, before he described the Witbier, a 4.5 percent ABV, 8 IBU interpretation of a popular Belgian style. The recipe calls for Belgian yeast; Hersbrucker hops, which contribute spicy, fruity, and floral notes; and lemon and orange rind and coriander seeds.

"It has a slightly dry and tart finish," he noted. "I think it will be very popular in the summer."

As he introduced the fourth regular, Murphy remarked, "I had a vision of what I wanted for an amber beer. I wanted it to be rich and malty, and so I used a variety of different malts, including some from the United Kingdom. But I also used Cascade hops to balance the maltiness." At 5.5 percent ABV, it's the strongest of the core beers; however, it is only 14 IBUs. "It's a hearty beer for crisp outdoor weather in the fall and for sitting by the fireplace in the winter."

I had read somewhere that Murphy's motto was "Respect Tradition—Love Adventure." His core beers are an example, to use a phrase from the 20th-century poet T.S. Eliot, of "tradition and the individual talent." He understands the styles well and makes them his own through his interpretation of aspects of the tradition. They are sessionable beers, high in neither alcohol content nor bitterness, but they have a complexity that infuses the basic stylistic characteristics. The love of adventure is most fully evident in one of the new seasonal beers and the Windward Series, which includes a number of one-offs. Among these are an 8 percent Baltic Porter, a Hibiscus Wheat Ale, and a British IPA, a 5.8 percent beer that uses English ingredients and has the earthy notes of that interpretation of the style.

At the end of our conversation, I asked Murphy to describe the differences between working in a production brewery such as Lighthouse and working in a brewpub. He replied using a metaphor that reflected his studies of the arts and creative writing: "I think it's the difference between acting in a film and on the stage. In a production brewery, you don't see the audience, and the goal is to make the beer the same all the time, just as a film is constant from viewing to viewing. In a brewpub, you are on the stage, and the audience is usually just a few metres away from the brewery. You're getting constant feedback." He also emphasized that he was not the only player on the stage and paid credit to the work of Kyle York, who started at Canoe as a bartender and was now an assistant brewer.

If the positive responses Murphy has been receiving over the last few years are any indication, he will, to use a theatre metaphor, be "treading the boards" of his stage, the Canoe brewhouse, for some time to come.

CHAPTER 2

VICTORIA'S PIONEER CRAFT BREWERIES

Vancouver Island Brewing Company,
Lighthouse Brewing Company,
Phillips Brewing and Malting Company

After Labatt shuttered its Victoria operations in 1981, it didn't take long for the capital city to acquire a new production brewery. Then Victoria mayor Peter Pollen approached a group of Victoria businessmen about opening a locally owned brewery in the now-vacant building. However, Labatt, wanting to keep competition for its beer to a minimum, demolished the structure. John Hellemond, one of those businessmen who had been approached, then formed a group of investors to build a new brewery. Named Island Pacific Brewing, it opened in 1985 in Saanichton, only a few blocks from where Category 12 now operates. It was renamed Vancouver Island Brewery in 1992 and **Vancouver Island Brewing** 25 years later.

Its first beer was Goldstream Lager, a European style that was a crossover beer to be sold on draft to both pubs and restaurants. At the time, only bottled beer could be sold at restaurants, and so the owners successfully lobbied the provincial government to change the law so that they could sell their products, which were available only on draft. Craft brewing pioneer Frank Appleton helped set up the brewery and develop the first beer, but it soon became apparent that a full-time brewer would be needed. German-trained Hermann Hoerterer was hired late in 1985 and developed the company's second and third beers: Piper's Pale Ale, named after a Victoria resident who had died a heroic death during the First World War, and Hermann's Dark Lager.

"In the 1990s, we reached a wide range of beer drinkers," said Barry Fisher, when I interviewed him in 2010. One of the original owners, he had been CEO from 1988 to 2008. "People at the University of Victoria Faculty Club would be drinking Hermann's Dark Lager, and downtown, younger professionals would have our regular lager, which was much more flavourful than the mainstream varieties."

Bottling began in 1992, and by the middle of the 1990s, the brewery had outgrown its small facility in Saanichton. In 1996, it moved to its current location on Government Street, just a few blocks north of the old Lucky Lager plant. Early in the new century, the brewery began offering its main beers in cans, but lacking a canning line, it initially transported its beer to Prince George, where it was packaged at Pacific Western Brewing. Canning began at the Government Street location in 2006.

By the beginning of the second decade of the 21st century, Vancouver Island Brewery produced four core beers. Given that many of its customers were crossover drinkers with limited experience with craft beer styles, offering something too different would have been difficult. "We used to offer a wheat beer, but a lot of people didn't like it," remarked Ralf Pittroff, a German-trained brewer who had visited the brewery while on a Canadian vacation, then returned in 1995 as a brewer and became head brewer in 2001. "The wheat beer was the same colour as the beer they drink, but it tasted very different."

People who tried Hermann's Dark Lager, a schwarzbier, were told not to be afraid of the dark. And in 2010, when Sea Dog was created to honour the 100th anniversary of the Royal Canadian Navy, it was presented as an amber ale. "It was really an altbier, which is a traditional

German style," Pittroff explained. "But *alt* means 'old' in German, and we thought that if we used that word it might scare people off."

The four year-round beers available in 2010 and for a few years after included Islander Lager, the latest in a number of successors to the original Goldstream Lager; Piper's Pale Ale; Hermann's Dark Lager; and Skyhopper Honey Brown Ale. Each was a solid, mainstream craft beer, but none could be credited with being adventurous, with pushing the brewing boundaries. Nonetheless, Piper's Pale Ale, Islander Lager, Hermannator Ice Bock, Hermann's Dark Lager, and Sea Dog Amber all picked up Canadian Brewing Awards gold medals. The brewery also won four silver and five bronze medals.

By the beginning of the 2010s, with Phillips creating very hoppy IPAs, Driftwood introducing Belgian-style ales, and Moon Under Water making German-style lagers, Vancouver Island was beginning to seem, as one experienced beer drinker told me, "like the beer your grandfather drank," a phrase used to describe the bland beers that dominated the beer scene before the beginnings of the craft brewing movement. Something had to change.

And it did—in the spring of 2016. Barry Fisher sold his majority interest in Vancouver Island Brewery to Bob MacDonald, the owner of Muskoka Brewery in Bracebridge, Ontario. When MacDonald had assumed ownership of the Ontario brewery in 2008, its sales were sluggish. He was instrumental in rebranding it and bringing about a significant increase in sales. Tim Barnes, who, as vice-president of sales and marketing at Surrey's Central City Brewers and Distillers, had been responsible for an over 300 percent increase of sales there, came on as Vancouver Island's president. Although Ralf Pittroff remained as head brewer, Danny Seeton, a member of Vancouver brewery Parallel 49's award-winning brew crew, was named production manager and director of research and development. Changes began to take place immediately: the lineup of beers was altered, and recipes for the old brands that were retained were revised. A clean, new logo for the brewery, which was renamed Vancouver Island Brewing (instead of

Brewery), was designed to appear on bottles and cans. "We discovered that we weren't relevant to the current craft beer consumer," Barnes remarked when the rebranding was complete in 2017.

The morning after I'd chatted with Daniel Murphy at Canoe, I walked up Government Street, past Chinatown, and past the site of the old Lucky Lager brewery to Vancouver Island Brewing, where I would meet two of the people who were responsible for reshaping the destiny of the Island's oldest production brewery. The building, which had been custom-built in 1996, didn't look much different from how it had looked when I last visited it nearly a decade ago. The most noticeable changes were the new VI logo on the side of the building and a growler-filling station in the front lobby.

I was met by Ralf Pittroff, now in his 23rd year with the brewery, and Danny Seeton, who laughingly noted that he hadn't even been born

when the brewery had been founded. (I learned that Tim Barnes had left Vancouver Island Brewing a few weeks earlier to take a position with the Calgary Airport Authority.) We proceeded to a second-floor conference room, which overlooked a very large room containing the bottling and canning lines, sat at a long table, and talked about the changes that had taken place. Pittroff began by remembering Victoria's beer culture in the mid-1990s, a time when, he said, they often had difficulty getting people to try such relatively mild beers as European lagers and low-hopped English-style pale ales. "People are very educated about craft beer now," he said. "They want new beers."

New beers—that's what Pittroff and Seeton had begun working on in the summer of 2016. "First, we cut any of our failing brands. Then we decided to make everything a craft beer and to make sure we used the finest ingredients," Seeton explained. One of the first victims was Islander Lager, known in the trade as a "value-priced" (i.e., cheap) beer, the kind of beer in which the "best-quality ingredients" aren't that top-quality and may include inexpensive alternatives to malted grain. Hermann's Dark Lager made the cut, although it acquired a new name, Dominion Dark Lager. A 4.8 percent ABV schwarzbier, it has a recipe slightly different from Hermann's. "We used some roasted wheat to soften the character and give it a lighter colour. It's not so malty as before, and the addition of hops late in the boil cuts the malt sweetness."

Two new lagers were added to the lineup. They are based on old styles, but they are definitely not "the beer your grandfather drank." Victoria Lager (4.8 percent ABV) is a Dortmunder export, a northern German beer that is a rich gold in colour, more malt-forward than many lagers and fuller-bodied. Juan de Fuca Cerveza (4.8 percent ABV) is based on a Mexican style (itself based on Austria's Vienna lager) that has recently become very popular among Canadian and American craft beer drinkers. Flaked maize and Vienna malts provide notes of corn and grain. In the 10 months since its release, Juan de Fuca has become

Ralf Pittroff (left) and Danny Seeton oversee brewing operations at Vancouver Island Brewing Company, the oldest craft brewery on the Island. ←

Vancouver Island's top-selling offering. As Pittroff noted, this beer is an example of the brewery's moving a little bit away from relative "safe" interpretations of styles: "It's not wild, but it is different."

Piper's Pale Ale was another beer that made the cut, but it, too, underwent changes. "We wanted to make it a traditional English ale, rather than trying to fit it into the American pale ale style, which is very popular along the West Coast." To do that, they used English ingredients: Maris Otter malts, which contribute rich, nutty flavours, and Fuggle and East Kent Golding hops, which add earthy/woody and spicy/honey characteristics, respectively.

"We wanted to give people an English pub beer," Seeton said of the 4.8 percent ABV, 27 IBU ale. What a perfect fit for Victoria, where English-style pub culture is alive and well. A cask-conditioned version of Piper's is being considered.

The new lineup of year-round beers does not embrace the high alcohol and extreme hopping that have been trendy over the last two decades. Royston Rye IPA, which has an alcohol content of 6.5 percent ABV and an IBU rating of 65, is the exception. The rye gives the beer spicy notes, and the hops provide citrusy flavours that balance the strong malt basis of the beer. Vancouver Island Brewing's entry into the session IPA market is named 19 IPA, a low-alcohol ale that has become very popular with people who like their beers hoppy, but not too strong. It's 4.8 percent ABV but registers 47 IBUs and is brewed with Chinook hops, a standby in craft brewing, along with such relative newcomers as Ahtanum, Mosaic, and Citra hops, and has flavours described as citrusy and floral.

Seasonal releases include Hermannator Ice Bock (9.5 percent ABV), a favourite winter beer for 30 years (and in 2017 also released as a limited edition that is barrel aged); Juniper Lime Ale (7 percent ABV), a summer release; and Burton Ale, brewed in collaboration with Courtenay's Gladstone Brewing, a 7 percent ABV tribute to the English brewery renowned for its IPAs.

Although its limited-edition, 650-millilitre bottle releases do take it beyond the middle-of-the-road landscape that has been its territory for over three decades, Vancouver Island Brewing does not generally range into the adventurous—some would say risky—territory of extreme beer. However, by reinventing its "old" beers and by creating new beers that are its interpretations of classic styles of days gone by, the brewery has definitely moved far beyond being the producer of ales and lagers that some people referred to as being "like the beer your grandfather drank."

Instead of walking a couple of blocks south to Phillips Brewing and Malting, the third oldest of Victoria's production breweries, I drove a couple of kilometres to an industrial area in the northern area of the municipality of Esquimalt to pay a visit to the second oldest, **Lighthouse Brewing**, which was founded in 1998. One of the company's first beers had been called Beacon, but unfortunately there wasn't any guiding light to help me find the place. I headed east along Devonshire Road past many buildings, none of them with a sign saying "Lighthouse Brewing," and I got lost. Just before I came to a building that housed a business called Signs Victoria, I happened to glance up a driveway, and there, behind the street-side building, was my destination. The brewery building didn't look much different from what it had in 2009 when I had visited then co-owner Paul Hoyne, brother of Swans' and then Canoe's Sean Hoyne. There were several loading docks, three or four visitor parking spaces, and a few steps leading up to the office area. However, there had been changes: Paul Hoyne had left the company; the front counter had been replaced by a retail area with a growler-filling station; and beyond the office area, the brewhouse had been expanded greatly.

During my first visit, Hoyne had told me that Lighthouse had been formed when he, Gerry Hieter (founder of Whistler Brewing), and Dave Thomas, a local restaurant owner, had decided to open a brewery that offered beers that were less mainstream than those Vancouver Island was brewing. "Because of Spinnakers, Swans, and Canoe, Victoria's beer drinkers had developed a palate for craft brews, but their beers were only available on premises. We would be a production-only brewery."

On August 18, 1998, Race Rocks Ale (named after an island in the Strait of Juan de Fuca that had a lighthouse on it) was delivered to Victoria-area bars. An amber ale, a style popular among American craft drinkers, Race Rocks marked a departure from the predominantly English styles available at Spinnakers and Swans. There followed three more beers: Beacon IPA, Keepers Stout, and the simply named Lager. "We weren't trying to shock or threaten drinkers, but to make really flavourful beers," Hoyne said. The lineup remained unchanged until 2008, when Riptide Pale Ale was introduced. Two years later, Fisgard 150 Bavarian Lager joined the lineup. Also unchanged when I met Hoyne were the recipes, which, he told me, were "written in stone."

In 2004, Lighthouse began to package its product. It was decided to use cans rather than bottles, something unusual in the craft beer industry at that time. "Cans are less expensive, they keep the beer fresher, they're easier to transport, and they're more environmentally friendly," Hoyne explained. Within a year the brewery's sales had doubled, and by 2010, annual production had reached 12,000 hectolitres. However, by this time, Lighthouse's solid, middle-of-the-road craft beers faced competition. Phillips Brewing and Driftwood Brewery had developed beers that pushed the craft beer envelope. Lighthouse entered the second decade of the 21st century faced with the need to change its beers and image.

In 2018, I met with assistant general manager Ben Thomas in the same small conference room in which Paul Hoyne had told me about the recipes being written in stone. "We needed a complete change if we were to appeal to the evolving beer culture," Thomas said. "In 2008, Riptide Pale Ale was a kind of ripple of the changes to come. Then, in 2009, we installed a bottling line. We could now do special releases and package them in 650-millilitre bottles."

Thomas referred to the years from 2010 to 2014 as "the era of the big shift, both in beers and attitude." First, Lighthouse hired Dean McLeod as head brewer. A New Zealander, McLeod had worked in Australia, where the craft beer scene had expanded both rapidly and in new and

exciting directions. Before
he left Lighthouse in 2016, he
developed over 40 new beer
recipes, including a Belgian
golden ale, several saisons,

Assistant general manager Ben Thomas (left)
and then head brewer Adam March stand
before shelves displaying the many types of
beers brewed and the awards won by Lighthouse
Brewing since it was founded in 1998. ↑

many barrel-aged beers, sour beers, a kolsch, and a Scottish ale. From 2011
to 2013, Lighthouse won two silver and two bronze Canadian Brewing
Awards medals, two of them for what might be called "different" beers:
Navigator Doppelbock and Overboard Imperial Pilsner. In 2012, a new
25-hectolitre brewhouse was installed, allowing the brewers to meet
increased demand for their beers and to put some new zip into the old
core brands. "We didn't really change the recipes that much, but the new
equipment allowed the true, original recipes to shine through. Our beers
got a lot cleaner," Thomas declared.

Major rebranding came in 2014. The can labels were redesigned to
resemble painted lighthouse towers, and the beers were grouped in series

given special names. The House Series included Beacon IPA, Race Rocks Ale, and Bowline Pilsner. The Explorer Series, which Thomas described as having beers that "were more exciting, more out there," included Tasman Pale Ale, Seaport Vanilla Stout, and Shipwreck IPA. "Shipwreck really got us into the IPA market," he remarked. The Uncharted Series was a group of beers that were "even more interesting and more out there." The most noteworthy of these is the Numbskull group of imperial IPAs, each one showcasing one hop variety. Sales increased, and in 2016, Lighthouse expanded again, installing a 50-hectolitre brewing system.

When I visited, Lighthouse's brew crew was led by Adam March, an Ottawa native who had never intended to enter the brewing profession. He'd been a Molson and Coors drinker when he went to St. Francis Xavier University in Nova Scotia to study business administration. "My roommate's father owned a homebrew shop," March told me. "So we began to homebrew and started experimenting with different styles." It was when he'd graduated and returned to Ottawa to work in product management for a tech firm that he realized he really wanted to be a brewer. So he enrolled in the two-year Brewmaster and Brewery Operations Management program at Ontario's Niagara College. "They had a 10-barrel brewery on campus, and once a week we spent a whole day brewing. Each week we'd learn about a different style. It was like working in a small professional brewery." Two years ago, after graduation, he joined Lighthouse. (Several weeks after our conversation, March left Lighthouse to take a brewing job in his hometown. Darrin Gano, who had worked for several years at the Labatt Brewing plant in Edmonton and who had joined Lighthouse in 2014, took over as head brewer.)

Before he described several of the brewery's beers, March emphasized: "Style is not as important as flavour." Race Rocks Ale (5.2 percent ABV) is still the flagship ale, but it is second in sales to Shipwreck IPA. Darker than most amber beers, it is brewed with Munich, crystal, and chocolate malts to give it a rich flavour, highlighted by coffee and chocolate notes. English hops balance the malt richness and create a clean, crisp finish. Shipwreck IPA (6.5 percent ABV, 65 IBUs), what March called the brewery's game-changer, is a hop-forward West Coast version of the style. "The Galaxy hops are the star of the show," he remarked, "and contribute some fruit, citrus, and tropical fruit flavours. It's lighter in malts than many IPAs, and it's not a palate wrecker."

Keepers Stout (5.1 percent ABV), which, along with Race Rocks, is one of the Lighthouse originals, is what March called a classic Irish stout. "We use dark but not overroasted malts, so the beer is not bitter. You'll taste some espresso and dark chocolate." Bowline Pilsner (5 percent ABV) is also a classic example of its style. More German than Czechoslovakian, it uses two of the so-called noble hops, Tettnang and Saaz, to create a beer that is lightly spicy and refreshing. Tasman Pale Ale (4.6 percent ABV, 22 IBUs) uses four Tasmanian and New Zealand hops. Among the latter are Motueka hops, which provide lime and tropical fruit flavours for this sessionable, light-bodied, North American–style pale ale. Citrus Shore Session Ale (4.6 percent ABV) also emphasizes flavour with the Mandarina hops providing a slightly sweet tangerine taste.

Metaphorically speaking, it could be said that a decade ago, the beam from Lighthouse was flickering. But now, through the recapturing of the original recipes' intent, the addition of several new and very sessionable beers to the core lineup, and the creation of such interesting "out there" one-offs as Numbskull ElDorado Imperial IPA (9.1 percent ABV) and Depth Charge Oak Aged Belgian Quad with Cognac (9.2 percent ABV), the beam is again shining brightly.

My third stop of the day was back on Government Street, south of Vancouver Island Brewing. I was a little early for my appointment at **Phillips Brewing and Malting** and decided to take a walk around the block, starting in the parking lot at the brewery's small retail store. Just as Lighthouse had, it looked pretty much the same as when I'd visited several years ago, except that the sign above the door now read "Phillips

Brewing and Malting." After I'd walked north on Government Street and turned left on Pembroke Street, I discovered something really different. At the east side of what had been a large parking lot and loading area stood two rows of large stainless steel tanks. It was a forest of fermenters, and their presence was an indication of the rapid increase in production Phillips had experienced in recent years. Construction was going on in another section of the parking lot. I continued my walk, and when I reached the intersection of Discovery and Government, I noticed that the windows of a building on the northwest corner were covered with brown paper and that official-looking notices taped onto the windows announced some kind of city hearing. The building, which had been the home of Nirvana Pet Resort, would become, when the very lengthy process of rezoning and permitting had been completed, Phillips Brewing's expanded tasting room and retail store. (The tasting room opened in April, several weeks after my visit.)

Phillips Brewing and Malting, after the renovations had taken place and the new retail space opened, would be much different from the small space in an Esquimalt warehouse where, in 2001, Matt Phillips had opened his eponymous brewery. When he was studying microbiology at Mount Allison University in New Brunswick, he and his buddies would frequently pile in a car and head to the nearest liquor store across the border in Maine, where they'd buy as many different craft beers as they could find. He also homebrewed. "There are a lot of connections between microbiology and brewing," he told me several years ago. "I loved the brewing process and experimenting and devising new recipes." He realized that he wanted to become a professional brewer and headed west, where the craft brewing scene was larger and more active than in the Maritimes. His first stop was Grizzly Paw Brewing in Canmore, Alberta; then Whistler, where he worked at Whistler Brewing at night and as a ski instructor by day; and then Victoria, where he first worked at Spinnakers.

"I'd dreamed of owning my own brewery for a long time," Phillips remembered. "I wanted to make interesting beers my own way. When my tenure at Spinnakers ended in the late 1990s, I decided it was time to make the step. Victoria was the place to do it; the water was excellent for brewing, and there was a very knowledgeable beer culture. There had been a slowdown in the craft brewing movement; quite a few breweries had gone out of business, and so there was a fair amount of used equipment around at a pretty good price."

Although equipment was fairly easy to come by, funding wasn't. Banks kept turning loan applications down, so he filled out several credit card applications, which were accepted, and then maxed the cards out. He purchased a seven-hectolitre system, and when he couldn't find a bottling machine, he cobbled one together himself. He set up his brewery in warehouse space in Esquimalt, where he brewed and slept (he showered at a nearby gym). Phillips Brewing opened for business in the summer of 2001 and produced 400 hectolitres of beer during the first year. Matt Phillips was the brewer, packager, salesman, and deliveryman. He'd often take the last ferry of the night from the Island to the mainland, park outside the liquor distribution centre and, when it opened, unload his bottles, head back to the ferry, and start the business all over again. His first beers were an espresso stout, a raspberry wheat, and an IPA. "At that time, these were esoteric beers; they were different, and you couldn't get anything like them around here."

The first few years saw Phillips walking the thin line "between success and bankruptcy." But business grew, and in June 2004, he moved his brewery—partly because he needed more space and partly because, after one of the tanks burst, his landlord suggested that he should relocate. Phoenix Gold Lager, which had been named for a brewery in what is now a ghost town in the province's Interior, was the best-selling product. In 2005, Phillips gained national recognition as his beers won three gold medals, two silvers, and a bronze at the Canadian Brewing Awards. One of the golds was awarded to Phoenix, which has since been retired. Production grew to 4,000 hectolitres the following year. The old blue step van that had made so many trips to Vancouver proved inadequate for the job and was retired, and in 2008, business was so brisk that Phillips moved operations to the present location.

I was in the small retail space looking at a painting that resembled the *Mona Lisa* but was a portrait of a blue buck that had given its name to what is now the brewery's top-selling beer, when Matt Phillips greeted me. He'd been 27 when he first started the brewery, and there was more salt and pepper in his hair now than when we'd first met in 2009. But his face still reflected the friendliness and youthful enthusiasm that I remembered. He led me through a door at the back of the retail space and up the stairs that led to his second-floor office. I glanced at the brewhouse, which was much more crowded with equipment than I remembered it having been. I noticed nearby a large copper kettle, which I learned was used in distilling gin and whisky for one of the company's newer branches, Fermentorium Distilling Company.

When Phillips had moved to Government Street in 2008, the website had reported, "Even though Phillips has moved to a bigger facility, the same small kettle setup and small brewing ensures the freshest ales and lagers hit your lips on a regular basis." Those days are gone forever. Although the beers are as good as ever, much more of it is made (the company does not release annual production figures). Each of the 23 fermentation tanks in the parking lot has a 240-hectolitre capacity. Two of them would hold more beer than Phillips produced back in 2001. In 2017, 73 different beers were brewed.

We discussed the changes that had taken place since I'd visited in 2009. In describing the brewery in the second decade of the 21st century, he used the terms "evolution" and "expansion." In 2012, Phillips began canning many of its beers, a move that led to a fresher, more easily transportable product. Two years later, the company created the Fermentorium, making a gin using BC natural ingredients and distilling whisky, which would be aged for three years before release.

In 2015, Phillips fulfilled a long-time dream when the brewery began making its own malt, the only Canadian brewery to do so. "Brewers want to control as much of the brewing process from beginning to end as they can. We have much more quality control, and we can also custom make malts for specific recipes." He contracted Vancouver Island grain farmers to supply barley and assembled a malting facility that can produce 20 tonnes of malt in a week. By the beginning of 2018, in-house malts—both base malts and specialty malts—met 60 percent of the brewery's needs. In 2018, a new 120-hectolitre brewing system, locally manufactured by Specific Mechanical Systems in nearby Saanichton, was installed. Not only did it increase the volume of beer Phillips could produce, but also it did so more efficiently and in a more environmentally friendly way. The next step in the expansion and evolution process would come when the large tasting room and retail area opened next door.

The brewery has increased not only its production and the number

Matt Phillips stands in a "forest" of fermenting tanks "planted" in what used to be the employee parking and loading area of the brewery that bears his name. Founded in 2001 with himself as the only employee, Phillips Brewing and Malting has grown in less than two decades into one of the largest craft breweries in British Columbia. ↓

of beer styles it puts out, but also its number of employees—there are now over 100 people to do what Phillips did alone in 2001—and range of distribution. Phillips's beers are available throughout British Columbia and in Alberta and Ontario. But equally important in Phillips's mind, as he notes with pride, is the fact the brewery has worked hard on being environmentally friendly. Malting in-house lessens the carbon footprint; no longer is malt shipped from the Prairies. The efficiency of the new brewing system enables less water to be used in the brewing process, steam to be recaptured for reuse, and carbon dioxide generated by fermentation to be captured and reused. Heat generated by the refrigeration plant used to cool the beers is also used to keep the offices warm. And, as is the case in many breweries, area livestock producers pick up the spent grain to feed their animals.

The number of year-round Phillips beers has increased from 4 in 2010 to 13 in 2018. Two of these, the top-selling Blue Buck Ale and the simply named Pilsner, have interesting backstories. The former had been called Blue Truck, after the retired delivery van, until Red Truck Beer Company of North Vancouver issued a cease-and-desist order, claiming that the names were so similar as to create confusion. Phillips decided to cease and desist and in the process created much good publicity for the beer and the brewery. A very convincing story about a legendary blue animal was created, and the beer was named in its honour. In June 2016, in order to publicize the release of its newly created Pilsner, the brewery announced that two lucky people who had won a draw would have bottles of the beer delivered to them by a trained bald eagle. When the government refused to allow the promotion, a drone decorated to look like an eagle made the delivery. A picture was released of the eagle, whose name was Hercules, standing in front of a control board, supposedly operating the drone. The event was published in newspapers and reported on radio and television across the country and in the United States.

"We love hops," Phillips commented, as we began discussing the beers themselves. "But we are more concerned with malts—we want to showcase them. We want our malts to perform better so that we can achieve a variety of effects." And, although the core beers could be grouped as either malt-forward or hop-centric, the malts do play an important role in all of them. The famous Blue Buck Ale (5 percent ABV), an amber ale, has been mistaken for a pale ale because it is hoppier than most versions of the style. However, its darker colour and medium body, along with a caramel sweetness and a hint of roasted malts, put it into the amber category. Cascade hops do provide a balance to the malty sweetness. Slipstream Cream Ale (also 5 percent ABV) has caramel and coffee notes and is lightly hopped. Medium-bodied, this copper-brown ale is both smooth and clean. Analogue 78 Kolsch and Pilsner (both 5 percent ABV), while they are light-bodied and have a crispness and what someone called "a tingle on the tongue," also have a malty sweetness.

The love of hops is exhibited in the seven core beers that are listed on the website as either pale ales or IPAs. At the end of my visit, Phillips would present me with a Hop Box, which contained four of the brewery's most popular hoppy beers. Phillips's flagship IPA, Hop Circle (6.5 percent ABV), first released in 2010, is both citrusy and resiny and has malty notes that make it seem more English than West Coast. Electric Unicorn White IPA (6 percent ABV) was released two years later and has lemon and coriander notes, along with the banana and bubblegum flavours found in Belgian beers. Bottle Rocket India Session Ale (4.5 percent ABV), released in 2013, is Phillips's entry into a style that has become popular in the last seven or eight years, the session IPA, a hoppy beer that is low in alcohol. It is definitely hop-forward, with no noticeable malti-ness. Short Wave West Coast Pale Ale (5 percent ABV), a 2015 release, is a medium-bodied, balanced beer, in which the malts and citrusy hops complement each other. Its piney, resinous notes maybe come from the use of Cascade hops, which over three decades earlier, had given California's renowned Sierra Nevada Pale Ale its distinctive flavour. Other hoppy beers regularly available include Citricity Grapefruit Zest IPA, Thunder Punch Unfiltered IPA, and Amnesiac Double IPA.

"We want our core beers to be consistent, high quality, and drink-able," Phillips remarked. "Our seasonal beers and special releases are sometimes a bit out there." There are a number of single-hopped beers, showcasing the qualities of specific hop varieties; sour beers; Belgian-style ales; and barrel-aged beers. Over 61 new beers have been released since 2015, and many bear very interesting names: Space Goat Dry Hopped Oat Pale Ale, Heifer Bison Blackberry, and Sky High Grand Fir Ale (brewed with fir boughs).

Matt Phillips is proud of all of the beers that have come out of his brewery, especially those that have garnered Canadian Brewing Awards—21 in all. But there is one category of beer for which he feels a special pride, Phillips Benefit Brew, which has been brewed annually since 2012. Members of the community (in British Columbia and, since 2015, in Alberta) nominate charitable organizations and then vote for one of 10 finalists. A special beer named after the winning charity is brewed, and all the proceeds are donated to the charity. In 2018, the winning charities were YamnuskaWolfdog Sanctuary in Alberta and the BC SPCA Wild Animal Rehabilitation Centre.

Our interview completed, Phillips showed me around the brewery, pointing out, among other things, the large, new, environmentally friendly brewing system. As we walked through the forest of fermenters that I'd noticed during my walk around the block, I asked him how long expansion would continue and how large the brewery might become. He replied, "The larger we get, the more cool things we can do; we can experiment. But we want to be sure to do things that make our beer better." I felt that, for Phillips, it wasn't just a matter of bigger is better. Bigger would be better only if the beers were even better than they are now.

CHAPTER 3

VICTORIA'S CRAFT BEER SCENE EXPANDS

Driftwood Brewery,
Moon Under Water Brewery and Pub,
Hoyne Brewing Company,
Île Sauvage Brewing Company

After 2001, when Phillips Brewing began operations, it was seven years before another brewery opened in Victoria. Then, between late 2008 and the end of 2011, two breweries and one brewpub appeared on the scene, all of them located within three blocks of each other in the Rock Bay district, several blocks north of downtown. In 2008, three former employees of Lighthouse Brewing began Driftwood Brewery; then in 2010, Moon Under Water, the capital city's fourth brewpub, began offering beer and food. A year later, Sean Hoyne, long-time brewer at Swans and then Canoe, started the brewery that bears his own name.

The day after I'd stopped in at the pioneer craft breweries, I visited what many people are calling the "brewery district." When I arrived at the block northwest of Hillside Avenue and Bridge Street, there was no parking available on the street or in the parking area between the buildings housing Driftwood Brewery and Hoyne Brewing Company. A semi delivering to a building on the south side of Hillside completely blocked the street. Smaller trucks were either loading or unloading in front of Driftwood; a farmer was loading his truck with very large containers of spent grain from Hoyne, and one of that brewery's trucks waited to get out onto the street.

Squeezing my compact car into a very small parking space I found a block away, I returned to the busy scene, mounted the stairs to the loading platform of **Driftwood Brewery**, stepped around a pallet loaded with just-delivered packages of hops, and went to the tiny office, which was once the business headquarters of the brewery. When Driftwood opened in 2008, it occupied less than half of the building; now it occupies all of it. In addition, it has warehouse space and an expanded office elsewhere in town. Entering the little office, I was greeted by Susie, a cocker spaniel who had been little more than a puppy when I had first dropped in at Driftwood near the beginning of 2009. I was also greeted by two of the three owners, Jason Meyer and Kevin Hearsum.

Meyer and Hearsum had met when they were brewers at Lighthouse; the third partner, Gary Lindsay, was also a Lighthouse employee, working in the sales department. There, the first two helped to make, while Gary helped to sell, Lighthouse's four products, the beers whose recipes were "written in stone." Meyer remembered that the work was fairly routine, but that part-owner Paul Hoyne had allowed the brewers after-hours use of the small test-brewing system. "This gave us a creative outlet, a relief from the routine. Then I'd go back to my home and homebrew on the weekends," Meyer recalled.

Being creative about beer had been part of Jason Meyer's makeup since the late 1980s, when he sampled Alberta's first craft beer, Big Rock Traditional Ale, and also began homebrewing, discovering and brewing styles that weren't commercially available, tinkering with recipes, always thinking outside of the box. He'd read Michael Jackson's *Great Beers of Belgium* and tried various Belgian styles when a non-beer-related job sent him to Europe, and he began making them himself. "I always liked pairing beer with food, and Belgian beers go really well with food," he said, remembering those days. "And I liked the fact that Belgian beers weren't rigidly defined by styles. You could be experimental, creative."

Early in the 1990s, one of Edmonton's leading homebrewers, Neil Herbst, set up Alley Kat Brewing, which produced far more creative and interesting beers than were being churned out at the gigantic Labatt brewery a few kilometres away. Herbst invited Meyer to become a member of his team, and so Jason got his start in professional brewing. There followed stints at McAuslan Brewing in Montreal and then Lighthouse, before Meyer and his two friends decided to strike out on their own.

"The people of Victoria had been enjoying a range of really good beers for a quarter of a century," Meyer remarked. "They had developed very discriminating palates. We felt that they would be prepared for something that was new to them, even if the styles were centuries old." However, the first beer Driftwood offered in the fall of 2008 was Meyer's version of pale ale, a style that has been popular in Victoria since Spinnakers opened in 1984. Driftwood Ale—now known as New Growth Canadian Pale Ale (5 percent ABV)—is a beer not dissimilar to Sierra Nevada's ground-breaking Pale Ale. The hops for the recipe came from Sartori Cedar Ranch in the Fraser Valley.

Before the end of the brewery's first year, Meyer and Hearsum had created two Belgian-style beers. White Bark Wheat Ale (5 percent ABV) is a straw-coloured beer that uses ground coriander and Curaçao orange peel; the wheat gives a slightly chewy feel. With Farmhand Ale, they moved into what, for most Victoria drinkers, was new territory. This dark gold, 5 percent ABV beer is a saison or farmhouse ale, traditionally brewed in Belgium for consumption by fieldworkers during the hot summer months. It has a tartness and a spicy taste, contributed in part by the fresh ground pepper it contains. The yeasts—"Belgian beers are all about the yeasts," Kevin Hearsum remarked to me several years ago—contribute fruity notes to the complex flavours.

The fourth of Driftwood's year-round beers, Crooked Coast (5 percent ABV), was an altbier ("old beer"), a German style that was developed before lager yeasts had been discovered. "We wanted something that used classic German hops (in this case Tettnang) and a beer that didn't require lagering because, at first, we didn't have the space to lager beers," Meyer explained, referring to the process of cold storage involved in making lagers. The dark wheat and Munich malts give this amber ale a rich caramel flavour, which is balanced by the crispness of the hops. Each of these beers is still on Driftwood's core list. Other year-round beers now include Naughty Hildegard, an ESB with 6.5 percent ABV, and Arcus, a 5 percent ABV German-style pilsner.

When we first met, Meyer had told me "In the 1980s, the early microbrewers were seen as radical; now we are. But if we're to succeed, we have to set our standards high—not sell something

In 2008, three former employees of Lighthouse Brewing, (left to right) Gary Lindsay, Jason Meyer, and Kevin Hearsum, founded Driftwood Brewery, which quickly became one of Vancouver Island's most successful breweries. ↓

just different, but something of high quality." The brewery's first full-year sales of 1,200 hectolitres indicated that they were doing that. In 2010, sales doubled, and Driftwood released a beer that would firmly establish the brewery as a force to be reckoned with in the British Columbia craft beer scene. In late October, Fat Tug IPA was greeted by the public with great praise. In 2011, only months after its release, it was named Beer of the Year at the Canadian Brewing Awards. It sold so well that expansion of the brewery became necessary in 2012. It also paid the bills for the development of such other releases as The Last Aurochs (weizenbock), Cry Me a River (gose), Entangled (hopfenweisse), and Clodhopper (Belgian dubbel).

"We'd always wanted to have an IPA," Meyer told me on my current visit. "But when we opened in 2008, there was a shortage of hops. We couldn't get the quantity of quality hops we would need. Even now, we adjust our recipe around what good hops are available. Our recipes aren't written in stone." The hops are certainly the star of the show in Fat Tug and include Cascade, Columbus, Centennial, Citra, and Amarillo, which have been leading ingredients in the very popular hoppy beers being brewed along the West Coast of Canada and the United States. They provide grapefruit, mango, melon, and passion fruit notes. "We pushed the beer to the edge, but not over," he said, referring to the 7 percent alcohol content and the 80 IBUs. "When you have big hops, you need a malt balance." The crystal malts provide caramel notes; the Carapils malts, body, a smooth mouthfeel, and head retention.

We chatted briefly about the term "local" as it applied to beer. "We use local ingredients when we can," Meyer remarked and mentioned Pilsner Doehnel, made with barley grown and then malted less than 20 kilometres from the brewery on the Saanich Peninsula, and Sartori Harvest, a fresh-hopped IPA using Centennial hops grown at Sartori Cedar Ranch on the mainland. "But," he continued, "our hop consumption is enormous, more than all the hops grown in BC. The ingredients for beer travel much better than those for wine, and hops and malts require different growing conditions. Most of our malt comes from the prairie regions. But what is local is our connection with our customers. The craft beer movement was born out of the idea of making beer that can be consumed as close to where it is made as possible." He went on to note that the majority of Driftwood's customers are on Vancouver Island.

We finished our conversation by discussing the philosophy behind Driftwood's beers. "We brew beers that excite us, beers that are fun to drink. We brew what we want. We don't study market surveys. The product is first; it's more important than branding. When we think of creating a new beer or altering a recipe, all of the brewers contribute to the discussion. We don't use the term 'head brewer' or 'brewmaster'—everyone is part of the team. And none of us is averse to breaking the rules, to trying something new. But we have to be constantly vigilant; we have to avoid the danger of hubris. We don't want to be yesterday's news; we don't want to rest on our laurels. That why it's important to always have creative, excited, talented people around."

Jason Meyer is proud of the beers his team makes and of the craft beer movement in general. "Craft beer delivers a high-end gastro experience at a reasonable price. It's democratizing, not snobbish. Beer has earned its place at the table with wine—literally and figuratively."

When I left Driftwood, it was time for lunch, so I walked three blocks down to Bay Street and over to **Moon Under Water Brewery and Pub**. When Don and Bonnie Bradley, who in the late 1990s had founded Bowen Island Brewing, opened the pub in 2010, people wondered why they chose an area that was considered a gritty industrial district. They emphasized the positive aspects of the location: the nearby businesses would be the source of a lunchtime crowd; the pub's being on the main route to the near suburbs of Victoria West and Esquimalt would entice people to stop on their way home after work to have a pint, have their growlers refilled, or pick up a couple of bottles. Moreover, it was a short walk from harbour-side condominiums, the harbour ferry, and the popular Galloping Goose hiking trail.

"I wanted an English-style pub," Don Bradley told me in 2011, "a place where people could enjoy good food and beer, where we weren't just selling alcohol, but a social experience." In fact, the name was chosen because it was what English author George Orwell called his ideal pub in a 1946 essay. At the Bradleys' Moon, people would walk up to the bar, as they did in English pubs, and order pub-style comfort food and English-style ales (brewed by Don's nephew Ron). These included a ploughman's lunch and an ESB.

Things had changed by the time of my 2018 visit. You could now order beer and food at your table, and since 2012, the Moon had new owners. ESB wasn't on the beer list, nor ploughman's lunch on the menu. I enjoyed a Potts Pils and a bowl of carrot-ginger soup, and then I visited with the new owners, Clay Potter and his mother, Anne Farmer. Potter headed brewing operations, assisted by Jeff Koehl and Patrick Sand; Farmer, the business office. Potter's stepfather, Steve Ash, ran the Moon's recently opened distillery.

Potter hadn't discovered beer the way many boys do, by sneaking "what their fathers drank" out of the fridge. Instead, every Friday evening, he'd sample an international beer that his mother had purchased at the liquor store. "Sometimes it was from Europe, sometimes from South America," he remembered. "By the time I was 19 years old and could legally drink, I had a pretty good idea of the different styles and flavours." He'd also become a homebrewer and learned how to make these styles himself.

He specialized in microbiology at the University of Victoria and had been considering a career in either medicine or lab research when, as a part of his studies, he interned at Lighthouse Brewing, where he set up a microlab. "I also worked in the brewery and washed a lot of kegs." He picked up a great deal of information about brewing, especially from Jason Meyer, who was then at Lighthouse. "He really showed me how brewing was done on a professional scale." As a result of his experience there, Potter changed his career goals. He wanted to become a professional brewer and enrolled at Heriot-Watt University in Edinburgh in

the postgraduate brewing program. "It was a very creative environment to learn in; people came from all over the world. Each of us wanted our own brewery someday." Part of the program included an internship in Bitburg, Germany. "We skipped our classes to go to Oktoberfest," Potter recalled with a chuckle. It was in Bitburg that he would develop a love for German beers, a love that would influence the direction in which he'd take Moon Under Water a few years later.

"Clay came back after his studies and began working at Turning Point Brewery in Vancouver," Farmer recalled. "He wasn't that happy there and hoped to find a way back to Victoria."

In 2012, Potter had the opportunity to return to his hometown, own a brewery, and brew German-style beers. Don and Bonnie Bradley had decided to sell Moon Under Water; Potter and his family made an offer and, in September of that year, assumed ownership. "We got in just in time," Farmer said. "It was just before the big boom. It would be really hard to be starting up now."

Then began the process of "reinventing the Moon." They'd keep the name, but they'd change the beer focus. "I knew that there was a niche for a German-style brewery in Victoria. The system that was in place here was a German-made one, so all it needed was a little tweaking. We had plenty of fermentation tanks for making lagers," Potter explained. They

In 2012, with the help of his parents, Anne Farmer (left) and Steve Ash (right), Clay Potter purchased Moon Under Water Brewery and Pub, fulfilling a long-held dream. ←

introduced Potts Pils, Creepy Uncle Dunkel Dark Lager, and Victorious Weizenbock. "They were kind of fusion beers, with German styles adapted to local tastes." As the motto on the website states: "European Tradition—West Coast Creativity."

The Moon's new beers became very popular, so much so that expansion of the brewhouse became necessary. "We started with six 25-hectolitre fermenters; since then we've added two more 25s and four 50-hectolitre tanks." Originally they packaged only in 650-millilitre bottles, but as popularity of the beers increased, they began canning their top three brands: Light Side of the Moon, a session lager; Creepy Uncle Dunkel; and Potts Pils. The beers didn't just become popular; they achieved national recognition, winning a gold, two silver and two bronze Canadian Brewing Awards medals.

Creepy Uncle Dunkel, a German dark lager, is a relatively unknown style but has become the Moon's best seller. "It's interesting," Potter observed, "that our dark beers are very popular on Vancouver Island and not so much in Vancouver, where Potts Pils and our IPA do very well." I was surprised when he said this until I remembered that Lighthouse's Race Rocks Ale, Hoyne's Dark Matter, and Vancouver Island Brewing's Hermann's Dark Lager (now Dominion Dark Lager) are also very popular. Dark Munich malts, along with a small amount of roasted wheat, give the beer a rich, nutty flavour. It has a clean, dry finish. Twice it has been awarded a Canadian Brewing Awards silver medal.

Potts Pils, which, along with Hoyner Pilsner, has been a leader in making this European lager style a much bigger player in the Vancouver Island craft market, is an example of what "European Tradition—West Coast Creativity" embodies. It's a northern German version of the style and was inspired by Potter's apprenticeship at Bitburger Brewery. "It uses Saaz hops," he noted, "but it's much hoppier than usual." It's

38 IBUs, very high for this style, and carries what Potter calls "a hop punch. People out here like hops, and they'll get them in this beer. This is not your father's pilsner." The website lists the ABV as 5.2 percent. Each year from 2014 to 2017, it took home a Canadian Brewing Awards medal: a gold, two silvers, and a bronze.

Light Side of the Moon Session Lager is Potter's response to a recent craft beer trend: the production of lower-alcohol beers and the creation of lagers that will appeal to those who still haven't been weaned from the fizzy yellow stuff manufactured by mainstream, industrial brewers. "When the people who worked in the district would drop in for a beer, they weren't that enthusiastic about dark or hoppy ales; they wanted a lighter lager," Potter explained. "And when we set about to can our beers, which was an expensive process, we needed something that would sell well. Light Side was the answer." It's not very strong—4.2 percent ABV— and not very hoppy, only 14 IBUs. The grain bill includes 40 percent roasted rice, a staple in most mainstream lagers, along with Citra hops and sweet orange peel. The result is a light-bodied, light-coloured, refreshing drink, perfect for someone stopping briefly on the way home.

Two of the brewery's IPAs, Tranquility IPA and Hip as Funk Farmhouse IPA, present an interesting contrast. The former, a 6.5 percent ABV, 70 IBU beverage, is completely in the West Coast style and uses Cascade, Centennial, and Columbus hops. "We needed an IPA," Potter explained. "Every craft brewery has one." The website description of the beer begins with a humourous take on the idea of tradition: "This is the style that started it all and we're not talking about Olde England here; we're talking circa 1990 West Coast at its finest. Citrusy, resinous, and piney, this beer is a throwback to the pioneers of craft." Hip as Funk (7 percent ABV, 35 IBUs) also gives another twist to the idea of tradition. It uses both North American and New Zealand hops that are popular with creators of West Coast IPAs, but saison yeast, used for centuries to make Belgian farmhouse ales. It also includes *Brettanomyces*, a yeast that has been around for centuries but has only recently become popular, for the tropical fruit and sometimes funky notes it creates in beer.

Other Moon beers include Berliner-Style Weisse, This is Hefeweizen (a Canadian Brewing Awards bronze medalist), Victoria's Sticke (an altbier based on a traditional Düsseldorf style), Victorious Weizenbock, and several barrel-aged sour beers released in the Crow's Nest series.

I asked this "local boy makes good (and good beer)" what the term "local" meant to him. Potter talked about using local ingredients and began with the water: "Victoria's water is very similar to that in Pilsen; it's very soft and wonderful to work with." He uses local hops for some of his single-hop releases and for the fresh-hop beer he brews each fall at hop harvest time. And he's used the malts of Saanich's craft maltster, Mike Doehnel, for his Doehnelles, a Dortmunder/helles lager. He's proud of being part of the local craft beer community, noting that he's very glad to be in the "brewery district," where Moon, Driftwood, and Hoyne breweries are gathered, and he mentions the co-operation and goodwill that exists among them. This sense of co-operation extends beyond the brewery district. Moon Under Water, along with Swans, Canoe, and Spinnakers, is a member of the Harbour Brewpubs Collective, which was started in the late spring of 2017. For four months in the late spring and into the summer, each brewpub creates a special beer, which is then available at all four places. Moon's first offering for the collective was called Rock Bay Table Saison.

Years ago, Clay Potter used to have to wait for Friday evenings when his mother came home from the liquor store to discover a new and interesting European beer. That's not the case anymore—when he has a thirst for a good German-style lager, he has only to go to the taps at the bar of Moon Under Water and draw himself a glass of an award-winning beer that he and his brew crew have created just a few metres away.

<hr />

I returned to Bridge and Hillside in the mid-afternoon. The semi was no longer blocking Hillside, the smaller trucks had left Driftwood's loading docks, and the bins of spent grain had been carted off to some local farm. Something had been added: on the corner stood a sandwich board with the words BEER FOR SALE HERE. A metre away, a door announced the same thing. The door opened into the retail store/tasting room of **Hoyne Brewing Company**. It was a very small room, containing a counter with some taps mounted behind it, a large cooler, a shelf of growlers, and another shelf with souvenir swag: hats, glasses, and coasters. Here is where people on their way home could have their growlers refilled with beer that had been brewed a few metres back of the counter or pick up two or three bomber bottles of different Hoyne styles. A person could also purchase a sampler tray, provided the total amount of beer sampled didn't exceed 375 millilitres per day. The little store didn't have a lounge licence that would have made it possible to sell beer by the glass or bottle. To obtain one, the space would have had to be enlarged and some seating and public washrooms added.

From the tasting room, I was led out a rear door to the office of Sean Hoyne, the head brewer and co-owner with his wife, Chantal O'Brien. Hoyne was one of the pioneers of British Columbia's craft beer movement. A professional brewer since 1989, he had, in 2011, achieved what is every professional brewer's dream: ownership of his own brewery.

Hoyne and his two brothers had been homebrewers in Montreal, and he continued his hobby when he moved to Victoria in the late 1980s to take a graduate degree in English literature, a field he'd switched to after a couple of years studying microbiology and biochemistry. One day when he and O'Brien were walking downtown, they passed a building that was being renovated and transformed into a brewpub. A sign stuck on one of the windows invited applications for the position of brewer. The couple decided that Hoyne, who had discovered there weren't many jobs for people with master's degrees in modern Irish literature, should send in an application. He did and was invited for an interview. He packed a six-pack with one bottle each of the styles he'd brewed at home, arrived at what would become Swans, and introduced himself to the person who was setting up the brewhouse and devising recipes.

The man was Frank Appleton, one of what could be called the founding fathers of the British Columbia craft beer movement. He, along with John Mitchell, had created Horseshoe Bay Brewing earlier in the decade, and he'd played a role in the founding of Spinnakers and Vancouver Island Brewing. "What have we here?" Appleton asked Hoyne, pointing at the six-pack. Finding out that it contained samples of the job applicant's beers, he got two glasses and a bottle opener and poured out the first bottle. It was an ESB, the English style that Appleton remembered fondly from his days in England. He liked Hoyne's version of the style as well as the beer in each of the other five bottles. By the time the last bottle was empty, Hoyne had earned the job of Swans' brewer.

Appleton didn't just award Hoyne the brewing job. That day and in the weeks ahead as they worked together, he gave him lessons and wisdom that would guide the young English major in his new career. "Frank instilled in me a love of the craft and history of brewing," Hoyne said. "He stressed the importance of respecting the integrity of the brewing process: you use the best ingredients, stay true to brewing traditions, and use available science. Quality is first and foremost; the beer must be honest, good, and flavourful. 'If you make good beer, the rest will follow,' he said." Appleton also emphasized that beer is more than just a beverage; it helps to forge a community. Among the memories awakened by sipping Hoyne's ESB were the feelings of camaraderie and good fellowship Appleton had experienced sitting in a London pub with friends, enjoying a round of Fuller's ESB. Appleton's advice served Hoyne well, and he established a strong reputation, first at Swans and later at Canoe, as the maker of excellent examples of classic beer styles.

At the end of the first decade of this century, Hoyne took the first steps toward making his dream of owning his own brewery a reality. He leased one-quarter of the building across the parking lot from Driftwood, one of whose owners, Jason Meyer, had been six years away from becoming a professional brewer when Hoyne began his career at Swans. Then he leased a 10-hectolitre brewing system that had been in storage since Hugo's Brewhouse, located in downtown Victoria, had ceased operations a few years earlier.

Now began the challenges and hard work. He was brewing on a much larger scale than he had at the brewpubs, and he was brewing for an unseen audience, not for people who were enjoying food, beer, and

One of the pioneers of the Vancouver Island craft beer movement, Sean Hoyne was the first head brewer at Swans and then Canoe. He opened Hoyne Brewing in 2011. ↑

camaraderie at a table only a couple of dozen steps from the brewhouse. At first, there were only two full-time employees, himself and co-owner O'Brien, and they were responsible for all phases of the operation, from ordering ingredients to the final delivery of the product to bars, restaurants, and liquor stores. "We had to get used to all the activities that weren't a concern in the brewpubs and to the increased volume of production. But I kept the same principles I had before, and I still do: make the best beer you can and don't let marketing and accounting steal the show." The principles worked. Hoyne Brewing now occupies half of the building, along with warehouse space elsewhere; a new 35-hectolitre brewhouse has been installed; there are 35 full-time employees; and the beer is distributed throughout British Columbia and Alberta. And, of course, it's of excellent quality, having garnered three Canadian Brewing Awards bronze medals.

The first four beers from Hoyne Brewing covered a range from light to dark: Hoyner Pilsner, Down Easy Pale Ale, Devil's Dream IPA, and Dark Matter. In addition to Hoyner Pilsner, the current core list includes two other lagers: Vienna Lager and Helios Dortmunder Golden Lager. "We are one of the first BC craft breweries to make lagers central to our portfolio. Lagers are exquisite in style; we want to make them a thing of beauty," Hoyne explained, his voice bursting with enthusiasm.

The Hoyner Pilsner (5.5 percent ABV) is a blend of German and Czech styles and ingredients. "We use German and Canadian malts and Czech Saaz hops, along with two German hops. The yeast is a Czech strain." When I pressed for more details, he laughed and remarked: "Beer is not to be obsessed over; it's to be enjoyed with friends." Suffice to say that this 5.5 percent ABV lager is a light gold in colour; the Saaz hops give it a crispness and the malts a slight sweetness. Because it comes, as do all the Hoyne products, in 650-millilitre bomber bottles, you can share one with a friend. The Vienna Lager (5.2 percent ABV) is darker in colour (a copper/gold) and maltier and fuller-bodied than the pilsner. Helios is the strongest of the three, at 6 percent ABV. Malt-forward, with bready and biscuit notes, it has a crisp hop finish.

The pride and joy of Hoyne's hoppy beers is undoubtedly Appleton ESB. "I always said that if I owned my own brewery, I was going to name an ESB, his favourite style, after him," he said. This 5.2 percent ABV version of the style emphasizes the English ingredients: Fuggle and East Kent Golding hops, varieties which have been used for a century and a half and more, provide earthy and slight citrus, floral, and herbal notes, while Thomas Fawcett Golden Promise malts create sweet and robust maltiness. "Let us all raise a glass to Mr. Frank Appleton and say thanks!" reads the website account of the beer.

With one exception, the pale and India pale ales are hybrids, using English and North American ingredients. Down Easy Pale Ale (5.2 percent ABV) includes Cascade North American hops and Maris Otter English malts, and Devil's Dream IPA (6 percent ABV) mixes Citra, Simcoe and Centennial North American hops with Thomas Fawcett Golden Promise malts. The exception is Wolf Vine Wet Hopped Pale Ale (5.3 percent ABV), which uses fresh Centennial and Cascade hops as quickly as possible after they are harvested on nearby Pender Island.

And then there's Dark Matter (5.3 percent ABV). Various descriptions I've read have categorized it as a brown ale, a stout, and a porter, or some mix of two or all of these. "We don't know what it is!" Hoyne laughed when I asked him about this award-winning and, along with the pilsner, best-selling of the brewery's beers. "We know it's not as robust as a stout, it's not as light as a brown ale, and it's not as sweet as a porter. It's a category of its own; it's elusive. But one thing you can say with certainty: it's dark, it's delicious, and it's drinkable." The other core dark beer is Voltage Espresso Stout (5.6 percent ABV), flavoured (or maybe charged!) with espresso made at Victoria's Habit Coffee. The website calls it a "breakfast stout."

While the website descriptions are not overloaded with specific details about each beer, they are poetic, the creations of a long-ago English major. Here, for example, are the words for Hoyner Pilsner: "On the third night, I handed my sweetie a tall, slender Pilsner. Perfectly poured. While holding it up and gazing either at it, or through it at me, she said softly, 'You are so fine to me.'" Hoyne explained the approach: "I love literature and writing; I want our literature to entertain as well as instruct." He went on to say that the descriptions were also a little tongue-in-cheek. "I dislike a lot of the shameless self-promotion on labels. Let's not toot our own horn; let's have fun."

In addition to the great satisfaction he gets from making award-winning beer, Sean Hoyne also takes deep satisfaction in continuing a tradition he learned from Frank Appleton: mentoring young brewers. "Over the past five years, several of our apprentices have become full-fledged brewers." He then described a program he instituted in 2017. "I challenged our young brewers to make their own beers. It could be any style they wanted: they created the recipe, brewed the beers, and came up with a name and a label. I called it the Young Lions series. I gave them a free hand and they decided to call the first one Carte Blanche, because it's what I'd given them, and it was a Belgian-style white IPA. We do this to honour and pass on the traditions, just as Frank taught me years ago."

~~~~~~~~~~~~~

I finished my tour of the brewery district by walking three blocks north on Bridge Street to what would, possibly by the early winter, be the home of **Île Sauvage Brewing Company**. The name translates as Savage Island, a reference both to the rugged wilderness that makes up so much of Vancouver Island and to the principal kind of beer the new company would create: beers fermented with wild yeast.

One of three owners and the head brewer, Stephane Turcotte is another University of Victoria English student turned brewer. He also had a master's degree in applied linguistics from the University of Nottingham in England. Armed with these degrees, he travelled to Busan, South Korea's second-largest city, where he taught English, met his future wife, and discovered that the Korean beer scene was pretty abysmal.

"Back home, I'd been a fan of the Trappist beers made by Orval in Belgium and I'd been a homebrewer," Turcotte said. "I liked making funky beers. After I'd been in South Korea for a while, I said to myself and some friends, 'I can make better homebrew than this,' and we decided to open a craft brewery. Our most popular beers were a blonde ale, a crossover, and an IPA." After two-and-a-half years, Turcotte returned home, earned an online diploma in brewing from the Siebel Institute, became a certified beer cicerone, did some work at the 4 Mile Brewpub, and started planning, along with his friends Ian Ibbotson and Tom Jones, to open a brewery that would reflect his love of funky styles.

When I arrived, there was no sign indicating there was a brewery soon to open in the building, the windows of which were covered in brown paper. Behind the unmarked door, however, stood rows of brewing tanks and oak barrels. All the brewing equipment was still encased in heavy plastic, and it appeared that the web page announcement "Coming to Victoria BC Early in 2018" had been optimistic. "Victoria requires a lot of paperwork, and it takes a lot of time," Turcotte, who was awaiting my arrival inside, explained.

I asked him the same one-word question I've asked so many people who are starting up a new brewery in places that already have a large number of them: "Why?" He explained that while other Victoria breweries were making Belgian beers (he singled out Driftwood for praise), Île Sauvage would concentrate on the funky beers—the saisons, kettle sours, barrel-aged beers, beers fermented with wild, airborne yeasts—that had become so popular over the last decade.

"Moreover," he went on, "we have a different focus. Most breweries emphasize their beers in their branding. We are going to emphasize the place where we serve our beers. We'll have a lounge where people will be served by certified cicerones, people who can tell them about the variety of styles available. They'll be able to taste these and then take some bottles home with them. That way, our beers will become known around town. We'll make the beer we want to drink, and I'm sure others will enjoy drinking it too."

As I drove home late that afternoon, I remembered a progressive pub lunch I'd enjoyed

Stephane Turcotte stands in front of the barrels that he will fill with Belgian-style ales when the construction of Île Sauvage Brewing Company is complete. →

with a friend several years ago. We'd started at Moon Under Water, stopped at Canoe and Swans, and ended up at Spinnakers, enjoying one course and an appropriately paired beer at each stop. I thought that, in a few months, it would be possible to do something similar within the confines of the brewery district, sampling a different pre-lunch or dinner beer at three stops and finishing at the Moon, enjoying a substantial meal with a good German-style lager to wash it down.

CHAPTER 4

BEER IN THE BURBS—
SAANICH, SAANICHTON,
VIEW ROYAL, LANGFORD

Victoria Caledonian Distillery
& Twa Dogs Brewery,
Category 12 Brewing Company,
4 Mile Brewpub,
Axe & Barrel Brewing Company,
Howl Brewing Company

After 1859, when William Steinberger moved Victoria Brewery from the east shores of Swan Lake to Government Street, the areas outside of the Greater Victoria core of Victoria, Oak Bay, and Esquimalt were without a brewery for nearly a century and a quarter. In 1983 and 1984, respectively, Prairie Inn and Cottage Brewery and Island Pacific Brewery—now Vancouver Island Brewing—opened in Saanichton. In the middle of the 1990s, Prairie Inn stopped making its own beer and Vancouver Island moved to Government Street in Victoria. It wasn't until 2014 that another brewery, Category 12, opened up in what used to be considered the hinterlands but were now expanding suburbs of Victoria. Category 12's operations were located just a few blocks from where Island Pacific's headquarters had been. In 2014, the owners of the Four Mile House, which had been built in View Royal before the brewery at Swan Lake had been put together, decided to begin brewing their own beer. A year later, the Loghouse Pub in northern Langford also installed a brewhouse, and in 2016, Twa Dogs Brewery opened in Saanich, close to the municipal border with Victoria.

I began my tour of the new suburban breweries at **Victoria Caledonian Distillery & Twa Dogs Brewery**. It was located less than a kilometre away from Swan Lake in a building that overlooked the highway to the airport and ferry terminal. If one didn't recognize the establishment's Scottish focus from the word "Caledonian," from the Latin word for what is now Scotland, and the phrase "Twa Dogs," the title of a work by Scotland's most famous poet, Robbie Burns, it would be evident when the visitor was greeted in the tasting room by owner Graeme Macaloney. He spoke with a Scottish accent that is often called a "burr." He wasn't wearing a kilt when I met him, but for ceremonial occasions at the distillery/brewery, such as the forthcoming Robbie Burns dinner, he does don one. It's made of the best Macaloney tartan available.

Macaloney, who grew up near Glasgow, Scotland, had become interested in fermentation during a summer job at a distillery that made Black & White Scotch whisky. He studied fermentation sciences, earning a bachelor's degree and a doctorate at the University of Strathclyde. "I couldn't find work in a distillery, so I got a job at a biomedical company. The processes for brewing beer, distilling whisky, and making antibiotics are quite similar. In fact, during the Second World War, distilleries in Great Britain made penicillin." His profession took him to Edmonton, Alberta, where he wasn't too impressed with the Canadian beer available at the time, "except for Big Rock Traditional Ale," he explained. He liked what they did with malted barley—which is also a major ingredient in Scotch whisky.

Gradually, Macaloney began to form a plan for the creation of a distillery and a brewery housed in a building that would become a destination for both tourists and locals. Victoria would be an ideal location—it had an established craft beer culture, and it was a very popular tourist destination. The name he chose, Victoria Caledonian Distillery & Twa Dogs Brewery, would emphasize that it was an integral part of the capital city and that it also embodied a proud Scottish tradition. The theme of the Robbie Burns poem "The Twa Dogs" expressed Macaloney's philosophy about the social values of beer. In the poem, a rich dog and a poor dog sit over a couple of pints, discussing their philosophies of life. They get to know each other and respect each other.

Funding for Macaloney's enterprise came from two sources: a grant from Agriculture Canada for over $2 million to develop a new process for aging Scotch and donations from 300 individuals. "They were just ordinary people who cared enough to support our business," Macaloney said. "Most are punters," he continued, using the British equivalent of the term *beer geeks*. "They don't just help financially; they want to pitch in at the brewery." He noted that one of them was helping on the bottling line that day.

Macaloney realized that if he was going to open a brewery in Victoria, he'd need a first-class brewer—the area's very knowledgeable craft beer drinkers would simply not put up with inferior brews. He didn't have to look far to find one. "The craft brewing community was very helpful to me; they recommended Dean McLeod, who was working at Lighthouse. He was interested in expanding his skills into the distilling area and was very happy to join our team. He's from Australia, and he's had international experience in New Zealand. And," he added with a chuckle, "he's of Scottish descent."

McLeod brought his skills and knowledge, which included awareness of the uses of newly developed New Zealand hops, to Lighthouse in 2010. There he was a leader in revitalizing what had become a somewhat middle-of-the road product line. His special-release beers, as well as his tinkering with the core beers, helped move Lighthouse back into the mainstream of the Victoria craft scene. "He's a certified beer judge and judges international competitions," Macaloney told me. "It's interesting

Nicole MacLean, brewer, and
Graeme Macaloney, owner,
stand in the distillery section of
Victoria Caledonian Distillery &
Twa Dogs Brewery. ↑

to watch him deconstruct a beer: he looks, smells, and tastes it and can tell you just what the ingredients are and what's good or bad about them. When he sets about to make a beer for us, he researches the style very carefully; then he tweaks the recipe and comes up with just what he wants."

Unfortunately, McLeod was on vacation, so I wasn't able to talk to him, and it would be a quarter of an hour before Nicole MacLean, the brewhouse's second-in-command, could join us. So Macaloney gave me a shortened version of the brewery/distillery tour that was a major element of the new brewery's business. "I knew how big beer tourism was becoming," he explained. "And so I planned for extensive tours, not only for visitors to the Island but also their Victoria hosts and other townspeople. It wouldn't be just a quick walk through the brewery and a sample at the end. We'd put on a wee bit of a show. We'd have trained, knowledgeable guides dressed in kilts"—Macaloney tartan, of course—"giving visitors an in-depth understanding of how beer and whisky were created, and we'd include several stops for tastings along the way. I travelled to distilleries in Ireland, Scotland, and Kentucky to see how their tours were run and used that information to develop ours."

There were three beer tours ranging from 45 minutes to an hour and a half, and costing from $15.95 to $39.00. At the end of the $39.00 one, visitors enjoyed a chocolate and beer tasting and were able to pick out a bottle of beer from the bottling line to take home. This was a major marketing tool for Macaloney. "We will be giving people an experience. When they learn about the beer, they'll enjoy it more fully. And they'll probably buy some product and, after they've left, share it with other people. Word-of-mouth advertising is very powerful." In my mind, I compared this to what a poetry reading might have been like had there been any in Robbie Burns's day. People would listen to the readings, which would probably be accompanied by the poet's accounts of the background of the poems, and later, they'd most likely buy copies of his books, get them autographed, and give them as gifts to their friends.

As we made the tour, Macaloney pointed to an area set with tables and chairs and located between the brewing tanks and two copper-coloured stills used in distilling whiskey. "When we applied for our lounge licence, we deliberately designated this space, along with the tasting room, as the tasting area. We can serve beer and liquor by the glass here. People can book the space for community events and parties, and in a couple of weeks, this is where we'll hold the Robbie Burns dinner. There'll be bagpipers, haggis, and some really good single-malt Scotch."

We had just finished the tour of the brewing and distilling facilities when Nicole MacLean joined us. She had grown up in Stirling, a university town located midway between Edinburgh and Glasgow, but had discovered craft beer and surfing during a vacation to Canada's West Coast. Upon returning to Scotland, she began taking university classes, one of which included a section on brewing. She was hooked and soon after began working at BrewDog, a well-known Scottish production brewery and brewpub chain. "I started on the production line and, after three years, was one of the lead brewers," she said. The pull of Canada's West Coast was strong, and she returned to Vancouver Island, wanting to be close to the Island's surfing scene and hoping to be able to use her brewing skills to land a job. She worked first at Driftwood and was now the head brewer at Twa Dogs, working under the guidance of Dean McLeod.

MacLean talked about four of Twa Dogs' beers, each given names from Burns's poems. She admitted that she liked malty beers but also noted how McLeod's knowledge of hops, particularly new varieties from New Zealand, gave each of the beers its distinctive flavour. Holy Willie's Robust Porter (6.5 percent ABV) is the darkest and maltiest of the beers. Blackprinz malts give the beer its dark colour and roasted, but not bitter, flavour, while pale chocolate malts add mild chocolate notes. Magnum hops balance the malt-forward quality of the stout. Mistress of My Soul Saison (6 percent ABV) has the spicy, fruity notes and dry finish characteristic of the style. The Motueka hops from New Zealand contribute citrusy notes. "You can smell the hops and taste the yeast," MacLean remarked enthusiastically. "There is a wonderful complexity of flavours."

Keekin' Glass Pilsner (5 percent ABV) combines a Scottish name (from a Burns poem) with the ingredients of a Czech-style pilsner. It's clean and crisp, but not sweet. "It's the perfect beach beer," MacLean, the surfer, enthused. "A friend who knows beer said this is what a pilsner should be." Drouthy Neibor is a 7 percent ABV, 60 IBU IPA that has a slight malty sweetness and pronounced citrus and pine flavour from the four different (and unnamed) hops used in the beer. It's an easy-drinking IPA, in spite of the alcoholic content and relatively high level of bitterness. The name, by the way, means "thirsty neighbour." Other regulars or frequently appearing beers include Silver Flood Belgian Wit (5 percent ABV), Jolly Beggar's Pale Ale (4.7 percent ABV), and Seas Between Us Red IPA (7 percent ABV).

"We want our beers to be sessionable, true to classic styles, interesting, and not faddy," MacLean said. But there were times when the brewers moved outside of these guidelines. One of these times had recently occurred when MacLean brewed a recipe she had created: Chili Chocolate Milk Stout. Cacao nibs contributed to the rich, malty flavour of the beer, and the chili, which was subtle, gave a slightly sharp, enjoyable contrast to the richness of the malts. I told her that this beer would be very popular in my adopted hometown of Albuquerque, New Mexico, where chili is the most popular flavour enhancer around. It would, I told her, be a great valentine drink—chocolates and chili, all in one drink. It didn't have a name when I visited. I wondered what Robbie Burns would have come up with.

~~~~~~~~~~~

As I drove out Highway 17, a road I'd taken many times to get to the airport and the ferry terminal, I thought about how, when we were children, the Saanich Peninsula was that distant place where many of the fresh vegetables and fruits we ate came from. It's still an agricultural area, and had I not turned off the highway at Keating Cross Road, I'd have passed the Saanich Historical Artifacts Society exhibit of old tractors, cultivators, wagons, and other farming equipment and the Canada Experimental Station, run by the Department of Agriculture. But, after I'd proceeded a half kilometre along Keating, I discovered the new Saanich, the home of warehouses, manufacturing buildings—including Specific Mechanical Systems, which made brewing systems—and strip malls, one of which housed **Category 12 Brewing**.

It was a long, low, unassuming building that was the home to MDC, a maker of equipment and clothing for military and law enforcement personnel; Keating CrossFit, a workout centre; and Old Victoria Water Company, a supplier of distilled, purified, and spring water. When I met Karen Kuzyk, co-owner (with husband/brewer Michael Kuzyk) and director of branding, I laughed and remarked that neither the outside of the building nor the tasting room looked like the sketch on the brewery's website. On the website, a woman who seems to have driven up in a Volkswagen bus knocks at the door of an ordinary-looking two-storey house. But from a manhole cover just outside the dwelling, a ladder descends into an Erlenmeyer flask–shaped subterranean chamber containing a brewhouse. The silhouette of a mad scientist (brewer?) hovers around the tanks. Here in the real brewery, the people who sat at the tasting room bar, sipping beer while talking about the recently completed hockey game in which Canada had defeated Sweden to win the World Junior Hockey Championship, could look through large plate-glass windows at the shiny tanks of a very modern brewery.

"We wanted good branding, so we used the idea of a dangerous, mad scientist and we chose the name Category 12 to suggest some mysterious

scientific project," Karen said. The humorous branding is carried into the names of some of the beers: Disruption, Transmutation, Unsanctioned, Subversion, and Insubordinate. "We wanted to start with two unusual beers, Disruption Black IPA and Unsanctioned Saison, two styles that are somewhat out of the mainstream. We're literally and figuratively on the fringes," she added, referring to the Central Saanich location and to their beers and branding.

Although certainly not mad, Michael Kuzyk had been a scientist, a microbiologist and biochemist, for many years, teaching at the University of Victoria and conducting research there and with private firms. He'd also spent over two decades as a homebrewer. "He liked big, hoppy IPAs, and I was a wine drinker. Then he introduced me to yeasty Belgian beers, and I was hooked. Now I'm a recovering wine drinker," Karen said with a chuckle.

A scientist by profession, Michael Kuzyk wanted to apply his training to more creative and enjoyable endeavours. With his wife, Karen Kuzyk, he founded Category 12 Brewing in an industrial area of Saanich, north of Victoria. ←

While the two enjoyed Michael's hobby, he was finding his life as a full-time scientist confining. He needed to find something that would combine his fields of biochemistry and microbiology with his love of homebrewing. "When our kids became old enough that they could fend for themselves after school, we decided it was time to make a change. We'd start a brewery that wasn't just doing what everyone in town was doing. Michael grew up in the central Saanich area, the rental was cheaper here than in town, and we could become part of the local community. The first thing we did when we decided to start a brewery was buy a microscope, a really good one. Michael is always the scientist."

Category 12 opened in December 2014, offering Greater Victoria's knowledgeable craft beer drinkers what the website called "Colossal West Coast and Belgian Inspired Beers," ales that were "crafted with delirious precision." The scientist might be mad, but the brews would be meticulously prepared. The website also offered a mock scientific equation for the creation of good beer: "(Sound Science + Good Taste)^4 x Art^8 = Great Beer^{12}." People must have agreed with the equation; six days after opening, Category 12 ran out of beer, and when Disruption Black IPA won a Canadian Brewing Awards gold medal in 2015, the brewery was hard pressed to keep up with a rapidly increasing demand. In 2016, Category 12 began its barrel-aging program and also created beers with new, often wild yeast strains and different flavouring adjuncts.

In the winter of 2018, Category 12's website listed 21 beers, 7 in the IPA/pale ale category, 10 in the Belgian-inspired category, 2 familiar craft beer styles—stout and blonde ale—and 2 that are difficult to define: Zombie Repellant Ale (an anti-pumpkin beer) and Raw Ale (a Scandinavian-inspired beer that included local red cedar bark). The various pale ales reflect Michael Kuzyk's love of hops. There are such familiar hop standbys as Amarillo, East Kent Golding, and Centennial, but there are also many of the newly developed or rediscovered varietals—Jarrylo, Ekuanot, Ultra, Huell Melon, and others, each delivering unique aromas and tastes. Among the Belgian-style beers are a golden strong ale, a dubbel, a witbier, a couple of saisons, and a quad. Bourbon and wine barrels impart their subtle notes to two beers. There's a Brett IPA and a Wild Saison. Flavour additives include loganberries, cucumber, cacao nibs, and grapefruit peel. "We like diversification into the unfamiliar," Karen told me. "We see it as a kind of duty to educate and to expand the knowledge of beer drinkers."

Two of the beers listed seemed like hybrids of the two types that Karen and Michael loved and decided to make the focus of Category 12. The terms "fresh-hopped" and "dry-hopped," most frequently found in discussions of pale ales and IPAs, were applied to a saison and a sour, respectively. "Brett" and "Wild," which you'd expect to describe Belgian-inspired creations, preceded "IPA." I imagined the mad scientist/brewer/artist in his underground bunker chuckling fiendishly as he concocted these unusual new brews and prepared to unleash them on the beer-drinking world.

As Karen was recounting the backstory of Category 12, we were joined by Michael. He hadn't crawled out of a manhole cover in the parking lot; he'd come through the door that led to the brewery. And he didn't look like a mad scientist; he looked like a hard-working brewer. He talked about being introduced to craft beers on a visit to Washington and Oregon, where he'd tried the brews of Northwest craft beer pioneers Pyramid Brewing of Seattle and Full Sail of Hood River, Oregon. "It was Storm Brewing [of Vancouver] that really turned me onto hops," he remembered and spoke of the influence of the creations of James Walton, the owner-brewer, who has been referred to as a mad scientist and nicknamed Captain Quirk. The discovery of Belgian beer came later.

Our discussion of Category 12 beers began with a description of Disruption Black IPA, one of the original two beers and the brewery's bestseller. Michael had wanted to create an unexpected version of the dominant craft beer style from British Columbia to California. Carafa malts provided the dark, almost opaque colour and the roasted flavours of espresso, coffee, and chocolate, but without the bitterness often found in dark beers. Munich malts created a full-bodied, smooth mouthfeel. Simcoe, Cascade, and Columbus hops contributed a pronounced but not overwhelming bitterness (77 IBUs) and also piney notes. That night, as I sipped a glass of Disruption (6.7 percent ABV), I read the notes on the bottle; they explained, in a few dozen words, the significance of the beer and its name: "While most of us languish in the concept of predictability, there are a selected few who are restless. They spend their days trying to hide a need to disrupt this culture of needless repetition.... Get ready to challenge what you think about dark beer.... It looks big and scary like a stout, but it drinks like an IPA."

Two pairs of contrasting ales and two unusual "hybrids" are among Category 12's hoppy beers. Pivotal ESB (5.2 percent ABV) is a slightly malt-forward English-style beer, while Critical Point Northwest Pale Ale (5.1 percent ABV) is more hop-forward. Insubordinate is a 4.5 percent session IPA, while Subversion is an 8.7 percent ABV imperial IPA. Wild IPA (6.9 percent ABV) and Brett IPA (6.8 percent ABV) have the spicy and funky notes, respectively, associated with Belgian beers. Both are limited releases in the Elemental Series, which focuses on "experimentation and innovation."

The second original beer, Unsanctioned Saison, fulfills the second half of the stated "mandate"—the creation of Belgian-inspired ales. The website calls it "discreetly sessionable," although, at 6.9 percent ABV, it is stronger than most beers to which the term "sessionable," [meaning a beer, more than one of which can be safely enjoyed at a sitting, or session] is applied. The Zythos hops provide tropical fruit and citrus flavours, the Caravienne malts contribute slightly toasty and caramel notes, and the yeast gives a clove and spicy quality. Two other saisons are on the list. Fresh-Hopped Saison (5.1 percent ABV) uses just-harvested Cashmere and Ultra hops that contribute tropical fruit and citrusy flavours, respectively. Wild Saison (6.3 percent ABV) is what might be called a very local beer: mixed wild yeasts, along with loganberries harvested just over a kilometre from the brewery, are used to create an ale that balances the flavour of the fruit with the spiciness of the yeast.

While he was discussing the beers, Michael referred to the sciences he'd studied, noting that biochemistry was the most important in the mashing and boiling, and microbiology during the fermenting process. He stressed the very important role of that tiny organism, yeast; not only did it produce alcohol, but also, unbeknownst to many people, it was the ingredient that determined what style the final product would be and how it would taste. Karen noted that was why the purchase of the microscope and setting up of a lab were crucial to the success of the brewery; without these, the great potential of yeast would probably not be fully realized.

A couple of weeks before my visit, the brewery had celebrated its fourth anniversary. In that short period, it had achieved national recognition and was now available in all Canadian provinces except Ontario and Quebec. Nonetheless, Karen spoke of this being, in many ways, a very local business. "We didn't start the brewery to go head-to-head with Driftwood or Phillips; and we didn't want to try to capture a huge slice of the West Coast–style IPA market. We're part of this neighbourhood. Michael grew up not far away, our brewing system was manufactured less than a kilometre away, and the loganberries for our saison were harvested even closer to the brewery." The sense of "localness" encompassed more than that. "We're part of the local community in a way that we wouldn't be if we were in the city. People come into the tasting room and visit with us and have a beer on their way home from work. We know each other's names. There's a real sense of connection between the brewery and the customers."

~~~~~~~~~

The next day, I visited the Victoria area's two most recently opened brewpubs. One was in a mid-19th-century building that I had first passed by when I was a small boy travelling on what is now called the old Island Highway on our way to Shawnigan Lake. The other was housed in a later 20th-century building half a kilometre north of what old-timers still called the new Island Highway. It was just one of a large number of businesses that have been established in the rapidly growing area in the northern part of Langford. Both brewpubs are, in part, a product and an illustration of the expansion of the Victoria area westward into what is now known as West Shore, which extends from View Royal west to Langford and south toward Sooke.

We never used to stop at what we called the Four Mile House on our way to the lake, although occasionally we'd stop at the Six Mile House, where my parents would go in for a quick 10-cent glass of beer. It wasn't until I began research for this book that I understood why we had never stopped. After the Second World War, the building, which was then known as the Lantern Inn, was a dine-and-dance establishment that rented its reportedly very small upstairs rooms for dubious purposes. Those dubious purposes are made explicit in the name of one of the beers of what is now called **4 Mile Brewpub**: Brothel Brown. Named the Four Mile House because it was four miles from Beacon Hill on a 19th-century stage route, the building had been in almost continuous use until the mid-1950s, at which time beer parlours opened within the Victoria city limits. It was vacant until 1979, when Wendy and Graham Haymes purchased the place, renovated it extensively, and operated it first as a tea house, then as a restaurant and, starting in 2014, as a brewpub. At one time, it was believed to have been haunted.

This building, more than 150 years old, has served as a road-house, tea room, restaurant, house of ill repute (reputedly), and most recently, the home of 4 Mile Brewpub. ✝

The Tudor-style building houses both a restaurant and a sports bar as well as the brewhouse. The top floor is a cozy, English-style pub/restaurant, with comfy armchairs and a gas fireplace. There is a four-seasons glassed-in sun porch on one side of the restaurant with a door leading to an outside patio. The bottom floor is the sports bar, which features several television sets, a keno screen, and a growler-filling station. Behind the bar (which has a full liquor menu that includes Labatt Blue as well as the in-house beers) is the brewhouse, visible from the parking lot through plate-glass windows, on which are painted short explanations of the brewing process.

I was greeted in the sports bar by brewers Steve Gray and Richard Edwards, who took me into the brewhouse and gave me a brief tour. It was a fairly standard brewhouse with one notable exception: the kettle was faced with brick. Gray explained why: "The owners had been thinking about turning the restaurant into a brewpub for quite some time. One of their relatives, Doug White, had trained as a brewer in England, and when they made the decision, he was in charge of setting things up." White turned to Alan Pugsley, who in the 1980s, had been his teacher in England and who had since become a consultant helping set up breweries around the world. Pugsley came to Victoria, which he said had excellent brewing water, and led the transformation of the establishment from a restaurant that served beer to one that made its own. He decided to install a Peter Austin Brick Kettle brewing system, one in which the heat generated by direct flame was contained by the brick insulation. It was, as well, easy to operate, clean, and maintain. White, who became the first brewer, had since gone his own way, and some of the original fermentation tanks had been replaced with tanks made by Specific Mechanical Systems of Saanichton.

Edwards was a chemistry graduate of the University of Victoria who had been a homebrewer before coming to work at 4 Mile Brewpub. He was in charge of the lab, managing the yeast, and maintaining quality control. "One of the first things I learned about professional brewing was that you had to have really good yeast to work with," he remarked. Gray, who like his predecessor Doug White, was a member of the owners' extended family, had been working at the brewpub and expressed an interest in helping White around the brewhouse. "I began working with him one day a week and then more. And now, here I am."

The tour over, we sat in the sports bar, where Gray and Edwards discussed the beers on the sampler trays that had been brought to our table. As would be expected from a brewpub, there were many different styles that ranged from light-coloured and lightly hopped crossover beers, to the darker Brothel Brown, to hoppy beers, to two rather unusual beers that were called porter and stout but that I categorized as "dark and different."

The simply named Pilsner (5.2 percent ABV) was German-style and used Hallertau and Saaz hops to give it a spiciness and a clean, crisp finish. Golden Ale (4.6 percent ABV) started with a malt sweetness that was then balanced by a crisp finish created by the Cascade and Willamette hops. Tangerine Dream Wheat (4.2 percent ABV) was an American wheat ale flavoured with citrusy hops, orange peel, and ground coriander.

The pale ale and the IPAs had either citrus additives or citrus notes supplied by the hops. In the West Coast India Pale Ale (6 percent ABV, 70 IBUs) these notes, along with tropical fruit flavours, came from the Amarillo, Simcoe, and Galaxy hops. Grapefruit IPA (5 percent ABV) added grapefruit zest, while Mandarin IPA (6.5 percent ABV) included orange along with Mandarina hops. Hazy Citra Pale Ale (5.5 percent ABV) is 4 Mile's take on the recently introduced "East Coast style," which is a hazy ale. The menu description states: "The huge amounts of dry hops and special British yeast strain combine to create a beer that tastes like...juice." Edwards noted, "I think we do well with fruit beers."

While the hoppy beers are definitely in the West Coast style, the dark ales are definitely in the British tradition. Brothel Brown (5.3 percent ABV) is full-bodied with chocolate and caramel notes. Then there's Candy Bar Stout (6.5 percent ABV). "We add vanilla, cacao nibs, peanut butter, and sea salt," Gray explained. It is a full-bodied beer and sweet, although the sea salt countered the sweetness slightly. The hint of peanut butter was there, but only enough to add another flavour. And finally, I tasted what Edwards called "dessert in a glass," Rice Pudding Porter (6 percent ABV). Spices, vanilla, and brown rice syrup made this not just your ordinary porter—or dessert beer either.

"Dessert" over, it was time to go. But, before I did, I jokingly asked the two if those small rooms on the second floor were occupied. They shook their heads and said that there were a couple of offices and some storage space, but that the ladies of the night had long since disappeared into the darkness. I wondered if, when what used to be called the Lantern Inn went dark in the wee small hours, ghosts cavorted in those upstairs chambers.

Location may not be everything for a brewpub, but it certainly is important. Both Moon Under Water and 4 Mile Brewpub are beside roads well travelled by people going home from work, people who may drop in either for a quick pint or to have a growler filled. Location is also important for **Axe & Barrel Brewing Company** in north Langford. It's at the edge of a shopping district that includes big-box stores, service stations, fast-food outlets, and smaller businesses, and just south of Western Speedway, an automobile racetrack and recreational fun park, and Bear Mountain, an upscale residential district and resort area.

Axe & Barrel opened in the late 1990s as a restaurant/sports bar called the Loghouse, a reference to its outside siding. A small, attached liquor store was later added. Ron Cheeke, who with his wife, Diana Kresier, is the current owner, joined the ownership group in in the 1990s and later bought his partners out. In 2014, citing the area's rapid population growth, which included many young professionals who had a taste for craft beer, he decided to rebrand the restaurant, revise the menu to include higher-end pub fare, undertake over $2 million in renovations, open a very large liquor store across the parking lot, and create a brewery in the space originally occupied by the original liquor store. (Early in 2018, he sold the restaurant and property on which the restaurant and brewery stood and then leased back the space that housed the brewery. The restaurant returned to its original name, The Loghouse.)

In 2015, the renovations complete, the brewery and restaurant were renamed Axe & Barrel, a reference, first, to the logging industry so important in the area during much of the 20th century and, second, to the containers that are so important for barrel-aging beer. Dave Woodward, who had worked for many years at the Brewhouse at Whistler and then become the founding brewer at Tofino Brewing on the Island's west coast, became the founding brewer. He told reporters that the beers he planned to create would be both good and sessionable. With the brewery well established, Woodward returned to his hometown of

Qualicum Beach to help in the start-up of Mount Arrowsmith Brewing, located in nearby Parksville.

Woodward was succeeded in 2016 by Andrew Tessier, who had won 37 Canadian Brewing Awards medals, including 22 gold, while working at Swans in Victoria, where I'd met him in 2009. A Victoria boy, he'd begun homebrewing in high school and, with his friends, formed the "Raging Grainies," which set up a brewing system in Tessier's basement. He remembered how, when a local homebrew supplier refused to sell him ingredients because he was too young, his father, a non-drinker, went to the supplier the next day and made the purchase. "We loved to make big, hoppy beers," he told me, adding that he used the Cascade, Columbus, and Centennial hops that had been the game-changing

ingredients in the early years of the West Coast craft beer movement. He turned professional in the 1990s, working first at Backwoods Brewing (now Dead Frog Brewery) in Aldergrove, in the Fraser Valley, and R&B in Vancouver and then at Propeller Brewing in Halifax, where he introduced many Maritimers to big, hoppy West Coast IPAs. In 2003, he returned home and to Swans, where one of the first things he did was to add an IPA to the core list.

When Tessier heard that his friend Dave Woodward was heading up Island, he decided to apply for the job at Axe & Barrel. "I was ready for a change; I wanted to explore new projects." At Swans, he'd not been able to use the brewing system to full capacity; most of the beer produced was for the brewpub, and very little was bottled for sale off premises. He welcomed the opportunity to work at a place where he could create beers that could be enjoyed by people at the tasting room in front of the brewhouse and in the restaurant next door, but also could be packaged for distribution off-site. He'd also enjoy the challenge of creating beer for a wider demographic, not just for young professionals, other city folks, and tourists, as had been the case at Swans. In Langford, he was on the fringes of Lucky Lager territory. "And, besides, it was a chance to work in a bright and airy place—at Swans there were no windows in the brewhouse. Here I can look outside and see deer grazing on the lawn." He also enjoyed the camaraderie with owner

Winner of numerous national awards, Andrew Tessier worked for many years at Swans in Victoria before taking over the duties of head brewer at Langford's Axe & Barrel. ←

Ron Cheeke; the two would often sit together sipping one of Tessier's brews and talking about beer and business.

To Tessier, brewing is an art. "There has to be a scientific base, but until the last three or four decades, the art was mainly ignored." Certainly his work at Swans demonstrated that Tessier was an artist. Not only did he win all those medals, but he won them for an amazing variety of styles, 13 in all. Included were a barley wine, Scotch ale, bitter, witbier, kolsch, and Bavarian lager. Interesting additives to some of the beers included coconut, raspberry, and honey. His winning ways followed him to Axe & Barrel when his King Kolsch was awarded a 2017 Canadian Brewing Awards silver medal.

As we worked our way through a sampler tray of Tessier's Axe & Barrel beers, the artist/creator described them. Langford Logger Lager (4.8 percent ABV), the brewery's first beer to be canned and one of the top sellers, was developed in response to locals who had grown up, as it were, with pale American-style lagers such as Lucky. This one, however, used German Hallertau and Czech Saaz hops and German Munich malts to give a crisp, light-bodied, clean mouthfeel. "It's a little hoppier than most European versions," he noted. "It's like some of the craft pilsners that are now being made in the States." West Shore IPA (6.8 percent ABV) continues Tessier's tradition, which started in his homebrewing years, of brewing big, hoppy beers. Like most West Coast versions, it has tropical fruit and piney notes. The simply named Stout (4 percent ABV), the first beer he brewed after moving from Swans, is a traditional Irish stout. It is described as having "roasted coffee and oven-fresh brownie notes." He noted that more stout is sold at Axe & Barrel than was sold at Swans when he was there.

Tessier's Witbier (5 percent ABV), one of his most popular brews at Swans, has also become a favourite at Axe & Barrel. The Belgian yeast provides spicy notes, while orange peel, coriander, and "a secret spice" add an interesting mix of flavours. Speedway RPA (5 percent ABV) is hoppy like an IPA, but this amber-coloured ale has a tang created by the rye. The award-winning King Kolsch (5 percent ABV), which started as a seasonal offering but is now available year-round, is a classic example of the style: crisp, clean, and light-bodied with a slight maltiness. Most of the beers I tasted were familiar and fairly traditional interpretations of well-known styles. But the most unusual and also most unusually named beer was Fruity Mother Pucker (4 percent ABV). This kettle-soured beer was indeed a lip puckerer. The mix of raspberries, blueberries, and strawberries produced a subtle mingling of fruit flavours.

After we'd finished our discussion, I walked across the parking lot, past the plastic dinosaurs, and into Liquor Planet, where I bought a six-pack of Langford Logger to take to a party that would be attended mainly by non–craft beer drinkers. That evening, one of them decided to try a Langford Logger. After a big swig, he paused for several seconds and said, "This isn't that bad; maybe I'll stop at Axe & Barrel and try a couple of their other beers." And that, from a lifelong and unrepentant Lucky drinker, was strong praise.

POSTSCRIPT: A NEW BREWERY OPENS

Two weeks after the manuscript for *Island Craft* was sent to the publisher, I learned that the Saanich brewing scene had expanded. **Howl Brewing Company** had opened in late June just north of the Victoria International Airport. Dan Van Netten and his wife, Alayna Briemon, had opened Howl adjacent to Fickle Fig Farm Market. Named after the title of a famous poem by mid-20th-century poet Allen Ginsberg, Howl is an outgrowth of a homebrewing hobby and the encouragement of friends. Van Netten, who brews along with his cousin Ben Van Netten, said that the brewery will feature rotating seasonals, brewing small batches of a variety of styles and using, whenever possible, local ingredients. During the first few weeks of operation, Howl beers have included Lands End IPA, Deep Cove Pale Ale, Old Tavern ESB, and a strawberry and a blackberry wheat ale.

CHAPTER 5

THE SOOKE BEER BOOM

Sooke Oceanside Brewery,
Sooke Brewing Company,
Bad Dog Brewing Company

The town centre of Sooke is only 36 kilometres from downtown Victoria. However, when I was a child in Victoria, it seemed very far away. Once, in the early 1950s, we did go to Sooke—very briefly. It was All Sooke Day, an annual July festival featuring logging competitions, barbecued salmon and beef, kids' games, and a best-baby contest. The contest was sponsored by the *Victoria Daily Times*, and my father had to represent the paper and award a small trophy to the proud parents of the winner. Then we got in the car, drove to Colwood Corners, and headed up the old Island Highway to the lake.

I didn't go back to Sooke until 2018, and my, how things had changed. It was now a district municipality with a population of 14,000. Businesses dotted Highway 14, with only a few stretches bordered by trees. Fourteen thousand cars drove this highway each weekday, many of them taking commuters to and from work in Victoria. The town of Sooke had also become a tourist destination—for sport fishermen, campers, or simply people making day excursions. Now, it is also a destination for beer tourists. They come into an area that for decades has been known as one of the Lucky Lager strongholds (the fellow who commented on the Langford Logger I gave him was from Sooke) to visit three microbreweries: Sooke Oceanside Brewery, which opened in 2016, and Sooke Brewing Company and Bad Dog Brewing Company, both of which began business late in 2017. On a rainy Monday morning early in January 2018, I drove to Sooke to visit these most recent additions to Greater Victoria's burgeoning craft beer scene.

Sooke's first craft brewery, **Sooke Oceanside Brewery**, is relatively close to the ocean, but it doesn't have a view of the sea—a forested hill is between the building it shares with a Shell gas station/convenience store and the seashore. Ryan Orr, who owns the brewery with his wife, Karri Jensen, had not been able to find a suitable oceanside location for a restaurant and brewery he was planning and had been approached by the owner of the Shell station to see if he'd like to rent the adjacent vacant space. After saying no twice, Orr agreed. A location that lives up to the brewery's name is still in the long-range plans.

Ryan Orr (left) is the owner and Garritt Lalonde the brewer at Sooke Oceanside Brewery, the first of three breweries to open in the town since 2016. ➜

Orr grew up in the Sooke area and spent many years as a chef in the Clayoquot Wilderness Resort in a remote spot midway up the west coast of Vancouver Island. "I wasn't really much of a beer drinker," he recalled. But when he tasted Driftwood Brewery's Fat Tug, he was impressed with its flavours, and as he discovered other craft beers, he was struck by the tremendous variety of flavours. "I began cooking with beer and thinking of how different craft beers could be paired with food." He also kept bees, made mead, and even went to a U-brew homebrewing store to make honey beer.

After many years of spending several months of the year away from his family, cooking at the wilderness resort, Orr decided it was time to live full-time in the Sooke area. Having a restaurant and a brewery there would enable him to combine his two interests and be with his wife and small children. Sooke was no longer a tiny village a long way from nowhere. Many young families had moved into the area to get away from increasingly congested city life. Quite a lot of them had a taste for craft beer. Sooke was developing a reputation as an artisan centre with craft shops, art galleries, organic farms, and the like. A craft brewery would no doubt find a very receptive audience.

Orr realized that to make a craft brewery a success, he would have to hire a professional brewer. The area's growing number of knowledge-

able craft beer drinkers would quickly recognize an inferior product. He hired Garritt Lalonde, whom he'd met on a tour of Vancouver Island Brewery and kept in touch with. Lalonde, who'd moved to the mainland to work at Surrey's award-winning Central City, was anxious to return to Victoria. The two spent a few years developing recipes and testing them on a half-hectolitre system Orr kept in his garage. They moved the system to the space next to the Shell station and prepared to open Sooke Oceanside Brewery. Three days after they opened in November 2016, they ran out of beer. The area's beer drinkers were ready for craft beer. Lalonde still uses the small brewing system to create special one-off beers, but now most of the brewing is done at Riot Brewing in Chemainus. "We're very hands-on up there," Orr emphasizes. "Garritt oversees all our brewing and is in charge of quality control and packaging."

Lalonde had been a fan of Kokanee lager (considered by many to be British Columbia's best mass-produced beer) until he tried Arctic Ale, an award-winning kolsch created by Swans' Andrew Tessier. That inspired Lalonde to become a homebrewer and, at age 20, to take a job at Vancouver Island Brewery. His work there and at Central City gave him the experience of working at a production brewery and also whetted his desire to run his own brewery, but on a smaller scale. Helping Ryan Orr start up SOB (as Sooke Oceanside Brewery is affectionately called by its local fans) was just what he was looking for.

Lalonde remarked that one of the biggest challenges SOB faced was making a go of it in a territory filled with Lucky Lager devotees. And so Bonfire Blonde (5 percent ABV, 15 IBUs), one of the first beers they created, was a crossover designed to help newcomers make the step from pale American lager to craft ale. Light-bodied, it uses kolsch yeast and Citra hops to create a crisp but still slightly malty beer in which the hops are not overwhelming. "We didn't want to dumb it down," Lalonde remarked. "But we wanted it to be approachable and non-threatening." The other initial offerings included Stiff Jab Pale Ale (5.4 percent ABV), a West Coast version of the style that uses Willamette, Cascade, and Centennial hops. It's not too bitter and has a good malt body and a crisp, dry finish. Renfrew Red Ale (5 percent ABV) uses eight malts, four varieties of hops, and Irish ale yeast. It is malt-forward and has a slight nip or tang. BoneYard IPA (6.5 percent ABV, 68 IBUs) is the strongest regular offering. A classic West Coast–style IPA, it has piney and floral notes. Lalonde said that SOB beers are generally malt-forward, that he likes to experiment a little after he's got the style right, and that the beers are well balanced. One of his experiments features an interesting additive; it's an IPA with cedar and juniper in it.

SOB has been successful not just with the young city dwellers who have moved south of Colwood Corners and the tourists but also with many of the local Lucky drinkers. "We have an account at the Empress Hotel in Victoria," Orr noted. "And we have another at the local Royal Canadian Legion in Sooke." And it's not just the crossover Bonfire Blonde that people are drinking; SOB's most popular beer is the Renfrew Red Ale, a style that many of the area residents may not have heard of before 2016.

As I left Sooke Oceanside Brewery, I noticed a sign beside a garbage can placed next to a picnic table: "Bears in area—make sure garbage is in bin." I thought that although the Sooke area was part of the southern Island's rapidly expanding West Shore, it was bordered by wilderness on one side and ocean on the other. Bear sightings were common; the *Sooke Pocket News*, an online publication, reminded readers: "We are guests in bear country." Cougar sightings were not unusual.

~~~~~~~~~~

My second stop was in the centre of town, half a block off Highway 14, at the home of **Sooke Brewing Company**, which had opened a year after Sooke Oceanside. Although the brewery is not in a big building, it is in an impressive one. A large cedar tree, debarked and polished, forms a rustic artistic column supporting the canopy over the entrance. On either side are columns faced with cobblestones. Inside, stumps form the base for some of the tables, and large slabs of finished wood, all of it local, serve as tabletops. There's a crosscut saw, known to loggers as a misery whip, on one wall, a reminder of the industry that long formed the economic base of the Sooke area, and on another, paintings of giant cedars and Douglas firs. Visible from the taproom is the 15-hectolitre brewhouse, fabricated by Saanichton's Specific Mechanical. The building and the land are owned by Carl Scott, who is also one of the brewery's founders. The building is leased by the brewery.

I was greeted by Yari Nielsen, another of the owners. He told me that the idea for a brewery in Sooke had been born when he and Scott, on a camping trip to the northern part of the Island, had visited Tofino Brewing. They thought that having a brewery like it in their hometown, Sooke, would be a good idea. Together with Anton Rabien, another Sooke native, Trevor Wilson, and John Adair, an award-winning brewer, they began to plan one. In 2016, they received the go-ahead from the district council, which believed a brewery would be good for the area's growing tourist business, and started a $2 million construction project.

Adair, a Victoria native, had been an award-winning homebrewer before he turned professional with Parallel 49 Brewing in Vancouver. Like many beginning pros, he began working at the end of the brewing process, on the packaging line, before moving up to becoming a brewer. He then became the first brewer for Gladstone Brewing of Courtenay, where he won Canadian Brewing Awards medals for his porter, dark lager, and Belgian ale. Wanting to broaden his brewing experience, he travelled to Scotland, where he worked for Six Degrees North, which specialized in Belgian-style beers. While in Scotland, he made two trips to Belgium, biking around the country, visiting breweries, talking to brewers, and discovering different ways of doing things. Then he returned home to be part, once again, of a brewery start-up. "I really loved hops when I started brewing. Tree Brewing's Hop Head really turned me onto hoppy beers. Now I've become really partial to Belgian beers; they make such a creative use of yeasts. I call yeast the unsung hero of brewing." He would use his love of both hops and yeasts in creating beers for Sooke Brewing Company.

Adair described Sooke Brewing's beers as "adventurous, but approachable and interesting." He doesn't have specific beers on his core list because he feels that to limit himself to one example of a specific style does not give patrons experience with the great variety of craft beers available. Instead, he chooses to always have on tap at least one example from each of four general categories: a sessionable, easy-drinking beer; a hoppy beer; a dark beer; and a Belgian-style beer.

When I visited, the easy-drinking beer was a Vienna lager (5 percent ABV). "This is our most approachable style," Adair told me.

"It's light and refreshing, and the Vienna malts give it a toasty, bready flavour." The IPA (7 percent ABV, 70 IBUs), a North American version of the style, with stone fruit, berries, tropical fruit, and pine flavours, has a bitter finish. The dark beer was an oatmeal stout. Although it is only 4 percent ABV, it is full-bodied and creamy. Roasted barley and raw oats give chocolatey, raisin, and cocoa notes. The Belgian category was represented by a blonde ale (6 percent ABV). The yeasty flavours characteristic of the style were balanced by the Hallertau hops, which gave a crisp and dry quality to the beer. Other early offerings have included a Belgian IPA, a German pilsner, and an FES (foreign extra stout). A barrel-aging program has begun, and a saison will be one of the first beers to come out of one of the wooden vessels that had previously contained gin or bourbon.

An impressive column made from locally harvested timber dominates the entrance to Sooke Brewing Company. ↓

John Adair gave me a tour through the brewhouse, where Carl Scott, Trevor Wilson, Anton Rabien, and Yari Nielsen, the other owners, were doing employee duties, two taking recently delivered beer kegs and passing them up to a loft where the other two were stacking them. We then retired to the tasting room, where I sipped a small glass of the Belgian Blonde as Adair discussed the importance of being local.

Although the 15-hectolitre brewing system was designed to be a production brewery and there were plans to can or bottle the beers, Sooke Brewing's success would depend a great deal on its being centred in Sooke. "Three of the owners are from Sooke, the owner of the building has a business next door, and the building was designed to say Sooke," Adair said. He noted that many BC towns of this size have a brewery, that the current boom of breweries was essentially local in focus. "When a brewery has a local connection, it becomes a focus for the community." Yari Nielsen had earlier remarked that Sooke needed a meeting place like the tasting room that we were sitting in, a place to visit and enjoy craft beer. Several days later, as I looked at photographs of the tasting room on Facebook, I saw that in its first few weeks, Sooke Brewing had indeed become a gathering place; the 25-seat room was jammed with people watching a game on the television set, playing board games, or just enjoying each other's company. When the warmer, drier weather arrived, the crowds of locals and tourists would no doubt spill out onto the 30-seat patio, enjoying beers that were designed to be "adventurous, but approachable and interesting."

***

Bad Dog Brewing Company, the most recent brewery to open on southern Vancouver Island, was just over a month old when I visited. From Sooke Brewing, I drove a few kilometres southwest into a semirural area not that far from the shores of the Strait of Juan de Fuca. Parking next to a sign that read BAD DOG BREWING, I was greeted by two barking and tail-wagging dogs that were anything but bad. In fact, they seemed to think that I'd come to visit them and not the brewery located in a small building a couple of dozen metres behind them. The building, which had been the woodworking shop of John Lyle, had been transformed into a commercial brewery when, he confessed, his "homebrewing hobby got out of control." But there's still some space left for carpentry equipment—the brewery is in an area zoned for home-based businesses, and only 640 square metres of the building can be used for making beer.

Lyle had begun his hobby that got out of control 15 years earlier, after he'd tried a friend's homebrew, enjoyed it, and thought, *If he can do it, so can I.* "I discovered that the beer I made was much better than what I'd been drinking before." He wasn't the only one who thought so; so did his brother-in-law Glenn Barlow, owner of Victoria's Cook St. Liquor, a mecca for people looking for a selection of hard-to-find craft beers. "He told me it was good as some of the stuff he was selling." And so, about five years ago, Lyle and his wife, Rosanne, began to talk seriously about starting a brewery. They first considered Victoria, but they couldn't find a suitable location and realized that, even if they could, the craft brewing scene in the capital city was getting pretty crowded. Then, the District of Sooke changed its zoning laws, and it became possible for the Lyles to create a brewery in the woodworking building.

Having decided to locate their new business on the family property, the Lyles began the process of wading through red tape, building the brewery, and developing recipes. "Because we were not serviced by city water and sewer service, we had to have our well certified as potable and build an acceptable septic field." But the biggest problem came with the equipment. The Chinese-built system they purchased from a Vancouver wholesaler had many things wrong with it and required over $8,000 of repairs (which were not covered by the dealer). Developing recipes was the easiest part; in fact, Lyle had been sharing his Honey Blonde with appreciative friends and relatives for a long time.

We walked up the driveway to the brewery, followed by Kona and Duke, the not-so-bad dogs. They weren't allowed to come in, as they were still very damp and smelly from their time spent playing in an early morning shower. Inside, I was introduced to the three other members of the four-person brewery team: Rosanne, who handled sales and other business details; and sons Chris and Paul, who handled cleanup and packaging duties. John Lyle had decided that, rather than distribute only in kegs or have a mobile canning company package his product, he would buy his own canning equipment. "It's much more convenient, and cans are more practical to distribute," he told me.

Bad Dog debuted with four beers, two of which could be called entry-level or crossover beers and two hoppier, but not too hoppy, beers. Within a month, a darker beer joined the lineup. 642 (4.5 percent ABV) is a session ale named after the prefix for Sooke telephone numbers. "We wanted to start with something that would appeal to local beer drinkers.

This is Lucky Lager and Bud Light country." Light straw-coloured and light-bodied, it uses pilsner malts, which give a slight sweetness with honey notes, and Saaz hops that balance the sweetness with a crisp, slightly tangy finish. Lyle reported that it had already converted several of the area's drinkers of mainstream beer and that the first batch had quickly run out. "It's as light as you can be in an ale," Lyle noted. Honey Blonde (5 percent ABV) is a dark golden ale that is maltier than the 642 and has a sweetness contributed by the 20 kilograms of British Columbia honey used in each batch. Cascade hops provide floral and piney flavours, while Hallertau hops create a crispness that balances the malt and honey sweetness.

Although Old Red (5 percent ABV) is lightly hopped, it does move into what is somewhat unfamiliar territory for drinkers of mainstream lagers. Crystal malts give this American-style Irish ale sweet, caramel flavours, and there is a slight hop bite. Tire Biter IPA (6 percent ABV) is, as the name suggests, Bad Dog's most aggressive beer. Amarillo, Cascade, Centennial, and Columbus hops provide grapefruit notes. However, it is relatively low in IBUs for the style, with 50. "I don't want it to be a palate wrecker," Lyle explained. Coco Ale (5 percent ABV), Bad Dog's "dark-side" beer, is neither a stout nor a porter. It is light-bodied but has a complex mixture of chocolate, coffee, and burnt toast flavours.

With the exception of Tire Biter, all of Bad Dog's beers are a sessionable 5 percent ABV or less. "I try to make beers that go back to basics, that don't go over the top," Lyle said. "They are beers designed to appeal to the average beer drinker." They certainly won't intimidate Lucky or Bud aficionados, but they will offer them very flavourful ales.

After my visit to Bad Dog Brewing, I made a short drive south to a viewpoint overlooking the Strait of Juan de Fuca. As I watched the waves roll onto the beach, I thought about the three brewery visits I'd just completed. My stops had marked a transition in my travels. Each

Bad Dog Brewing is a family affair. From left to right, Paul, John (co-owner and brewer), Chris, and Rosanne (co-owner) Lyle are watched carefully by Kona (left) and Duke, who had an influence on the naming of the newest of Sooke's breweries and its beers. ←

of the earlier breweries I'd visited had been one of many options for craft beer fans in the Greater Victoria area. From now on, I'd be visiting smaller towns and cities like Sooke, where the craft breweries and brewpubs would be integral parts of their communities, offering not just a variety of non-mainstream beers but also centres where people could listen to local musicians, look at local art hanging on the walls, and visit with friends. Sooke, as well as many of the places I would soon visit, was located in a place that could be considered a Lucky Lager stronghold. While that value-priced product manufactured far from Vancouver Island by an international megabrewer would probably never be completely displaced, the new breweries and brewpubs were offering members of their local communities flavourful alternatives that frequently had been brewed just a few dozen metres from where they were being enjoyed.

PART II

MID-NORTH ISLAND

From the Cowichan Valley to Campbell River

CENTRAL, WESTERN, AND NORTHERN
VANCOUVER ISLAND

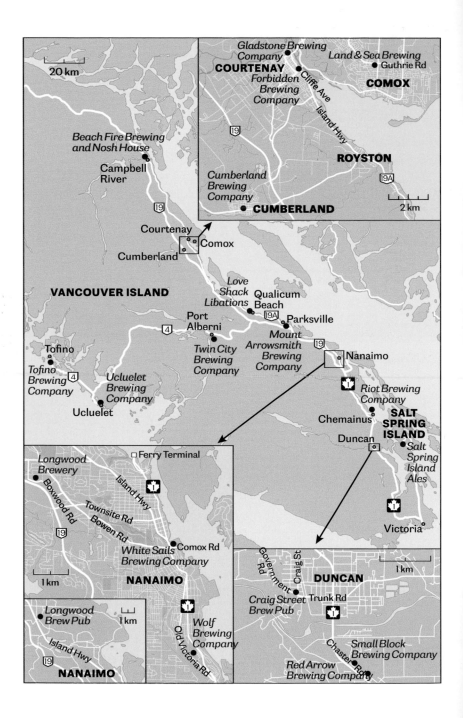

A few years ago, I heard the saying "Go north, get Lucky"—a "command" that was jokingly addressed to beer drinkers in the central and northern parts of Vancouver Island. Shortly after that, I read an article stating that Lucky Lager outsold all other alcoholic beverages in Nanaimo, the Island's second-largest city. Around the same time, I found out that the Cowichan Valley was proudly referred to as the "Valley of Lucky Lager" and that the small city of Cumberland had been declared the "Lucky-est town in British Columbia." Bob Surgenor of Comox had wanted to challenge Lucky's dominance north of Nanaimo, and in 2009, he created a brewery that would, he told me, "offer Lucky Lager drinkers something different—but not too different." By 2012, Surgenor's brewery was out of business.

Harley Smith, now co-owner of Longwood Brewery, remembered the time when someone walked up to the bar at Longwood Brew Pub and asked him what he had that tasted like Lucky. Smith's reply: "Nothing, I hope!" Smith did, however, have several alternatives to offer, lagers and ales that had been brewed just a few metres from the bar. Longwood was not alone in offering a variety of good locally made beers. Beginning in the late 1980s, breweries or brewpubs in 11 different central and upper Vancouver Island centres have offered their patrons locally made lagers and ales that didn't taste like Lucky.

CHAPTER 6

ISLAND HOPPING FROM DUNCAN TO CHEMAINUS VIA SALT SPRING ISLAND

Craig Street Brew Pub,
Red Arrow Brewing Company,
Small Block Brewing Company,
Salt Spring Island Ales,
Riot Brewing Company

When we were children, the Malahat Summit, 352 metres above sea level, marked for us the dividing point between the lower Island, which was known and familiar, and all points north, places unvisited and unknown. We usually never reached the summit, leaving Highway 1 at the Shawnigan Lake cut-off to complete the trip to our cabin. I remember going to Duncan, 61 kilometres from Victoria, only two or three times, and then only on very short day trips. Once we made an overnighter to Port Alberni.

As I began the second part of my travels, which would take me to 17 breweries and brewpubs located north of the Malahat Summit, I remembered my youthful unfamiliarity with the central and northern parts of the Island. In 2010, I'd stopped in Duncan and Nanaimo to visit three breweries. Since then 14 new breweries had sprung up, some of them in places I'd never spent any time in: Chemainus, Qualicum Beach, Tofino, Cumberland, and Courtenay. This would be as much a journey of discovery as that long-ago trip to Port Alberni in the family's 1949 Plymouth.

My first stop was in Duncan, a city of just under 5,000 people, but the commercial centre of the Cowichan Valley Regional District, which has a population of just over 80,000. I parked beside the old Esquimalt and Nanaimo Railway station house, the building in front of which we'd alighted from the train on one of those day trips. Stepping onto the sidewalk, I noted a trail of red footprints that led toward and then past a plaque that explained that they marked a pathway to the 40 totem poles in the downtown area. Created by contemporary Cowichan Indigenous artists, they had given the town the name City of Totems and were very popular tourist attractions.

The footprints led me to Craig Street and my destination, **Craig Street Brew Pub** which, when it opened in 2006, became the first brewery ever to operate between Greater Victoria and Nanaimo. The rain had been falling steadily during my walk, and as I sat at a table enjoying a hearty bowl of soup, I was pleased to see and feel the light and warmth from a log-burning fireplace at the end of the room. The brewpub is a four-level affair. The brewhouse, bar, and restaurant are on the main floor; the mezzanine level has a small, snug-like pub. The third floor houses the library—not really a library, although there are low bookshelves along the walls. Here are two of Craig Street's televisions sets, and the library is crowded

On a grey, drizzly day, Liz Steward (co-owner) and Warren Hulton (brewer) each enjoy a pint in front of Craig Street Brew Pub's cheerful log-burning fireplace. ➜

on Vancouver Canucks game nights, as it is when local musicians are invited to perform. During warmer weather, the fourth level, a rooftop deck and barbecue area, is open.

I'd visited the brewpub in 2009 on another rainy day and had met Liz Steward (co-owner along with husband Lance) and then brewer

Chris Gress (now brewer and co-owner of nearby Red Arrow Brewing). Steward had then talked about the skepticism of many Duncan residents who wondered why anyone would want to open a brewpub at the eastern entrance to the Cowichan Valley. But the Stewards' decision wasn't a whim. The pair had operated Just Jakes, a respected local restaurant, for nearly 15 years. Great fans of Spinnakers, Canoe, and Swans in Victoria, they knew that the Duncan government liquor store ranked in the top 25 percent in the province for sales of imported beers. They felt that the area was ready for this kind of restaurant and bar—and, as Steward remarked, "We wanted to give Lucky drinkers the taste of something different!" She confessed that the brewery did keep bottles of Lucky on hand but would tell a patron who ordered one that he or she

would have to sample Craig Street beer (for free) before the Lucky was served. "We converted hundreds of mainstream drinkers during our first year," she laughed.

If converting Lucky drinkers was a challenge, just getting the brewhouse assembled was a bigger one. When Steward sat down to talk with me during my 2018 visit, she recounted the adventure of getting equipment. "We bought our system through a broker. There was a new one sitting unused in the Dominican Republic; the person who went down there to inspect it said that it was really great, so we bought it. But then the ship that was bringing it to Canada got lost at sea . . . for over three months! It finally showed up in Vancouver. But there was a dockworkers strike and so nothing could be unloaded. When everything finally arrived, Chris, our brewer, was so happy that he ran out and hugged the tanks. The whole delivery process took over five months."

When Chris Gress left Craig Street to assume the role of co-owner (along with Liz and Lance Steward) of Red Arrow Brewing, his duties were taken over by Warren Hulton. Hulton, a self-confessed consumer of Lucky and Bud before he began making craft beer, had worked with the Stewards for nearly four decades, first when the three of them were at Victoria's Keg restaurant and then in Duncan, where he worked in the kitchen of Just Jakes and then at the brewpub. "I began to help Chris by keeping an eye on the brewing operations on weekends. Bit-by-bit I learned about brewing from him." Gress's influence on Hulton is strong. "I brew our four core beers according to the recipes Chris developed. But the seasonal beers I'm doing are my own." These have included a citrus kolsch, containing orange and lemon peel, and Craig Street ISA, a session pale ale made with Citra and Mosaic hops.

The four core beers include Cowichan Bay Lager, Arbutus Pale Ale, Shawnigan Irish Ale, and Mt. Prevost Porter. About the lager, Hulton said, "Chris created it to ease the Lucky drinkers into craft beer. He made a light, German-style lager that's very crisp and clean."

In 2006, it was very unusual for a craft brewery to have a lager on its core list because it took up so much tank space. "It was so popular that, within a year, we had to install another conditioning tank so that we'd always have it available," Steward recalled.

Arbutus Pale Ale is also a light-bodied beer. An English-style ale, it's only mildly hoppy (although Hulton has upped the hoppiness). It was Gress's way of introducing the people of the Cowichan Valley to hoppier beers.

Shawnigan Irish Ale features what Hulton called "heavier, bolder malting." It's what Gress called, when I talked to him several years ago, "a beery beer." He added that it doesn't seem heavy because of the natural carbonation. Mt. Prevost Porter, Gress enthused at that time, "is such a neat beer. It's great in beer-culture markets, but harder to sell here. So I was really surprised when I took it off our list for a while and people asked to have it back." Dark in colour and medium-bodied, it has coffee notes and a dry finish.

With the exception of Porter, which is 5.6 percent ABV, each of these beers is 5 percent. "We want good beers that people like," Hulton commented. "They're true to style; we don't go crazy."

When Craig Street opened in 2006, its beers received an enthusiastic response from people relatively unfamiliar with craft beer. Of course, given the popularity of mainstream pale lagers in the area, it wasn't surprising that Cowichan Bay Lager was the most popular. The core beers remain popular, and people look forward to Hulton's new seasonal beers. Remarked Steward, "Our customers are much more knowledgeable now about craft beer and have had lots of experience with so many good beers here, around the Island, and on the mainland."

"People really know what they're drinking, and they know what's good and what's bad. It keeps us working to brew the best beers we can," Hulton added.

~~~~~~~~~~

As I retraced my way along the red footprints to the car and then drove to the edge of town to **Red Arrow Brewing**, I recalled what Liz Steward had said about why she and husband Lance decided to start Craig Street Brew Pub and then later, along with brewer Chris Gress, to open a production brewery. "We wanted to grow," she had remarked about both decisions. Opening the brewpub next to their restaurant Just Jakes marked their entry into the craft beer scene that had been growing for over two decades in Victoria but hadn't really begun in the Cowichan Valley. Starting up Red Arrow marked a new growth phase. The three of them would have to learn the processes of operating a craft brewery the annual production of which would be at least four times greater than that of the brewpub. Moreover, they'd have to master the logistics of distributing their product. The three of them had played an important role in the growth of a craft beer culture in the area, but the Cowichan Valley was not large enough to support a production brewery by itself. Gress would have to create very good beers, which he did (two Canadian Brewing Awards bronze medals in 2016), and the beers would have to be made available fairly far afield. (By 2018, Red Arrow products were distributed through British Columbia and into Alberta.)

I pulled in to the parking lot of Red Arrow and walked around the red brick, ivy-covered building, previously the home of a motorcycle manufacturing business that had given the brewery its name. In the border along the wall was a sign that read: ZEUS HOPS, indicating the spot where recently planted rhizomes would soon begin to grow into bines that would reach the top of the building by the late summer and bear hops that would be used in the brewhouse inside. In the middle of the courtyard, the site of the beer garden in better weather, stood a totem pole that had been carved by a Cowichan artist and that had come with the building. At the edge of a rooftop crouched a gargoyle, which had also come with the building and had come with a name: Christopher. Its presence and its name had been quickly seized upon by the new occupants and used in their publicity. At the edge of the parking lot stood a food truck with the sign JUST JAKES ON THE GO. During the warmer-weather months, this would be its permanent home, a place where visitors to the tasting room could purchase snacks and light meals to enjoy with their beers.

My brief tour of the outside completed, I escaped the rain, entering the tasting room. There were a few tables where patrons could enjoy Red Arrow beers. However, because the brewery was without a lounge licence, they could enjoy a total of only 365 millilitres of beer, poured into taster glasses and served on a wooden tray painted red and shaped like an arrow. Most of the area was taken up with the largest gift shop/retail store I'd see in my visits to Vancouver Island breweries. There were glasses of different shapes and sizes, beer coolers, T-shirts, hoodies, and baseball caps, and in the glass-doored refrigerator case, a very large selection of Red Arrow ales and lagers.

Chris (the owner-brewer, not the gargoyle) was busy back in the brewery for a few minutes. So I took a stool at the edge of the tasting room, gazed at the riches of swag around me, and thought about our first meeting, nearly a decade ago, at Craig Street. Then, he had told me about his entry into the craft beer business. He became interested in microbreweries in the early 1990s when he'd moved from northern Saskatchewan to Victoria, met Swans' first head brewer, Sean Hoyne, and was inspired to build a pilot brewery in his backyard. There he made beer for his Camosun College friends, the Brew Engineers as they called themselves, and listened to their feedback. While he was working at a Victoria bar, he kidded a group from Duncan that there was no good beer there. In the group were Liz and Lance Steward. When he learned from them about plans for a brewpub on Craig Street, he applied for the brewer's job, got it, and with the help of Hoyne, set up the brewing equipment and began considering what beers to create.

"I noticed that in Duncan people seemed to be drinking either Lucky or imports," Gress had remembered. "So I visualized a colour spectrum of beers from light to dark. I decided to be right down the middle in the interpretation of styles. I could push the envelope and be creative when I brewed limited-edition seasonal beers. At first I was pretty traditional."

His business in the brewery behind the door in the taproom finished, Gress joined me and brought the story of his brewing career up to date. As the time passed at Craig Street, he'd become more creative, blending yeasts and experimenting with hops although, he admitted, Duncan had not, at that time, become a hop-based beer culture. He had to make sure he didn't go overboard.

As his creativity blossomed, so did a dream—a dream held by so many professional brewers—to start his own brewery. "I wanted to do my own thing, to grow as a brewer." At first he considered opening a brewery in Victoria's Rock Bay area. However, when the Stewards expressed an interest in supporting him if he'd start his new venture in Duncan and told him that they knew of other people who'd be interested in investing, he decided to build his brewery in the City of Totems. He knew the people of the area and had attracted a loyal following among them, the Stewards were well-respected citizens of Duncan, and the area had excellent brewing water. Now, all he needed was a place to house his new business. That's when he and the Stewards learned that the building that had been home to the Red Arrow Motorcycle Company was available for lease. "The building had a great deal of local history:

the place itself, the motorcycle business, the totem pole celebrating Indigenous cultures. It had the space we needed and plenty of area for parking. And it was almost right next to the highway. Over 30,000 cars drive past every day." Duncan's first production brewery opened in 2013.

Our conversation moved to the topic of "local," a word and a theme that is becoming increasingly important for craft brewers. "It's important to be part of the local community," Gress said. "We want our brewery to be part of a community and its history." He spoke about the totem pole and the building, pointed to the Red Arrow cycle leaning against a wall of the tasting room, and then explained one unusual but very significant way that the brewery and the community are linked. Every spring, Red Arrow gives out small hop rhizomes to anyone who wants to take and cultivate them. In the early autumn, the people harvest the hop cones and bring them to the brewery, where they become ingredients in an annual release called Fresh Hop Co-op Ale. "Local hops and local people—it's about us being involved with the community and the community being involved with the brewery."

There are five core beers on Red Arrow's list: Kustom Kolsch, Old Style Lager, Sweet Leaf IPA, Piggy Pale Ale, and Midnite Umber Ale. The first two represent Red Arrow's lighter beers; the kolsch is an old German-style ale that has recently become very popular among craft beer drinkers, while the second is Gress's interpretation of a pale American lager, a style that has long been a favourite in the Cowichan Valley. Pilsner malts give the kolsch a slight sweetness, while Mount Hood hops provide spicy and herbal notes. Gress refers to this 5 percent ABV, 25 IBU ale as "an unassuming beer." The lager (5 percent ABV, 20 IBUs) balances biscuity and caramel malt flavours with tangy, crisp hop notes. "Sometimes you just want something refreshing and clean," Gress remarked.

Chris Gress relaxes in the tasting room of Red Arrow Brewing, the Duncan production brewery he co-founded with Lance and Liz Steward of Craig Street Brew Pub. ←

Sweet Leaf, the brewery's strongest (6.3 percent ABV) and hoppiest (65 IBUs) offering, is a Northwest-style IPA, which the website describes as floral and fruity. It uses Cascade, Citra, Chinook, and Zythos hops, which contribute tropical fruit aromas and flavours, and Zeus hops (the variety soon to begin climbing the trellis placed outside against the brick walls), which add a grapefruity flavour. "It's an expensive beer to make," Gress commented, "but we want to bring the best flavours forward."

Piggy Pale Ale and Midnite Umber Ale, each a 2016 Canadian Brewing Awards bronze medal winner, both exemplify Gress's idea that a beer can be created to match a story or that a story can be created to match a beer. Piggy is a hybrid of British and American styles with Fuggle hops giving earthy notes found in British versions of the style and Centennial and Cascade hops contributing the piney and floral qualities of North American West Coast versions. It was created as a tribute to the Cowichan rugby team, which is named the Piggies. And therein lies the (Piggy) tale, which is narrated on the label. "Our storied club has a rich history of fantastic rugger and countless shenanigans. It represents an impressive list of characters past and present, who define the playfulness and humour required to be part of the Cowichan Rugby Football Club family. Opposing teams know that it's going to be a hard game. They also know that every drop of blood and sweat left on the field will be replenished back in the clubhouse with the help of a pint of some fine ale. We took our love of the game and pitched it into this Pale Ale. Pouring a light golden orange, this Piggy has a medium hop aroma, balanced maltiness and just enough gumption to bring home the game."

Midnite Umber Ale is ruby-brown in colour, medium-bodied, and smooth. Apricot, toffee, and brown sugar notes highlight this 5.1 percent ABV, malt-forward beer. Having created the beer, the brewers gave it a story. The label depicts a fierce gargoyle crouched atop a ruined column, its fangs bared, the tips of its wings thrust aggressively forward. Behind it, storm clouds are gathering and seem about to obscure a red-orange moon. "Every brewery needs a guardian. Meet ours, Christopher, the all-seeing gargoyle. . . . As the bell tolls in the darkest hour, Christopher is always keeping a watchful eye."

After I'd said goodbye to Gress, I walked through the patio area and waved farewell to Christopher, who didn't look half so looming and fierce as he did on the label. As I entered my car and drove a few hundred metres north to my next destination, I remembered a sign that had been posted beside the entrance to the Craig Street brewhouse when I'd first met Gress. It read: WHEN I GREW UP IN NORTHERN SASKATCHEWAN, MY GRANDFATHER TOLD ME THAT IF I COULD FIND A JOB THAT I TRULY ENJOY, ONE: I WOULD BE A LUCKY MAN, AND TWO: THE JOB WOULDN'T FEEL LIKE WORK. HE WAS RIGHT. I DON'T JUST ENJOY MY JOB, I LOVE IT. It was clear after my conversation with him at Red Arrow that, even though he had devised new recipes for the beer created at the new brewery, the passion and devotion for the job he loved remained as intense as ever.

When I arrived at **Small Block Brewing Company**, Duncan's newest craft brewery had been open less than three weeks (they served their first beers on St. Patrick's Day). Located in a recently built light-industry complex just a few blocks north of Red Arrow, it is owned by Cate and Aaron Scally, two homebrewers who had visited Duncan a few years earlier, fallen in love with the Cowichan Valley and soon moved there. Aaron was not able to attend our meeting as he was halfway around the world performing helicopter maintenance for Thai Aviation Services. "He's loved mechanics all his life," Cate told me. "In fact, he took a Volkswagen engine apart when he was only five years old—he didn't put it back together though."

It was an accident that prevented Aaron from doing mechanical work that indirectly led to his starting up Small Block. "We'd always liked craft beers. I loved Okanagan Spring Pale Ale, Shaftebury Cream Ale, and Granville Island Maple Cream," Cate said, referring to three of British Columbia's early craft beers. "When he hurt himself, we both began homebrewing. People really seemed to like our beer, and when we

moved to Duncan, we thought we'd turn our hobby into a profession."
Aaron's loves of brewing and mechanical activities were joined when
they chose the name for their new venture. "A small-block engine is the
foundation of homebuilt cars," Cate explained.

I asked her whether there had been any Lucky Lager drinking in her
past. "Oh, gosh, no!" she exclaimed in mock horror. "But," she continued,
"I've been accused of ruining some Lucky drinkers since we opened this
place. Some of them don't want anything to do anymore with Cowichan
champagne." The term "Cowichan champagne," she explained, was a local
nickname for Vancouver Island's widely
consumed pale North American lager.

Small Block's Nail Head Pale
Ale is being packaged in cans for sale
both at the brewery and in other
locations. However, neither Cate nor
Aaron intends their new business to
be only a production brewery. "The people of the Cowichan Valley are
very supportive of local businesses. Just as a car can be built around a
small-block engine, we'd like to help create a community around Small
Block Brewing. Already we've had some people approach us about
holding a benefit night in our tasting lounge, and a local musician came to
us with the idea of holding jam sessions here, which we're already doing.
We have game nights, another way of bringing people together. And
while they are here, people will be able to look at work by local artists;
we're going to turn the walls of the lounge into an art gallery."

Although Cate and Aaron had received many compliments for
their homebrewed ales, they realized that they had neither the experience nor the time to take on brewing duties at Small Block; they needed
someone with a professional brewing background. They didn't have
far to look. Zach Blake, a Cowichan Valley native, had been brewing for
three years just down the road at Red Arrow. Before that, he'd worked
at a local liquor store where he'd become familiar with the growing
number of British Columbia craft breweries and the proliferation of

Zach Blake (brewer) and Cate
Scally (co-owner with husband
Aaron) await the arrival of patrons
in the tasting room of Small Block
Brewing, the newest of Duncan's
three craft breweries. ➜

styles, some traditional and some new interpretations of old styles. He was a homebrewer with agricultural roots and frequently grew his own hops. In fact, at one time, he'd even considered making his living as a hop farmer. In addition to several weeks apprenticing under Murray Hunter at Salt Spring Island Ales and three years working for Chris Gress of Red Arrow, he'd taken correspondence courses on brewing from the University of Oklahoma and had recently attended a seminar in San Diego on the uses of yeast in brewing.

"The idea of brewing on a smaller scale than that of Red Arrow appealed to me," he said. "I'd have a chance to work on specialty beers and seasonal releases. I learned so much at Red Arrow, and here there'd be a real chance for me to grow creatively."

Cate, Zach, and I sat in the tasting room, which already had a few paintings (artistic renditions of car logos) and took sips of samples of the four core beers. Cate explained the names given to the ales, and Zach provided tasting notes. Hornet Blonde Ale, named after the 1950 Fabulous

Hudson Hornet race car, is Small Block's crossover beer. Rounded and light-to-medium in body, it's slightly more bitter than most blonde ales, Zach explained. The Magnum, Opal, Saaz, and Hallertau hops give it "a nice hop snap." Dagmar India Session Ale, a tribute to the bumper of the 1956 Cadillac Eldorado, has a fresh-bread taste contributed by the Maris Otter malt. Cascade hops provide grapefruit and pine notes, while Citra hops add lemony flavours.

Nail Head, the name given by hot rodders for a Buick engine they like to use in building their cars, is the title given to Small Block's pale ale. "We want our pale ale to be balanced," Zach explained. Amarillo hops introduce stone-fruit flavours, while Northern Brewer hops give cedary and earthy notes. Miss Lead, as the 1951 Mercury Eight, the Lead Sled, was called, gives its name to the oatmeal stout. In order for it to have the smooth, creamy mouthfeel of an English stout, Zach used English malts and "built" (i.e., chemically altered) the water to resemble that used by English breweries in the famous brewery town of Burton-on-Trent. The English malts create roasted, chocolate flavours, while the yeasts create date and cherry notes.

Zach referred to these four beers as good, solid core beers. But he went on to remark that he'd like to offer some limited-edition brews that were somewhat different. He spoke of beers created with locally foraged ingredients and others fermented with wild yeasts. Already he was planning cask nights in which he could present patrons with a variety of styles. The first would be held just over a week after my visit, and the beer would be a version of the Dagmar ISA called Hop, Skip, and a Mango. An ESB, which would certainly appeal to the valley's contingent of British expatriates, was in the works.

Cate told me that within a few weeks each of the four core beers would be available in cans that could be purchased at the brewery and area liquor stores. "The trend toward more in-house sales of beer is growing," she said. "Already people are coming in, trying our beers, and taking some home. Our location makes us easily accessible to people in the valley. We want to remain small, to make the brewery and tasting room the focus of our operations."

The number of people arriving each day at the tasting room is growing. You could say that, even though it is patrons who are doing the arriving, Small Block's engines are all revved up, and they're about to take off.

~~~~~~~~~

The next morning, I took the ferry from Crofton (a 20-minute drive north from Duncan) to Salt Spring Island. Although our family had a slight historical connection with the island—my maternal grandfather had owned land there early in the 20th century—I hadn't been there until the early 1980s. When I returned nearly three decades later to interview Murray Hunter, the part owner of Gulf Islands Brewing—now called **Salt Spring Island Ales**—the area was well on its way to becoming a centre for craftspeople and artisans, painters and authors, organic farmers and estate wine makers.

In the mid-1990s, Hunter, the owner of a Salt Spring Island brew-on-premises business, decided to sponsor a bus trip for his patrons to Victoria's Great Canadian Beer Festival. On the way home, he and his friend Bob Ellison discussed the idea of opening a brewery on the island. For five dollars, the local school board sold them plans it had for a 185-metre-square barn. They then built their brewery on Ellison's farm at the foot of Mount Bruce. It was set in a grove of cedars, some of which supplied the building's siding. They sold their first batch of beer in 1998.

Why, I had asked Hunter when I talked to him in 2009, did he want to start a brewery on an island with a population of not much more than 10,000 and from which they'd have to transport much of their product via ferry to craft beer–savvy Victoria? "We felt that there were a sufficient number of people here with educated beer palates—people who drank beer to enjoy the flavour, not the alcohol. We also wanted to give something back to the island, to buy local products, and to create beer that reflected the lifestyle of people here, somewhat laid back, not too assertive. And there's a spring on Bob's farm that's pure and clean and ideal for brewing beer. We are truly a cottage brewery."

Hunter and Ellison sold the brewery to Becky Julseth and Neil Cooke-Dallin in 2009, and they, in turn, sold it in 2016 to Michael Forbes and Ian Laing, two Victoria entrepreneurs. However, the idea of the local, cottage brewery using local ingredients continues. The web page displays the brewery's tag line, "Drink Beer with Nature," the phrase referring to the use of locally sourced hops (which Julseth introduced in 2013), organic malt, and such other nearby ingredients as heather, honey, nettles, and even mussels—along with the fresh spring water.

A few kilometres along Fulford-Ganges Road, I turned left at Furness Road and drove past TANDMGems and Alchemy Farm Flowers to the base of Mount Bruce and the parking lot for Salt Spring Island Ales. I walked past the portable toilets for the use of visitors to the brewery and up a steep set of stairs to the tasting room. Unfortunately, I was unable to talk with the two head brewers; Heather Kilbourne was on maternity leave, and Tim Rennie had left a few minutes before our scheduled interview to catch a ferry to Vancouver. Kelly Pearson, an Australian who was working her way around the world and had been at the brewery for a few weeks, showed me around. On a flat area just outside of the ground-floor brewery stood four shining, newly installed fermenting tanks, one of which, Pearson told me, contained nettle ale, which had been brewed the day before and the name-giving ingredients of which she had foraged in a wilderness area the day before that. Not far from the new fermenters were the four old "Grundy" tanks, probably made in England well over five decades ago, and now looking very dingy and useless beside their replacements.

The brief tour over, Pearson kindly offered me bottles of some of the brewery's main products, which a few days later I enjoyed and made the tasting notes that, along with the notes on the brewery's website, formed the basis of my descriptions of the beers.

Salt Spring Island Ales offers six year-round beers, three of them winners of Canadian Brewing Awards medals, all of them using some, if not all, local ingredients. Golden Ale (5.5 percent ABV, 12 IBUs), which has earned three gold medals, features local hops. It is a nice balance of toasty, nutty malt flavours and citrusy hop notes. The simply named Bitter (5.5 percent ABV, 40 IBUs) is a true-to-style rendition of the classic English session ale. Earl Grey India Pale Ale (7 percent ABV, 45 IBUs) is an English version of the style that takes its name from the oil of bergamot, an ingredient in the famous British tea which gives a hint of citrus to the beer. Odd Fellows India Pale Ale (6 percent ABV, 45 IBUs) is another English version, which was named to honour the well-known international service organization and which won a Canadian Brewing Awards silver medal. Dry Porter, winner of a silver medal, is 5 percent ABV and 38 IBUs, and has espresso stout and chocolate notes. Heather Ale (5 percent ABV, 15 IBUs) was originally brewed for the world-famous Butchart Gardens and used heather petals from the plants there. Now available in six-packs of cans and, along with the Golden Ale, the brewery's most popular regular offering, it is lightly hopped.

~~~~~~~~~~

Back on Vancouver Island, I made a leisurely drive north along Highway 1A to Chemainus. Originally, this road had been part of the Trans-Canada Highway and had run through the centre of the town of just under 4,000. However, nearly a half century ago, the main road was rerouted around the town, causing many local businesses to lose customers. Then, in 1983, the sawmill, which had been operating for 120 years and employed 700 people, closed down. Many people predicted the town's demise. But Chemainus began a program of reinventing itself with a push to make the town a tourist destination. Murals depicting the area's geography, history, and economy were painted on the sides of buildings, the number reaching 40 by the second decade of this century. Boutique shops opened, street markets and drama festivals were held, and on November 10, 2016, **Riot Brewing Company** opened. Chemainus had become not only a tourist destination, but also a starting point for the area's many outdoor sports, including scuba diving, kayaking, mountain biking, and hiking. Chemainus had proved itself to be, in the words of the town's advertising tag, the "Little Town That Did."

Riot Brewing is located at the north edge of the town in Chemainus Village Square, a recently created complex of buildings designed to resemble the industrial and mercantile structures of a century earlier. In addition to the brewery, there are a large and local grocery store, a bar and grill (which carries Riot products), a liquor store, a drug store, a credit union, a fitness centre, and Green Aura Cannabis Dispensary.

I walked past Riot's patio area, where dogs were welcome and often given treats shaped like its lightning logo and made from the brewery's spent grain, and took a seat just inside the entrance. As I awaited the arrival of two of Riot's owners, Aly Tomlin and Ralf Rosenke (the third, Morgan Moreira, lived in Vancouver), I noticed a mobile made of brightly coloured beer cans turning slowly in a gentle air current. It was made, I learned, by a local art teacher and patron of the tasting room and was seen as a symbol of the interrelationship between the less than two-year-old brewery and the town. The colourful designs on the can had been created by world-famous punk rock and skateboard artist Jimbo Phillips of Santa Cruz, California, and reflected two of Tomlin and Rosenke's lifelong passions, punk rock and skateboarding. Their third passion, craft beer, could be found inside the decorated cans stacked in a cooler next to the bar.

Rosenke and Tomlin came from the back, joined me, and recounted the long and very difficult journey that had ended with their opening the brewery in Chemainus Village Square. Tomlin had been a home-brewer, had worked in a liquor store where she became familiar with the wide variety of international beers, had won a week's course at the world-famous Siebel Institute brewing school, and had joined R&B Brewing in Vancouver, where she worked her way up to assistant head brewer and then general manager. Rosenke, her life partner, had been a member of the founding board of the British Columbia chapter of CAMRA (Campaign for Real Ale) and had written articles on craft beer for Vancouver-area publications. When Tomlin was let go from R&B in 2010, the two decided to start their own brewery. At first they hoped to open one in Vancouver, where craft brewing was just about to enter a tremendous boom period. Then they considered Duncan before settling on Chemainus.

Seven difficult years preceded the opening day of November 10, 2016. The Duncan area was not hospitable to the idea of a new production brewery/tasting lounge. Craig Street Brew Pub was well established in the downtown area, and Red Arrow, a production brewery, was well into the planning stages. Tomlin and Rosenke worked menial jobs, cleaning parking lots and houses, earning just enough money to keep body and the dream alive. Banks were not encouraging; friends and potential investors were skeptical. "But Ralf and I believed in us," Tomlin stated emphatically, a smile spreading across her face.

The pair was just about to give up the quest when three events occurred. First, they received a call from an official at the Municipality of North Cowichan. He had heard of their hopes and their struggles and told them that Chemainus would like them to open a brewery there. Second, a local developer was creating a commercial centre and would construct a building to their specifications. The location would have city water and sewage, essential to a brewery, the building would have ceilings high enough for brewing equipment, and needed drainage could be installed before concrete was poured. Third, Morgan Moreira, who had worked with Rosenke at a Vancouver auto upholstery company, came into an inheritance and, interested in his friend's planned enterprise, decided to become an investor. Other investors followed; even previously reluctant banks loosened their purse strings.

With investors, municipal support, and a building underway, Tomlin and Rosenke needed both a name for their brewery and a brewer to make their lagers and ales. They chose the name Riot, Rosenke told me, because that's what their life together had been. "We wanted people who came to our brewery to have a riot as well. Not a wild destructive time, but something lively and fun." The punk rock/skateboard visuals would reflect who they were and would make them different from other brewers. But who would their brewer be? With craft breweries opening at an astonishing rate, it would be difficult to find a good one. Then someone called them: Fabian Specht, who'd been a homebrewer and had worked at Sailor Hagar's Brew Pub in North Vancouver, Howe Sound Brewing in Squamish, and Central City/Red Racer in Surrey. The idea of working as his own boss in a smaller production brewery in a small town by the sea appealed to him. He joined the team.

As we were chatting, several people dropped by to order either a pint to be enjoyed in the tasting room or a six-pack or growler to take home. Patrons and owners didn't just greet each other by name; they chatted about the brewery and about local affairs. After one such short conversation, Tomlin commented on how important the relationship with community was, especially for a brewery in a small town. "It's not just a place to drink beer; it's a meeting place. The community has embraced us, and we want to do everything we can to give back to the community."

Rosenke and Tomlin then led me on a circle tour of the brewery. "Here is where we hold our musical events and other activities," Tomlin said as we reached the back of the tasting room. Then we entered a hallway leading to the brewery, perhaps one of the most interesting hallways I've walked through. On the doors to the washrooms were silhouettes indicating not only male and female but also transgender. WE DON'T CARE, a sign proclaimed. This simple gesture greatly pleased the LGBT community and also served as another indication of how Riot Brewing had reached out to and embraced the community. On the wall facing the washrooms was a giant calendar on which the name of the month and the dates of the days of the week could be written. Already nearly half of the days for the current month had been filled in with events that either would occur here or were being sponsored elsewhere by Riot.

Just inside the entry to the brewhouse stood an old barber's chair just like the one I remember from nearly seven decades ago when I'd sit on a board placed across the armrests and get a 25-cent haircut. It was the main prop for one of Riot's most interesting tasting room events—"Beer and a Cut." For $25, customers could, to use an old haircutting expression, "get their ears lowered" and also enjoy a pint of one of Riot's beers—presumably after the cut, so that bits of hair wouldn't float around at the top of the glass. Profits from the event are donated to a local community organization. Other "Beer and a..." nights included a yoga night and a painting night, with instructors on hand.

Riot Brewing's Fabian Specht (left), head brewer, and Ralf Rosenke, co-owner, share their affection for good beer with co-owner Aly Tomlin. ←

Fabian Specht greeted us and showed us through the brewery before we ended our circle tour and returned to our table in the tasting room. Along with Tomlin and Rosenke, he talked about the beers on Riot's core list. "We're alcoholics, so we make low-alcohol beer," Tomlin had joked. The alcoholic percentages by volume range from 3.8 to 6. "We also emphasize classic styles brewed well," Rosenke added. These included an English dark mild, a pale ale, an IPA, a helles lager, and a saison. Lipside Lager (4.8 percent ABV, 18 IBUS) is Riot's entry-level beer, a Munich-style helles that is named after a skateboarding technique. It's a medium-bodied beer with caramel and bready notes and a honey-like sweetness that is balanced by herbal and spicy hop flavours. Life Partners Pale Ale (5 percent ABV, 32 IBUS) is a West Coast pale ale, hop-forward but with a firm malt background. Fruity, citrusy, spicy hop flavours are balanced by the caramel, toasty malt notes. Junk Punch IPA, named after a blow delivered to a vulnerable part of the male anatomy, is the strongest core offering (6 percent ABV, 70 IBUS). A bold, hoppy character, with citrusy, piney, herbal, and spicy notes, is complemented by the biscuity, toasty, slightly sweet flavours contributed by the malts.

The two other year-round beers are also classic styles, but certainly lesser-known than the first three. Working Class Hero is an English dark mild, a favourite session beer style in English pubs. Only 3.8 percent ABV and 14 IBUS, it is an almost opaque brown colour. Full-bodied and rounded, it has a low hop presence, with the East Kent Golding, a British varietal, giving earthy flavours. It is rich, but not too sweet, with roasty, biscuity, and nutty notes. It is an ideal session beer, for cold, damp winter evenings sitting in front of a fireplace. (Shortly after my visit, Working Class Hero won a gold medal at the World Beer Cup.) The other, Sorry We Took So Long Saison, is Riot's interpretation of a traditional Belgian beer that was served to field workers during the summer. Typical of the style, Sorry has spicy and yeasty flavours. It's designed to be thirst-quenching, not overwhelming. At 4.2 percent ABV and 19 IBUS, it is closer to the Belgian originals than many modern versions, which are often above 6 percent ABV. At the higher percentage, long ago workers would have been in considerable danger when they returned to the fields. Riot's saison is a perfect summer complement to the winter seasonal, Working Class Hero.

Although the core beers have been very well received by both experienced craft beer drinkers and local people who had been "raised" on the industrial pale lagers of mainstream brewers, it was a seasonal lager that won a silver medal at the 2017 Canadian Brewing Awards (held just over six months after Riot opened for business) and put Riot Brewing on the Canadian beer map. Good Vibrations Classical Pilsner (5.3 percent ABV, 32 IBUs) is a crisp, clean interpretation of the German lager. However, it wasn't just the medal that gained Tomlin, Rosenke, and Specht national attention; it was also the story that was told about the brewing of the pilsner. During the eight-week fermentation period, Specht had classical music played to the fermenting wort, connecting speaker nodes to the sides of the tanks. The strains of the classical music (I wondered if it had included Handel's *Water Music*) provided vibrations that may have improved the taste of the beer and could even have created an artistic ambience that assisted the fermentation process.

As I prepared to leave, both Tomlin and Rosenke embraced me. He remarked that people were big on hugs at the brewery, and Tomlin added that she, Rosenke, and Specht even hugged the brewing tanks. I thought their gesture symbolized the philosophy of Riot. Not only did the brewery make very good beer and provide an enjoyable place to drink it, but also the owners had embraced the community, just as the community had embraced them.

I thanked Tomlin, Rosenke, and Specht for the conversation, the tour, and the gift of several bottles of their beer for me to take home. I told them that I'd certainly had a riot.

CHAPTER 7

CRAFT BREWERIES MOVE INTO NANAIMO (AKA LUCKY TERRITORY)

Longwood Brew Pub, Longwood Brewery, Wolf Brewing Company, White Sails Brewing Company

Nanaimo, the second-largest city on Vancouver Island, with a population of just over 90,000 and an area population of just over 146,000, was founded in the mid-19th century. It was a coal-mining centre for nearly 100 years and then a forest-products one. Always it has been a commercial centre and a large port—business and shipping have given it its two nicknames, first the Hub City and later the Harbour City. Seven breweries operated here between 1864 and 1917, and although after that there was no locally made beer until 1984, there was no shortage of beer drinkers. I remember being told early in my beer-drinking days that Nanaimo had more beer parlours per capita than any other Canadian city.

Although Lucky Lager has been and remains the most popular beer, the city has not been without its craft breweries and brewpubs. Cheers

Downtown Pub and In House Brewery operated from 1984 to 1987, and Bastion City Brewing Company did business for a year in the late 1990s. Fat Cat Brewery operated from 1999 to 2010. Currently, there are three breweries and one brewpub in the Harbour City: Longwood Brew Pub, established in 2000; Wolf Brewing Company, the successor to Fat Cat, in 2011; Longwood Brewery, in 2013; and White Sails Brewing, in 2015.

I arrived at **Longwood Brew Pub** late on another misty, moisty morning. Located in an upscale shopping centre 10 minutes north of town, it shared the sprawling area with well over a dozen shops, services, and other restaurants. A person who hadn't been to the Harbour City for a few decades would quickly discover that this wasn't an old-style Nanaimo beer parlour. Just inside the front entrance, behind floor-to-ceiling windows, stands a stainless steel, 10-hectolitre brewing system. On the main floor, cherry-wood walls, jatoba flooring (made from Brazilian cherry wood), and a wood-burning fireplace give the large restaurant an air of elegance. Downstairs, cozy booths and tables grouped around another fireplace, a pool table, and a dartboard evoke the atmosphere of an English pub. There are a couple of televisions sets, but as Barry Ladell, one of the original owners, told me on a visit I made several years earlier, "We're not a sports bar; people come in here to talk with each other."

As I sat in one of the booths in the pub, a lunchtime crowd had begun to gather. A few men sat at the bar watching an English soccer game on the television. I would learn later that most of them were regulars and British expatriates for whom a pint of extra special bitter and an old-country soccer game were the next best thing to being back home. At the tables, many older couples gathered, spouses and friends, enjoying a lunch out. From the room behind the fireplace came the sounds of billiard balls clicking against each other.

Ladell and Harley Smith, who was then the brewer, were no longer at Longwood Brew Pub. The former had departed to pursue other endeavours; the latter to become part owner and head brewer at Longwood Brewery, related to but independent of the brewpub. Today,

I'd be talking with one of the co-owners, Mike Campbell, and the current brewer, Graham Payne. Campbell, his partner, John McPhail, and Payne had been with the brewpub since it had opened nearly 18 years earlier. McPhail, Longwood's first employee, had been the manager of the pub; Campbell, who had been in the restaurant business since he was 15 years old, had started as a bartender and worked his way up to a management position; Payne had been a bartender.

Campbell discussed the changes he'd seen in the craft beer scene over the years. "There are a lot more craft drinkers than there were when we started, and they know their beer. They understand

Located in an upscale shopping centre on the northern outskirts of Nanaimo, Longwood Brew Pub is the oldest brewpub north of Victoria. ↓

the various styles, and they can spot a badly made beer right away. And they don't drink as much during a visit as people used to. British Columbia's laws about drinking and driving are very strict. They now eat more when they visit. And so the quality of the food and the service must keep pace with good beer. Our approach is summed up in our motto: 'Good company, great food, amazing beer.'" He also noted how important it was to include as many locally sourced ingredients as possible in both the beer and the food. "People on Vancouver Island are very loyal to local businesses. We've had Lucky drinkers come in, and when they discover how local our beer is, they're very happy to try it. Quite a few of them become converts to craft beer."

For Graham Payne, becoming knowledgeable about craft beers involved a learning curve as steep as, if not steeper than, that encountered by those he served drinks to. "I was a Coors Banquet beer drinker from the mainland who came to the Island on a vacation and never left. I didn't discover craft beer until I began working here. I remember one day a customer asked me how many IBUs [International Bitterness Units] there were in one of the beers we had on tap. I didn't even know what an IBU was, so at the first opportunity I rushed back to the brewhouse and asked Harley Smith to explain to me. I had to ask Harley a lot of questions, and then I asked if I could help him when he was brewing. That way I'd learn the answers to a lot of the questions customers were asking me and I wouldn't have to keep running to him. I started as a volunteer, then worked one day and then two days a week, and finally became a full-time assistant. When Harley moved to the production brewery, I took over here. But I still ask him questions!"

Payne regularly brews a range of beers that vary in colour from light to very dark and from relatively low in alcoholic content (5 percent ABV) to fairly high (7.5 percent ABV). Czech Pilsner and Longwood Ale (each 5 percent ABV) are designed to be crossover beers, different enough in taste to distinguish them from the lagers of the megabrewers, but not so different as to threaten or even scare away people new to the craft beer scene. The Czech Pilsner is a crisp, clean lager, given a tang by the

Saaz hops. Longwood Ale is a golden-coloured, light-to-medium-bodied blonde ale, with biscuity malt notes. "It's the beer that built the business here," Campbell remarked. "People who don't like ales because they think they are too dark love this one. For a lot of people around here, this was their introduction to craft beer." The blonde ale, which is lightly hopped, provides the base for another of the brewpub's very popular beers: Raspberry Ale (5 percent ABV, 15 IBUs). After primary fermentation, the berries are introduced, initiating a secondary fermentation. They also create a red hue that gives the beer its unusual colour and introduce a tart and sour tang, which is balanced by the maltiness of the base beer.

Longwood Brew Pub offers an India pale ale, as virtually all breweries and brewpubs along the Canadian and American West Coast do. The Big One, as it is called, is a 6.5 percent ABV, 65 IBU English version of the style. Northern Brewer and Styrian Gold hops are the stars of this ale, providing bitterness, herbal, woody, and mint aromas, and a spicy, earthy taste. Though the style is English, the hops are local, having been grown a few kilometres from the brewery at Cedar Valley Hop Yards. Another English-style hoppy beer is the ESB (extra special bitter, 5.5 percent ABV, 26 IBUs), the expats' favourite for sipping while watching soccer games. The recipe derives from one developed by John Mitchell and Frank Appleton, who created the beers for two of British Columbia's pioneer craft breweries: Horseshoe Bay Brewing and Spinnakers. To the malty base, the Fuggle hops give an earthiness characteristic of many English hop-forward beers.

Two dark beers and two named after non-English countries that are part of the United Kingdom round out the roster of core beers. Steam Punk Dunkelweizen (5 percent ABV and 19 IBUs) is something of an oddity among ales. It's a wheat beer that is dark in colour, suggesting a full-bodied beverage, but it is light-bodied. The chocolate and black malts provide the dark colour as well as roasted flavours, while the Tettnang and Perle hops add spicy and herbal notes. Stoutnik is a Russian imperial stout with an alcoholic content of 7.5 percent ABV. Roasted and chocolate malt flavours are balanced by the earthiness of the hops. In the

Irish Red Ale (5.5 percent ABV, 24 IBUs), the rich, sweet malt tastes are balanced by the spicy tang of the Tettnang hops. Scottish Ale (6.2 percent ABV, 11 IBUs) is a full-bodied, rich beer with a complex variety of tastes. Malts provide coffee notes, a smoky touch, and a slight sweetness, while Nougat hops contribute some bitterness along with woody and resinous notes. The heather petals introduce tea-like flavours.

While all of the beers available at the brewpub are brewed there, some are also available in cans packaged at Longwood Brewery, which I visited after having enjoyed lunch and watching, along with the people at the bar, the last few minutes of the soccer game.

~~~~~~~~~~

I made my second Nanaimo stop at **Longwood Brewery**, which opened in 2013 on the west side of town in an area dominated by light industry and service businesses. I was greeted by Harley Smith, who had made the beer at Longwood Brew Pub for many years before he, wife Tracy McLean, and others had founded this related but independent production brewery. In it are produced the (slightly different) packaged versions of some of the beers available at the brewpub, as well as several others. "At the brewpub, we'd been packaging and distributing many of our beers for several years. We wanted to expand because we needed more capacity to meet the demand for our products," Smith noted. "Central City and Steamworks on the mainland had started as brewpubs, and they'd done the same thing." He explained that the brewpub and brewery each operated under separate licences and that at first, because of British Columbia's liquor laws (since changed), the brewery couldn't sell its packaged beer at the pub.

I'd first met Smith at the brewpub nearly a decade ago. He'd been standing at a counter, affixing labels to bomber bottles of Longwood's ales. He was from Toronto, where he began his career as a professional brewer (at Amsterdam Brewing Company) and met his wife, Tracy McLean (at a brewpub, of course). McLean is now Longwood Brewery's business manager and is referred to by people who work in the brew-house as "the lady upstairs."

Smith had come to Nanaimo from Steamworks, a waterfront brewpub in Vancouver. At Longwood, he began to brew beers that stuck fairly close to familiar styles. "If you know the history of beer styles, you won't be surprised by ours," he told me several years ago. "We're not big on aggressive beers; we don't go to extremes." With the exception of a dunkelweizen and a Czech pilsner, he focused on English styles.

During my 2018 visit to the production brewery, Smith discussed the changes he'd seen in his 30 years of brewing and the differences between making beer for consumption in-house and for distribution. "Since I started at Amsterdam in Toronto, the changes are like night and day. There are so many more craft breweries and so many more drink-ers of craft beer—drinkers who are really knowledgeable. The range of styles around now is wonderful. I credit Phillips Brewing [in Victoria] for leading the way. They made so many different beers available in packaged form. And there have been changes in provincial law that have helped the growth of breweries. Breweries can now have lounge licences where people can enjoy beer by the glass, and brewpubs can distribute their own packaged beer.

"At a brewpub, you don't get stuck in one area. You can make such a wonderful variety of beers. You create your own recipes and then see the customers appreciate what you're created. Consistency isn't the main object, like it is in production breweries. In a brewpub, you're filling a glass with the customer sitting right there. In a production brewery, you're packaging for someone you may never see. You have to strive for consistency from batch to batch of a style, and you've got to make sure that the packaged product is airtight and kept refrigerated."

A few hours earlier at Longwood Brew Pub, Graham Payne had mentioned that the Crow and Gate Pub, which was located in Cedar, an agricultural area just south of Nanaimo, would soon be holding a cask night, featuring a beer Harley Smith had brewed from ingredients all grown or produced in that area: grain, hops, and honey. The pub, in fact, was located right behind the Cedar Valley Hop Yards, where the hops had been harvested. When I heard that, I was reminded of an advertising tag line that had been prominently displayed on Longwood Brewery's website: "Introducing the Terroir of Beer . . . an Obsessively Local Product." I asked about the concept of "local," and Smith replied, "We say 'community sourced'; the term 'local' has been overused." He noted that inclusion of community-sourced ingredients is very prevalent in Washington State and that what happens there usually happens soon after in British Columbia. "Sixty percent of our ingredients are Island grown," he went on. "And that doesn't include the water! We ask the community to support our beer, and if we want that, we have an obligation to support the area growers." He admitted that getting ingredients sometimes took a considerable effort, but that it was worth it.

He listed the area ingredients and their suppliers. Cedar Valley Hop Yards, which I'd visited a couple of days earlier, supplied, of course, the hops; Carawood Farms of Courtenay, the barley (which was malted by J.

White Malting in Nanaimo); Farmship Growers Co-op of Yellow Point (just south of Nanaimo), the beets used in Beetnik Root Stout; McNab's Corn Maze and Produce Farm in Yellow Point, the pumpkins in Full Patch Pumpkin Ale; and the farm of Jill and John Edwards of Yellow Point, the quince in Quinceotica Harvest Lager. "I visit our suppliers regularly to watch things grow and to establish a relationship with the people who grow them. You know, there's a sense of pride watching a field of barley or row of hop bines grow."

Smith described the core beers made at the production brewery as "solid and approachable. We don't want you to have just one," he remarked with a chuckle. "But many of our seasonal beers are outside the box. When we make them, we feel we can go down any path." The five core beers are Stoutnik, Berried Alive Raspberry Ale, The Big One IPA, Steam Punk Dunkelweizen (each of these also brewed at the brewpub by Graham Payne), and Island Time Lager. The brewpub and brewery versions of the first four are very similar.

Harley Smith, a co-owner of Longwood Brewery and one of the veterans of the Vancouver Island craft brewery scene, stands beside a board listing the beers available in the tasting room. Most of these use what he refers to as "community-sourced" ingredients. ←

Island Time Lager (5 percent ABV, 18 IBUs) is the newest of the beers on the core list. The website description calls this German-style pilsner an "Obsessively Local Brew" and goes on to emphasize that all ingredients are from Vancouver Island. The hops are showcased, with the Mount Hood, Magnum, and Perle hops from Cedar Valley Hop Yards contributing herbal, spicy, and fruity notes. "Lagers are the unsung heroes of beer," Smith stated. "They represent a growing part of the market, but no one really talks about them. They are the real workhorses." The dark gold-coloured beer is crisp and a little bitter, with the malts in the background giving the lager a slightly mellow roundness. Unsung heroes though lagers may be, Island Time is Longwood Brewery's top seller.

Two of the brewery's seasonal beers are definitely outside the box. Quinceotica Harvest Lager (5.5 percent ABV with minimal IBUs, according to the website) uses an ancient but, in North America, almost unknown fruit. Pear- or apple-like in appearance, it is virtually inedible raw, but sweet and citrusy after it's cooked. When local farmers Jill and John Edwards invited Smith to take as many of their ready-to-harvest quinces as he needed, he readily accepted their offer. The people at Footless Rooster Hobby Farm, who had a juice press, turned the fruits into liquid, which was added to already fermented blonde ale to begin a process of secondary fermentation. The light-bodied result was a tart beverage with citrusy flavours. When I tried it, I wrote down in my tasting notes, "This is like a beer cocktail." Then I added, "It's the ungose gose," a reference to the tart German wheat beer.

Beets are certainly much better known than quinces, but they would seem an unlikely flavour additive for beer. That certainly didn't bother Smith, who, when locally harvested beets were delivered to the brewery, had them diced and pickled and then added to Stoutnik Russian Imperial Stout to create what the label calls "a 'mash up' of Nanaimo's farm community and our brewery's desire to source locally." The dry stout's malt richness is countered by the pickled beets. The result isn't like the liquid found in canned beets, but a subtle mix of flavours: roasted barley, beets, and the liquid from the pickling. And it isn't purple in colour, although the label is, with a beet in the upper corner seeming to fly into space just as the Sputnik does on the stout label.

Good beer with local ingredients—that's what Longwood Brewery makes. Smith repeated in different words what I'd heard at the brewpub a few hours earlier. "If I say that this is local, people will try one of our beers. And some of them may even be turned into craft beer drinkers." He paused, smiled, and then added, "If we're lucky!"

~~~~~~~~~~

Late the next morning, I visited **Wolf Brewing Company**, which had begun its existence as Fat Cat Brewery in 2000 and become Wolf Brewing in 2011. The story of the founding of Fat Cat sounds like a brewer's version of the Book of Job. In the months leading up to its opening and for a couple of years after, owners Bunny Goodman and Rob Haseloh faced challenge upon challenge. After they had purchased the equipment of the recently defunct Bastion City Brewing, they found that they would have to quickly dismantle it and move it to storage facilities. When they arrived at the new building where they had leased space for the brewery, they discovered that the walls separating their area from other businesses had not been erected and that the concrete floor had been poured in such a way that water and spilt beer could not easily flow into the drains. Goodman had to battle the hydro company, which insisted that the power had been hooked up. It had—but to another building. On the first day of brewing, work came to an abrupt standstill as police cars screeched into the parking lot and officers converged on the unit next door. Their neighbours were operating a sizable grow-op, making good money from a plant related to hops. There were other difficulties, but Fat Cat seemed to have nine lives and pushed ahead. Finally, at the end of the new century's first decade, the number of lives had become very low, and Goodman and Haseloh decided to put their brewery up for sale.

Two couples who had often talked of opening a business together, Corinne and Travis Findlater and Jennifer and Dean Lewis, acquired the space, the equipment, and the beer that was still in the tanks. Travis and Dean, who had been friends since kindergarten, had been homebrewers. Corinne and Jennifer were stay-at-home moms. Although Rob Haseloh and Glen Lamontagne, who had apprenticed with him, helped them keep brewing operations going, the new owners decided to rebrand, changing the cat into a wolf, tinkering with recipes, and expanding distribution to cover a larger part of Vancouver Island. After a year, the Lewises bought out their partners, and they remain the owners of the Island's longest-running production brewery north of Victoria.

Three main elements characterize the transformation of a fat cat into a wolf. The cartoon-like labels of Fat Cat were replaced by labels featuring scenes painted by local artists: for example, for Golden Honey

Ale, Alex Walton's painting of whales towing Noah's ark; Sue Coleman's of a sunset along the coastal shore, for the Scotch Ale; and Linny D. Vine's of an old Volkswagen bus travelling along a country road, for Black and Tan. The facilities were expanded and updated: the old tanks and hoses that had come from Bastion City were replaced by gleaming new tanks;

the small window through which product was sold to customers disappeared, a tasting room with a lounge licence in its place; and the entire brewery was enlarged, taking over the space that nearly two decades ago had been busted for selling another agricultural product.

Kevin Ward, English-trained head brewer of Wolf Brewing, stands beside a board advertising the brewery's most popular ale. ↑

Perhaps the biggest change came with the hiring of a new head brewer, one with extensive experience in the profession. Kevin Ward was a native of Liverpool, England, where he grew up cheering for the famous soccer club (and still feels guilty when he sneaks a couple of hours away from the brewhouse to watch its games), helping his mother make wine, and brewing beer, at first from a kit she gave him. "I travelled around the world for a while, working at restaurants along the way," he remembered. "When I got back to England, I was bit by the food and wine business." He became involved with a group that acquired country pubs and transformed them into high-end gastropubs. "At each place we featured locally grown produce and locally brewed beer." He honed his brewing skills: "I'd work free for any brewmaster who would teach me. I learned the wonderful things malt could do."

I asked Ward how he ended up working at a brewery located halfway around the world from his hometown. "I was on holiday in the Lake District when I met this girl from a place called Nanaimo. We got married and stayed in England for 13 years before she decided it was time we moved to Canada. When we arrived, I visited every brewery on the Island, but there weren't any jobs available. Then I heard about Wolf, visited Dean and Jennifer, and told them I'd work six months for free and that after that they could hire me if they wanted." They did—and after only three months. "My getting a job here was really lucky.... oops. I arrived at the right time at the right place." He'd never heard of Lucky Lager before his arrival, and he has yet to taste it. "No corporate beer has been in my mouth for 15 years," he proudly announced. During our conversation, a young couple came to the taproom, which was now open. They were out-of-towners who, having a two-hour break between duty visits with relatives, had decided to sample some locally made beer. "It's what we like to do when we travel."

While Ward talked to them, I sat at the end of the bar, eavesdropping as unobtrusively as possible. Where were they from? Had they visited any other Island breweries? What kinds of beer did they like to drink? When he found that they enjoyed beers that were lighter in both colour and alcoholic content, he offered them each a small tasting glass of Golden Honey Ale, the brewery's best seller. As they sipped, he gave them a brief description of the beverage, pointing out the medium bitterness and the floral notes contributed by the Cascade hops. "It's a balanced beer," he pointed out. "Notice how the malts add caramel notes. And it's got local ingredients. We use raw honey from Fredrich's Honey Farm—it's just a few kilometres from here. You get the flavour of the honey, but not the sweetness." He then walked to the counter where the rolls of beer labels were and tore off a couple for the guests. "Even our labels are local; they have paintings on them by Vancouver Island artists."

His visitors finished their samples, had a growler filled with the Golden Honey Ale, and departed for their next family appointment. "I enjoyed talking with them," Ward said. "I try to be in the tasting room as often as I can. When we were opening the brewpubs in England, I found that people wanted to learn as much as possible about the food they were eating and the beer they were drinking. Meeting the people who prepare the food and the beer makes the experience of visiting more enjoyable."

Ward had wanted me to enjoy some samples of the beer he'd been brewing, but I had to regretfully decline. I had a full day, followed by a long drive, ahead of me. So he said he'd give me a bottle each of Wolf's core beers that I could take with me and enjoy at my leisure. I happily accepted and then asked him to tell me about the products I'd be leaving with.

My education began with a discussion of Wolf Pilsner. Although Ward had grown up with a fondness for malt-forward English ales, he had created a beer that appealed to craft beer newbies and pilsner fans. The 5.4 percent ABV light-gold lager was a German version of the style, using one German malt (Barke pilsner) and one noble hop (which Ward didn't identify) to create a crisp, clean beer with what he called "a lovely grain taste." Both the Golden Honey and the Wolf Pilsner are very sessionable beers. The brewery's popular IPA is sessionable as well, Ward told me. "It's a West Coast style; we wanted something that was flavourful, something that would have taste and some bitterness without destroying a person's palate." In fact, the numbers, 6 percent ABV and 50 IBUs, are relatively low for the style. Cascade, Centennial and "two secret hops" are used in the creation of an ale that has a mixture of peach, passion fruit, pine, and citrus flavours.

Two ales, an English porter and a Scotch "wee heavy" are excellent examples of Ward's love of malty, darker, English-style beers. About the porter (6 percent ABV), he joked, "We built a new brewery so we could brew this beautiful beer more often." It's a dark, robust porter with chocolate and espresso notes and has, in the brewer's words, a "wonderful" dry finish. "It's smooth, creamy, and balanced. You experience the coffee first, then the creamy chocolate, then the dry finish."

The darling of Ward's eye is the Scotch Ale, sometimes referred to as a "wee heavy" because it is fuller-bodied and more alcoholic than Scottish ale. It is sweet, malty, and 7.4 percent ABV. "The recipe calls for Maris Otter as the base malt to give it body, and five specialty malts. I use two brew kettles to make it," Ward said. "After the initial boil, I transfer half of the wort into one of the old kettles we acquired from Fat Cat. It produces higher BTUs [British thermal units] that caramelize the sugars. Then I return it to the main kettle. It has caramel, toasty, and bready flavours. And, if you really want to taste everything the malts contribute, you have to drink it at room temperature." While we were talking, a customer came in to have two growlers filled with the Scotch Ale. He didn't need any education about it, as it was one of his favourite beers. He had other errands to perform before he arrived home, so, by the time he took the growlers out of the car, the wee heavy would probably have reached an ideal drinking temperature.

Since his mother gave him a beer-making kit long ago in Liverpool, Kevin Ward had travelled many miles and developed a knowledge of beer and brewing that is both wide and deep. One of the most fortunate events of his life was his running into a young woman from Nanaimo during his travels. And the decision the two made to return to her hometown has been a fortunate one (dare we say a lucky one) for the Harbour City's growing population of craft beer lovers.

~~~~~~

White Sails Brewing is not only Nanaimo's newest brewery—it opened in 2015—but also the only one in the revitalized downtown area. It is in a building that overlooks Maffeo Sutton Park, the Harbour Front Walkway, and a bay in which are docked many small sailing vessels. In fact, the sails of these and other boats around the Nanaimo waterfront were the inspiration for the name of the new brewery. The building is on the site of a legendary hotel, the Newcastle, which had been built by Union Brewing in the last decade of the 19th century. A few years ago the place, which had housed what the locals called a "dive bar," had been gutted and completely redesigned and made into an attractive, desirable downtown destination. Just past the entrance stands a very large electric fireplace, in front of which sat a young couple who'd come in from the rain and were enjoying both the light and the warmth as they sipped their pints. At one end of the large tasting room, where local musicians set up on music nights, a young woman sat at a table

Tyler Papp, White Sails Brewing Company's head brewer, and his assistant Mike Nemeth take a break from working on the brewing equipment. →

working on her computer. Along one wall stood the bar, and behind it was a small kitchen. The 15-hectolitre brewhouse occupied the opposite end of the building behind floor-to-ceiling glass walls.

I was greeted by Teighlor Overton, tasting room manager. A Nanaimo native, she'd been working in the hospitality industry in Vancouver when she heard of the new brewery about to open and decided to return home. "White Sails is the fruition of a long-time dream of the owners, Brad McCarthy and Monty McKay," she said. "They felt that even though Nanaimo had three breweries, there was definitely room for a fourth, especially downtown." She explained that there had been both great growth and many changes in the Harbour City over the past decade. A lot of young families had moved from Vancouver to escape the congestion, the crowds, and the high cost of living on the mainland. Many had brought with them their knowledge of and appreciation for craft beer.

McKay, who was a district administrator for the Purolator courier company, and McCarthy, who owned UVin, which served the needs of local amateur winemakers, and Oceanside WineWorks, a similar business in nearby Parksville, had always made it a point to visit brewpubs in the cities they visited. They were impressed not only by the variety and high quality of lagers and ales these places served but also by their neighbourly atmosphere. "Monty and Brad wanted to create a comfortable place," Overton explained. "It would be a safe place where university students,

young families, retirees, people who worked downtown, tourists, and craft beer lovers could gather, enjoy conversations—that's why we don't have any TVs—listen to music, or just sit quietly by themselves sipping a beer or looking out the windows toward the water."

McKay and McCarthy realized that, in addition to a great location and a building with a welcoming environment, they needed to serve top-notch beer. Nanaimo's increasingly large number of knowledgeable craft beer drinkers wouldn't come to a tasting room that didn't offer very good ales and lagers; they had options. The new brewery would need a very skilled and experienced professional brewer. They found one in Tyler Papp, who'd begun his career working in Calgary for Brewsters, a well-known Prairie brewpub chain, and then at two award-winning breweries from the British Columbia Interior: Mt. Begbie Brewing of Revelstoke and Fernie Brewing. Not only were Papp's brews enthusiastically received by White Sails patrons, but also they received international recognition. In 2017, Snake Island Cascadian Dark Ale was named the best black IPA in the World Beer Awards competition; Mount Benson India Pale Ale was named the top Canadian IPA in the same competition.

At the time of my visit, Papp was tied up helping his new assistant, Mike Nemeth, learn the ins-and-outs of the White Sails' brewing system. But he took a few minutes away from his duties to discuss the brewery's core beers. "I really like hop-forward beers, West Coast–style ales with citrusy and piney notes." Four beers, each named after a local landmark, are available year-round. Departure Bay Session Ale (4.6 percent ABV, 25 IBUs) is a light-bodied, crisp wheat ale with citrusy notes. Mount Benson (7 percent ABV, 60 IBUs) is a medium-bodied, West Coast–style IPA in which the malt balances the hop bitterness and complements the fruity, citrusy hop flavours. Yellow Point Pale Ale (5.5 percent ABV, 35 IBUs) is an English-style pale ale with malts providing caramel flavours that are balanced by the citrus notes of the hops. Snake Island Cascadian Dark Ale (6.5 percent ABV, 80 IBUs) is a medium-bodied beer with chocolate and coffee malt flavours, along with citrus and piney notes from Pacific Northwest hops. White Sails also offers seasonal releases such as a Belgian witbier and a California common (a.k.a. steam) beer. Friday cask nights provide Papp with the opportunity to use locally sourced ingredients, including some obtained by foraging in nearby uncultivated areas.

Even on the grey, rainy day of my visit, White Sails was busy, and when I left in the late afternoon, the tasting room had begun to fill up. "It really gets busy on Fridays when we have live music," Teighlor Overton remarked. I guess you could say that, after just over three years in business, Nanaimo's youngest craft brewery is going full sails ahead.

CHAPTER 8

THE HIGHWAY 4 ALE TRAIL FROM GEORGIA STRAIT TO THE PACIFIC OCEAN

Mount Arrowsmith Brewing Company,
Love Shack Libations,
Twin City Brewing Company,
Ucluelet Brewing Company,
Tofino Brewing Company

Driving north from Nanaimo, I remembered the old Yogi Berra saying: "When you come to a fork in the road, take it." Soon I'd be coming to a fork. Highway 19 would continue north to what one of my friends calls "the C towns"—Cumberland, Courtenay, Comox, and Campbell River. Highway 4 began just east of the fork, on the shores of Georgia Strait, and ended at Tofino, on the shores of the Pacific Ocean. When I reached the fork, I chose Highway 4. From its eastern terminus to the western one, it traverses the relatively "empty" middle section of Vancouver Island. The total population of the four main towns along its 172 kilometres is just under 41,000 people, with the largest, Port Alberni, at 17,743 and the smallest, Tofino, at 1,932. Along many stretches of the road, rugged mountains, dense forests, and glistening lakes give travellers an idea of what most of the terrain must have been like before the European invasion.

Although logging, commercial fishing, shipping, and service and government businesses are central to the area's economy, in the last half century, tourism has become increasingly important. The coasts and the interior regions are important destinations for outdoors enthusiasts, practitioners of what have often been called "the silent sports," such non-motorized activities as kayaking, surfing, and swimming; hiking, climbing, and bicycling; and whale, bear, and on some of the beaches and café patios, people watching. In recent years, four cities along the highway have become destinations for beer travellers. In 2011, Tofino Brewing opened on the shores of the Pacific; in 2017, Love Shack Libations started up just north of Qualicum Beach; and in 2017, Twin City Brewing in Port Alberni and Mount Arrowsmith Brewing in Parksville began operations. While each of them depends heavily on the support of local beer drinkers, they would probably not be financially profitable without the patronage of tourists, of whom there are well over a million annually.

I started my journey west to the Pacific by driving east into the town of Parksville, which I hadn't visited for over half a century. Then it had been a sleepy little village; now it's a small but busy city, a commercial centre, and a four-seasons tourist destination. My first stop was in a business/industrial area at **Mount Arrowsmith Brewing**, named after the peak that dominates the horizon to the west.

The idea for opening a brewery in Parksville was born when two locals, Matt Hill and Dan Farrington, who had spent many years working away from their hometown, realized that their city was the only place of its size in British Columbia that didn't have a craft brewery. Hill had left town to attend Royal Roads University just outside Victoria and, after he'd earned a degree in hotel management, had worked for two years in Thailand. Farrington hadn't journeyed as far afield but had spent much of his time at sea, as a commercial diver and later as a captain of pilot boats. He wanted to do something that wouldn't keep him away from home at least six months of the year. The two noted the growing population, including younger people who liked craft beer, and the fact that the citizens were very loyal to local businesses, especially those that provided locally made products. As well, there were plenty of tourists all year round. Conditions were excellent for opening a craft brewery.

What they needed were some investors and a professional brewer. Three members of Matt Hill's family came aboard as financial backers, as did Dave Woodward, a Qualicum Beach native and professional brewer who'd left his hometown two decades earlier and was ready to come back. I'd first met Woodward in 2010, when he was running the Brewhouse at Whistler and was regaining his energies after the frenetic pace of making enough beer to meet the demands of the thousands of athletes and tourists who had descended on the area during the 2010 Winter Olympics. Woodward had told me then that he had originally intended to become a stonemason, a trade his grandfather had followed. However, his part-time job at a brew-on-premises business convinced him that "making beer was as interesting as chipping stone." He earned a degree in brewing at the University of Sunderland in England and apprenticed at a microbrewery in that country for two years before returning to Canada. He was a friend of Iain Hill, at the time the brewmaster at Vancouver's Yaletown Pub, and Hill recommended him for a job that had opened in Whistler.

Woodward was at Whistler from 2005 to 2010, when the opportunity to return to Vancouver Island arose. A new production brewery was being built in Tofino, and the owners, who at the time knew little about the actual making of beer, had advertised for an experienced person to set up the brewhouse, design recipes, and make beer. Woodward took the job at the opposite end of Highway 4 from his hometown of Qualicum Beach and guided Tofino Brewing through its first few—and highly successful—years. He next accepted the job of opening another brewery, this one a brewpub—Axe & Barrel, in Langford, just outside Victoria. Then, when he heard from a relative who knew someone who knew someone who knew that Hill and Farrington were looking for a brewer for their new business in Parksville, he decided to head back up the Island.

Each of the stops along the way from the brew-on-premises to the head brewer's position and a partnership at Mount Arrowsmith has been a learning experience, Woodward told me when I met him in Parksville on my current trip. The brew-on-premises work and the schooling and then apprenticeship in England provided him with a deepening understanding of the process of brewing. The Brewhouse at Whistler, he noted, was a very corporate environment. But the people who drank his beer were just a few metres away from where he made it, and he benefited greatly from their feedback. "When I got to Tofino, it seemed like Whistler was 30 years earlier: high-end restaurants, lots

ISLAND CRAFT

of tourists, and raw nature all around. It was a great experience designing the brewhouse and setting up the brand new equipment. We used to forage for wild ingredients for some of our beers. I'd read about how Captain Cook had sent his men ashore to gather spruce tips to make an anti-scurvy beer, and so we gathered some and used them in an ale we made. And we gathered seaweed for our Kelp Stout."

He honed his skill at setting up a new brewery when he moved to Langford, where he would once again make beer for a brewpub. Because this one was in strong Lucky Lager territory, he made sure that there was a good sessionable lager on the beer list. "By the time I came to Mount Arrowsmith, I'd had a lot of experience setting places up, and I wanted to construct a brewhouse that made the best use of the space so that the brewing would be both cost and labour efficient." As he showed me around, explaining why he'd placed certain pieces of equipment in certain places, I remembered his showing me around the cramped brewhouse in Whistler. "The owners there wanted to have a space for two pool tables and so they took space away from the brewhouse, which was right next to the pool room." I remembered that there wasn't much elbowroom as we walked between the tanks but that, on the other side of the wall, patrons had plenty of room to bend their elbows as they lined up their shots or hoisted their pint glasses.

Dave Woodward, who had originally intended to become a stonemason, honed his skill as a brewer and designer of brewhouses for over two decades before becoming a partner and the head brewer at Mount Arrowsmith Brewing Company. ←

During our short tour of his new brewhouse, Woodward talked about the changes he'd seen in the craft beer scene over the last two decades. Foremost, he said, has been the explosion in the number of breweries opening. "I relate it to the locavore movement, where people like freshly created foods from locally grown or raised products. And when you visit a local brewery, you know the beer you drink is made there. You can talk to the brewer, find out about the beer, and give feedback." The second important change he commented on was the proliferation of styles. "People want interesting new beers." He mentioned two of Mount Arrowsmith's special releases as examples: Spruce Tip IPA and Grand Cru Imperial Belgian Wit.

The brewery opened in April 2017 and just over six months later was named Brewery of the Year at the annual BC Beer Awards. One of its five year-round beers, Arrowsmith Blonde, won a gold medal. Woodward described the beer as a crossover or entry-level ale. "We wanted a beer that was true to style, full-flavoured, and sessionable." More fully hopped than some blonde ales, this 4.8 percent ABV beer has grapefruit notes that balance the malt flavours. Although the other core beers have different flavours, they, like the Blonde, are true to style and very sessionable. Comfortably Chum, a 5.5 percent ABV hefeweizen, is named after a salmon whose Indigenous name forms part of the name for Qualicum. The French and Belgian yeasts provide a complexity of flavours, including banana and clove notes, while the Hallertau hops contribute a crisp spiciness.

Salish Sea Pale Ale (5 percent ABV) is a West Coast version of the style that is, Woodward noted, also somewhat like an English ESB. Piney and citrusy notes and grainy, nutty malt flavours make this an interesting combination of British and American styles. Jagged Face IPA (7.2 percent ABV), which takes its name from the Indigenous appellation of Mount Arrowsmith, is a strong but flavourful West Coast interpretation of the style. The Munich malts contribute a rich toffee flavour, while the Citra, Centennial, and Amarillo hops provide contrasting citrus and tropical fruit notes. Low Pressure Porter (6 percent ABV) is the darkest of the regular offerings. Woodward said that it was designed especially for the British expatriates who live in the area. Full-flavoured, it is prevented from becoming cloying by the addition of West Coast hops.

It's been a long time since Dave Woodward put down the hammers and chisels used to cut stone and picked up a brewer's paddle and started mashing malts to begin the process of making beer. Since then, craft beer lovers from Whistler to Vancouver Island have been glad that he did, particularly the people who have been enjoying his creations at

Mount Arrowsmith Brewing. The local boy had travelled far since he'd departed for England. Having made good, he returned home. And, as his award-winning beers prove, he's making very good beer.

~~~~~~~~~~~~~

On the way to Dashwood, a small community just north of Qualicum Beach, I chuckled as I remembered a friend's response when I'd told him that one of the breweries I'd be visiting was called **Love Shack Libations**. "That sounds more like a place that sells potions for teenagers who want to get lucky," he responded and then began to hum the Clovers' 1959 hit "Love Potion No. 9." I replied that it had nothing to do with getting lucky, whether the word was spelled with a lowercase or uppercase L. Love Shack Libations was a very small brewery that had opened in 2017 and had made a name for itself locally with its bottle-conditioned beer.

Except for Wednesday evenings and Saturday afternoons, when a sandwich board next to the highway announced that it was open, Love Shack Libations was difficult to find. It was set off the road in the end unit of a small strip mall and was surrounded by more prominently visible neighbours, such as an auto tech garage, a renovation company, a coffee shop, and a tree service business. The term "nano" describes nearly every aspect of the brewery: there's a one-hectolitre brewhouse and a tasting room that seats only 14 people; production is small, just over 100 hectolitres in the 10 months after it opened early in 2017; and distribution is limited to a few local bars and restaurants and a small liquor store in the area.

Dave Paul, the co-owner with wife Rachel, and the brewer, had worked, like Mount Arrowsmith's Dave Woodward, in the liquor business (as a waiter and bartender) in Whistler. However, when Rachel, whose parents lived in Dashwood, said that she'd like to move back to the Island and that her mother and father had said they could build a home on their property, the couple and their young daughter left Whistler. "We lived briefly in a tent, and then I built a 12-by-16-foot place that we could live in while we were building a home. We called it the Love Shack."

Not only did Rachel's parents provide the Pauls with a place to build their home, but her mother started Dave down the path that would lead him to open a brewery in a space not a great deal bigger than the tiny house. "One Christmas she gave me one of those beer-making kits," Dave remembered. "So I made some beer; it was something new to do. It tasted pretty good, and it was cheap. A while later, I built myself an all-grain brewing system and developed 16 different recipes.

Except for a sandwich-board sign at the edge of the road on the two days a week that Love Shack Libations is open, this sign on the door is the only indication that there's a nanobrewery in the small, industrial strip mall in Dashwood, just north of Qualicum Beach. ↓

Rachel really liked my DPA, a Cascadian dark ale, and she suggested that we open a brewery." They did and named it after the cramped little place on her parents' property.

ISLAND CRAFT

"I make beer for both the locals and the tourists," Dave said. "It's mainly local people who come in late Wednesday afternoons. Some of the people in the businesses right around here will stick their heads in the back door and ask what's going to be available on Wednesday. Saturday is for the locals and the tourists. In the winter, we get snowboarders stopping by after they've spent an afternoon on the slopes, and in the summer, lots of vacationers who've come to the beaches will drop in."

DPA (6.2 percent ABV, 55 IBUs), the brewery's best-selling beer, stands for Dave Paul Ale, or Dark Pale Ale. "It's somewhere between an IPA and a Cascadian dark ale." Chocolate, brown, and crystal malts give it a malt richness, while the Chinook, Cascade, and Citra hops give it bitterness and citrus, piney, and fruity flavours. "It's tasty," Dave commented, "and it's not as bitter as most IPAs are." RPA, for Rachel Paul Ale, or Rye Pale Ale, at 6.4 percent ABV, is a little stronger than DPA, although slightly less bitter. The grain bill includes just over 15 percent rye, which gives a spicy quality to the beer. Galaxy, Mosaic, Mount Hood, and Amarillo hops provide contrasting tropical fruit and citrus notes.

Crafty Cream Ale and Killer Kolsch are lower in alcohol (5.5 and 4.8 percent ABV, respectively) and are designed to appeal to people who either are new to craft beer or don't like the stronger and hoppier ales. "I use Munich and Vienna malts, along with flaked corn, in the cream ale to give body and colour, and Centennial and Citra hops to provide fruity and citrus notes. It's a smooth, easy-drinking ale." When I asked why he would name his kolsch, one of the lightest and most delicate of all ales, "Killer," Dave laughed. "Well, I liked the alliteration, and I've always thought that a kolsch would really kill your thirst on a hot day." He went on to say that it would fill the role of a lager on the beer menu, but that it's "a cheating lager," that is, it doesn't have to be fermented for as long as a lager, or at such cold temperatures. It's crisp and clean and delicately carbonated. The pilsner malt gives it a light colour and body, and the Glacier and Vanguard hops, grown in nearby Maple Bay, are spicy and help create a clean, crisp finish.

The darkest beer is Precious Porter (5 percent ABV, 30 IBUs), the name another reflection of Dave's love of alliteration and a tribute to his and his children's love of J.R.R. Tolkien's *The Lord of the Rings*, in which the evil Gollum refers to his magic ring as his "Precious."

"It's dark and delicious, with chocolate and coffee notes," Dave remarked enthusiastically. "But it's not heavy, it's not strong, and it's not bitter. It's ironic, but this dark beer is my third gateway beer."

When I asked Dave Paul to describe the house style of his beers, he quickly replied: "Bottle conditioned, with love." I asked him why he used the not rare but relatively infrequent technique of bottle conditioning, a process in which fermented beer is transferred not to conditioning tanks but directly into bottles, where carbonation takes place. It turned out that he'd made a virtue out of a necessity. "It costs a lot of money to buy conditioning tanks, and that was money I didn't have. I'd bottle conditioned my beers when I was a homebrewer, and if I did it now, I'd save a lot of money. And besides," he said, "conditioning this way gives the beer a silkier, softer mouthfeel and deeper, more complex flavours."

"Love beer, Love Shack"—that's the message on Love Shack's answering machine. And it's clear that Dave Paul loves making good beer. As our conversation came to a close, I told him about my friend's comment on love potions and getting lucky. He laughed heartily and then remarked: "I love it!"

On a drizzly Sunday morning, driving west along Highway 4, I passed Cameron Lake, its surface a steely grey, dimpled with raindrops. A lonely paddle boarder, clad in a dark wetsuit, moved slowly across the water. At the end of the lake stood giant cedar trees, some of them over 300 years old. Soon after, I headed down a long hill into Port Alberni, a deep port and a forest products, commercial, and business centre serving an area population of just over 25,000. Some of the streets bear the names of the daughters of a long-ago city father, and I turned on one called Margaret, drove half a block, and then parked in front of what had once been a government liquor store but was now the city's first craft brewery and brewpub: **Twin City Brewing**.

Owner and head brewer Aaron Colyn is a Port Alberni native who had been taking a course on microbiology, part of his pre-med studies, and had become fascinated by the processes of fermentation, particularly as they related to making beer. He began homebrewing and regularly visited such Vancouver Island craft beer meccas as Phillips Brewing in Victoria and Longwood Brew Pub in Nanaimo. "The idea of practising medicine lost its appeal. I realized that I wanted to make a career of brewing," he said.

Back home in Port Alberni, he began to formulate plans to open a craft brewery. "I knew that this was primarily a lager town, but I didn't want to offer brews that were just clones of what many people were already drinking. I wanted to expose them to what was going on outside the Alberni Valley. I wanted to say to people, 'Try this beer; it's an alternative to what you're used to.' We didn't want to dumb down our beers, but we didn't want to frighten people. I knew that in a smaller community, we couldn't be a niche brewery offering specialties most people had never heard of. We would offer a standard range of craft ales."

Colyn didn't just want to create beers the local people would respond positively to; he wanted to create a place where they could come and enjoy them, an interactive community centre, what he referred to as a "third place." The term signified somewhere that wasn't home or a workplace, but a place where people could meet, interact, and in the case of Colyn's proposed venture, enjoy good craft beer. But were the people ready for such a place and for beers quite different from what many of them were familiar with? "People here are used to buying local and growing local, so I was hopeful," Colyn remarked. "Then I started a funding campaign on Indiegogo. One hundred people contributed 100 dollars each. The money was helpful, but what was most encouraging was the fact that 75 of the contributors were from this area. I knew then that we had a real chance." Colyn went ahead with his plans, and in March 2017, just over a year before my visit, he opened Twin City Brewing Company, the name a reference to what, before they amalgamated in 1967, had been the towns of Alberni and Port Alberni.

On this early Sunday afternoon, Twin City Brewing Company was very busy. Members of a young family were helping themselves to slices of a hot-out-of-the-oven pizza, a couple in the corner shared a charcuterie plate, and one person sat alone reading a newspaper and munching on a giant pretzel.

Colyn invited me on a tour of the brewhouse, which had been made by a Chinese company. "We worked very carefully with them and were very specific about what we wanted. I'd heard unhappy tales about people who'd had bad experiences with equipment made outside of Canada. But we did our research, and we're very happy." I noticed that the fermentation tanks had the names on them of the streets I'd driven by. When I pointed this out to Colyn, he laughed and said, "It makes this place even more a part of the neighbourhood."

Aaron Colyn, owner-brewer of Twin City Brewing, stands beside a painting that reminds patrons of the Alberni Valley's logging heritage. To his left is a photograph of the brewery building when it used to be a government liquor store. ←

Each of the four tanks held one of the four core brews of Twin City Brewing. "When we opened, we wanted to have something light, something West Coast, something clean and smooth, and something sweeter and maltier."

Swedish Gymnast Blonde Ale was the representative of the first category. Colyn explained that a Swedish gymnast could perform many different manoeuvres and that this beer could be many things. It was a 5 percent ABV, 30 IBU, light-bodied beer that was part blonde ale, part India session ale, and part American wheat beer that used only Citra hops, but "lots of them."

The name of Run of the Mill IPA (7 percent ABV, 51 IBUs), the West Coast representative, did not signify something average, but referred to the lumber mills that had been a mainstay of the area's economy for decades. "We wanted something that was traditionally West Coast, so we used the hops that have been the standbys for West Coast IPAs: Cascade, Columbus, and Centennial." The aromas and tastes are what one would expect from these hops: grapefruity and piney.

The maltier and sweeter, but not too malty or sweet, representative is Tickity Boo, a 5.5 percent ABV, 35 IBU, English-style pale ale. The name comes from the British expression meaning "everything's alright or okay," and it must be for this beer, because it's Twin City's top seller. Not only the name but also the ingredients are English: Maris Otter malts contribute biscuity and caramel flavours, while Fuggle and East Kent Golding hops add an earthiness. "It's very much like an ESB [extra special bitter, a popular English pub beer], but we didn't want to frighten people by putting the word 'bitter' in the name."

When he came to discuss Porter Alberni (5.5 percent ABV, 27 IBUs), the ale that represented the clean-and-smooth category, he made to me what was a surprising statement: "When people ask us for something like Lucky, we give them this!" When I remarked that I thought the Swedish Gymnast Blonde would have been what they were given, he explained: "The Blonde is also a crossover, although it's very hoppy. But this one is clean and smooth and not too strong." There are roasty, coffee, and chocolatey flavours, but the beer is not aggressive. Although dark in colour, it is light in body; it's flavourful, but not cloying. It's been said that people who are introduced to porters and stouts are often told, "Don't be afraid of the dark." Colyn said that any nervousness a person had would quickly disappear after the first sip of Porter Alberni.

As patrons of Twin City Brewing have become more familiar with beer styles quite different from the pale American lagers that dominated, and still do dominate, the Alberni Valley beer-drinking scene, Colyn has offered on a limited basis some extremely different brews. Among these are Peach Mango Smoothie IPA, Strawberry Hibiscus Sour, and Pineapple Coconut Sour.

When we returned to the tasting room, the number of people at the bar waiting to be served had grown, and Colyn briefly excused himself to help out, filling a growler for a customer who had just walked in the door and looked as though he might be old enough to have come into the building to buy beer when it was a liquor store. Colyn had a short conversation with him before he returned to my window table. "He ordered the Blonde Grisette, our new seasonal. It's like a very light saison. He was interested in knowing about the ingredients and how we brewed it." Colyn agreed when I suggested that such a discussion probably wouldn't have happened in this town a few years ago. "We've got a great range of people stopping by," he said, pointing around the room: families, young couples, and retirees, and what looked liked surfers coming home after a weekend on the West Coast (if the surfboard on top of the Volkswagen bus parked outside was any indication). "We love tourists," Colyn said, "but we're here mainly for the townspeople."

On the outskirts of Port Alberni, I noticed two interesting signs, each of which made implicit statements about the landscape I was passing through. The first was a tsunami hazard zone warning, reminding people that the area had the potential of being inundated by tidal waves generated by earthquakes far away. I remembered that, in 1964, the then twin cities of Alberni and Port Alberni had suffered enormous damage when a tsunami caused by the famous Good Friday Alaska earthquake rushed up the narrow Alberni Inlet, destroying homes and other buildings in the low-lying areas. An elaborate warning system had been developed, and just a few months before my visit it had been activated to alert people of a possible threat.

The second sign announced that there would be no services along Highway 4 for the next 83 kilometres. I'd be passing through an almost unpopulated, magnificent wilderness along narrow roads containing frequent pull-offs for slow-moving vehicles. There were a few 10 percent grades and many curves with signs recommending maximum speeds of 35 kilometres an hour. The recent precipitation had left snow on the higher elevations of the mountains, while along the roadside the buds on some of the alder trees hinted that the much-delayed spring might soon be arriving. There were several scenic rest areas and parking lots for trailheads and, in one spot, for the headquarters of a zip-line company.

Where Highway 4 took a sharp right turn on its way to Tofino, I made a left and followed Peninsula Road to Ucluelet, a town that, although it has a permanent population of just under 2,000, as does Tofino, has often been considered the poor stepbrother of its more famous sibling. Such a comparison causes the people of this village, named after the Indigenous term for a place with a safe harbour, to bristle. There is a safe harbour, where dozens of charter fishing boats are moored. The town has quaint shops and easy access to the many outdoor recreation spots the West Coast has to offer, including the magnificent Long Beach, 16 kilometres of sand and surf, and in the winter, prime locations for storm watching. A

The future home of
Ucluelet Brewing
was once an
Anglican church. ✝

few months after my visit, the town's first brewery, **Ucluelet Brewing Company**, was scheduled to open. It was the chance to see the building that would become this brewery and, with luck, to meet the owner, Dennis Morgan, that drew me to the town. The building was easy to spot. Right on the main street, it still bore a resemblance to what it had been until 2010, Saint Aidan's on the Hill Anglican Church.

I had walked around the outside of the building and was just about to drive to Tofino, when I saw a man cross the road, come to the front door of the building, and open it. Dennis Morgan, who would be meeting with contractors the next morning, had come to take a brief look around. Two decades ago, when he had come to the area to work with the national park service at the Pacific Rim National Park Reserve, he had brought with him a love of craft beer that he'd acquired while attending graduate school at the University of Oregon in Eugene, a craft beer mecca. After a developer friend of his had purchased the now-vacant church, the idea of making the building a community gathering place came up, and soon after, Morgan, with the help of a family inheritance and several investors, began developing a business plan and then renovations that would make the centre into a brewery and lounge. He was originally going to call the place Resurrection Brewery but found out that a brewery in the United States already had claimed the name. It would now be named after the town.

He invited me inside, pointed out where the tasting room would be, indicated the stairs down to the basement where the brewhouse would be, and then led me out to a deck where warm-weather visitors could enjoy a beer and a wonderful view. The deck looked over Ucluelet Inlet, the shore of which was lined with small fishing boats and pleasure craft, and to the wooded hills across the water. I remarked to him that, when the brewery was open, it would provide a view that only Spinnakers, on the shore of Victoria's harbour, could challenge. Morgan said that he certainly hoped so, but emphasized that before visitors could enjoy that view, there was a great deal of work to be done. He hoped that, sometime in the summer of 2018, the deck would be complete and beer for patrons to drink while sitting admiring the view would be in the serving tanks.

Late in the afternoon, I drove to Tofino, noticing several tsunami hazard and tsunami evacuation route signs in low-lying areas, and stopping for half an hour to walk a little of the shoreline of Long Beach, taking in the magnificent grandeur of the waves, and wondering how cold the wetsuit-clad surfers were. I passed Industrial Way, where tomorrow I'd visit Tofino Brewing Company, and checked into my hotel, before strolling through the town, noticing the artists' galleries, surfboard shops, and souvenir stores. I'm sure that at least half of the people on the streets were tourists, and I wasn't surprised when I read a brochure claiming that close to a million people visited Tofino every year.

Tofino Brewing Company is still housed in the large industrial building it has occupied since opening in the spring of 2011. However, when I pulled into the parking area, I noticed a tremendous change. On my September 2011 visit, it occupied a small amount of the space; large rollback doors then opened into an area that served as a growler refill station, small tasting bar, and 10-hectolitre brewhouse with two fermentation tanks. There had been a short lineup at the self-serve growler station as people, most of them locals, waited their turn to fill glass containers. Now, the brewery occupied nearly all of the building; there was a 50-hectolitre system, with seven 90-hectolitre fermentation tanks. People could enjoy beer in the 35-seat tasting room and either have growlers filled or purchase bottles or cans stacked in the large glass-doored cooler. In 2011, nearly 50 percent of sales originated in the brewery; now, Tofino's ales and lagers were available throughout British Columbia and in Jasper, Banff, Edmonton, and Calgary, Alberta.

When I'd first met the founders, Bryan O'Malley and Chris Neufeld (then both in their mid-20s), they'd confessed that apart from the fact that they liked craft beer, they knew little about brewing and selling it. O'Malley told me that he'd been a bartender and that in the 1950s, his grandfather had owned a brewery in Quebec. That was it. "But," Neufeld said at the time, "we both thought a brewery would be a good fit for the town. Tofino was a small community that focused on local products and supported local businesses. There were a growing number of tourists who knew about craft beer, and a lot of them would seek out a local brewery. We felt that visiting a brewery here would give visitors another thing to do during their stay."

Bryan O'Malley, co-founder of Tofino Brewing Company, sits in front of the recently expanded brewhouse. →

At the time of that visit, I'd commented on the lineup at the growler-filling station. O'Malley offered an explanation. "The beer drinkers from around here really like the idea that they can get their beer right where it's brewed. They also appreciate that growlers are reusable. And the tourists like to take a growler back to their hotel and, when it was empty, bring it home as a souvenir. For the first few weeks, the lineups were huge, and a couple of times we ran out of beer. We had to close the doors." He added another reason for focusing on growlers: "We were strapped for cash and we couldn't afford a bottling or canning line." It wasn't until January 2013 that a bottling line was installed. By that time, the brewery had established accounts beyond Tofino; now the product could be distributed much more widely. The expanded brewery, which opened in November 2017, includes a canning line.

During my visit this morning, O'Malley commented, "At first we thought that our beer would be just for young people like us, craft beer lovers who certainly didn't want to be seen drinking mainstream pale lagers. When we had what somebody called 'macro drinkers' stop by, we'd just say, 'Give us a try.' We weren't out to convert people, but we did end up converting quite a few. Now we get locals and tourists, quite a lot of them beer tourists; we get older people and younger people, surfers, people who like to shop at the small stores downtown—all kinds of people."

In 2011, knowing that they couldn't do the brewing themselves, O'Malley and Neufeld advertised for a professional brewer. Dave Woodward, who now brews beer near the eastern end of Highway 4, responded. The two young owners visited him at the Brewhouse at Whistler, liked what they saw there, and brought him on board. At first, given the limited size of the brewhouse, they could brew only two styles at a time. Always on tap was Tuff Session Ale, the term "Tuff" coming from the nickname for Tofino, where the people in the logging and fishing industries were tough people who led tough lives. Rotating styles included an IPA, a wheat beer, and a pilsner. Before he departed in 2015 to start up a brewery in the Victoria suburb of Langford, Woodward taught Bryan O'Malley how to make beer, and O'Malley now oversees the brewing operations of the expanded brewery.

As we sat in the tasting room, our conversation turned to the beers Tofino presently brews. "We brew beers that we like, and we hope other people like them too," O'Malley began, making a statement that I've heard from many craft brewers in many different places. Then he became more specific: "We have drinkers with so many different favourites that we try to have a range of styles available at all times." These included two of the ales originally offered in April 2011: Tuff Session Ale and Hoppin' Cretin IPA. The former, the brewery's best seller, is a 5 percent ABV, amber-coloured, malt-forward ale. Toasty and caramel flavours dominate this rounded ale but are kept from becoming cloying by the introduction of Warrior and Cascade hops, which contribute to a clean, dry finish. Hoppin' Cretin IPA (7.5 percent ABV) has what the website calls an "assertive hoppiness." The unnamed hops provide citrus, tropical fruit, and piney notes without overwhelming. The malts give a slight caramel undertone.

Tuff Session and Hoppin' Cretin are available all year, as are three other beers: Blonde Ale, Tofino Lager, and Kelp Stout. The 5.5 percent ABV Blonde Ale is the brewery's gateway beer, an introduction to craft beers for locals who grew up with Lucky and tourists who haven't yet ventured into the darker, sometimes more bitter styles. Straw-coloured, it's light-bodied and has a crisp, dry finish. There are earthy hop notes, a malty sweetness, and a subtle honey-like flavour. Tofino Lager (5 percent ABV), the brewery's entry into the resurgent field of light-bodied lagers, uses Czech hops to achieve a crispness. There is a slight malt sweetness, but the hops prevent it from becoming too strong. The label proudly announces that it is "Tuff City Brewed."

Being very far from where the main components of beer are grown, Tofino does not include locally sourced ingredients (except, of course, water) in most of its ales and lagers. There are, however, two exceptions, ingredients that come from the sea that surrounds the little town on three sides and the trees that cover most of the neighbouring hills. Kelp Stout (6 percent ABV), the only one, O'Malley proudly stated, brewed in North America, uses a locally harvested and processed ocean plant. "We used to pick and process it ourselves, but it became too labour-intensive and time-consuming. So now we get it from Canadian Kelp Resources, a small local operation." It's a smooth, full-bodied ale with chocolate and coffee notes and hints of brine introduced by the unusual local additive.

The land provides the local ingredient for Spruce Tree Ale (6.5 percent ABV), a spring and summer beer. "We pick the spruce tips every spring from trees along the shore," O'Malley said. Added to the golden-ale base, the tips help to create a beverage that the website describes as "fresh and juicy." The citrusy characteristics remind one that Captain James Cook, who used lime juice to prevent scurvy on his ships, had his crew harvest Vancouver Island spruce tips to make a beer that would also fight that dreaded shipboard affliction.

As our conversation wound down, I told Bryan O'Malley about something another Brian, Brian Lock of Santa Fe Brewing in New Mexico, had told me several years ago. He had said that having the name of a world-famous tourist destination on the label of his beers was one of the greatest marketing tools he could ask for. I asked this Bryan whether the same held true for his beer company. "Yes, it certainly does!" he responded enthusiastically. "People come here, have a great time, enjoy some of our beers, and take some home with them to share with their friends. Then, when they see our beers at liquor stores, they remember the experience they had here and buy it. For people who haven't visited here, seeing a beer with the name Tofino on it conjures up pictures in their minds of wonderful beaches and forests, and these mental images may get them to buy the beer."

As I prepared to leave, O'Malley gave me a few bottles and cans of Tofino beer to take with me. "When you try them, you'll remember the sea, the beaches, and the forests around here." I shared some of them with family in Victoria, but one I took back with me to my current home in Albuquerque, New Mexico. When I sipped a glass of Kelp Stout and tasted the subtle briny tang, I imagined myself on a beach near where the beer was born.

CHAPTER 9

CRAFT BEERS FROM CUMBERLAND TO CAMPBELL RIVER

~~~~~~~~~

Cumberland Brewing Company,
Forbidden Brewing Company,
Gladstone Brewing Company,
Land & Sea Brewing Company,
Beach Fire Brewing and Nosh House

After leaving Tofino, I returned along Highway 4 to that fork in the road where it runs into Highway 19 and drove north along what, a day earlier, had been the road not taken. My first stop was **Cumberland Brewing Company** in Cumberland, the westernmost of the three contiguous towns of Cumberland, Courtenay, and Comox. During the 1950s, after the end of the coal-mining era that had sustained the area since the late 19th century, Cumberland had garnered some attention as the hometown of world-class track-and-field athlete Terry Tobacco. It became much more famous (craft beer lovers would say "notorious") at the beginning of the 21st century, when Labatt Brewing declared it the "Lucky-est town in British Columbia." The per capita consumption of

Lucky Lager there was reportedly greater than in any other city, town, or village in the province.

As I drove into the centre of what the locals call "the Village," I thought that Cumberland must look just as it did well before I was born. Along the three-block downtown, the buildings were well maintained but didn't have that "modern retro-chic" that the "old towns" of so many cities have acquired in order to attract tourists. All of the stores and businesses, I later learned, were locally owned; only the gas stations at the edge of town were parts of corporate chains. It was easy to find my destination, Cumberland Brewing Company, because on the side of the 60-year-old building that housed it was painted a large sign reading "Cumberland Brewing Company Entrance." I opened the gate and walked past a stroller parking area and the entrance to the warm/ dry-weather beer garden and into the tasting room, behind which were the 12-hectolitre brewhouse and the kitchen.

I'd arrived early for our interview, and Darren Adam, one of the co-owners, and Mike Tymchuk, the head brewer and husband of the other co-owner, Caroline Tymchuk, hadn't yet arrived. Anders Petersson, an assistant brewer, gave me a brief tour of the brewery and tasting room. One of the points of interest was a collection of nearly 200 growlers on shelves, gifts from patrons who had been to breweries all across Canada and the United States. Another point of interest was a chalkboard by the serving counter that read: BEER IT FORWARD. People could pay for beer for friends who might be dropping by at another time or just for any future patron.

Mike Tymchuk arrived just as Petersson had finished showing me around. Tymchuk had moved to the Comox Valley in 2010, shortly after leaving Wild Rose Brewery, a Calgary company he'd co-founded in the mid-1990s. He'd begun brewing at Spinnakers in Victoria, where he'd originally been hired as a cook, and then moved on to Penticton, Saskatoon, and Calgary, with stops along the way as a brewery consultant in China, Japan, and the Philippines. "After I left Wild Rose, I needed time away from the brewing scene. Caroline and I moved here, discovered that Cumberland didn't have a pizza place, and so we started Riders Pizza."

While Tymchuk was discussing his brewing background, Darren Adam showed up. He'd come to the Comox Valley over a dozen years ago. An airline mechanic, Adam would fly his own plane to the mainland every Monday, work on planes, and return home on Friday. But he found the commute both wearing and time-consuming and was wishing he could spend more time in Cumberland. One day, he'd come to Riders for dinner and had ended up spending several hours talking with Tymchuk. He was fascinated by his brewing biography,

Mike Tymchuk, head brewer, and Darren Adam, co-owner, stand in front of the large wall sign pointing to the entrance of Cumberland Brewing Company. ↓

and, when he returned home that night, he told his wife, "I want to open a brewery with the fellow who runs Riders." It wouldn't happen right away, but in 2014, he became a partner in what, at the time, was the only brewery north of Nanaimo and the first one ever to operate in Cumberland. The brewery's opening increased the business at the pizzeria, and in a couple of years both places were so busy that Riders moved to a building across the street.

Although Cumberland Brewing has a few accounts in the area, it was intended right from the start that most of the beer would be purchased at the tasting room. "If you want our beer, you have to come here!" was a slogan Adam had made up soon after the opening. "The people around here really wanted a brewery," he said. "I remember overhearing a woman who'd come in with her mother, an out-of-towner, saying, 'This is our brewery.'"

Tymchuk elaborated on the idea of "local": "There's a long tradition of community breweries. I remember hearing an old saying that 'Every neighbourhood needs a bakery, a butcher store, and a brewery.' This is a place where people feel welcome when they come here. They know that they're visiting a local business that provides local jobs. In the summer, there are over 60 people working in the brewery, tasting room, and pizza place. I think we've done what many small breweries have done for their towns; we helped give Cumberland a shot in the arm. And we've gotten a big, warm hug from the community." That community ranges from young families who have pushed their strollers to the "Village local" to hikers and mountain bikers who have just come off of one of the area's many trails.

When I'd spoken with Tymchuk several years ago at Wild Rose in Calgary, he'd told me, "We open markets; we don't dive into existing ones." That had also been the case in Cumberland. It wasn't just a matter of there never having been a brewery in Cumberland or that there wasn't one in the three contiguous towns. It was also a matter of deciding what attitude to take about the tremendous area sales of Lucky Lager. Adam explained, "We've never seen such a mythology about a beer or a brand loyalty like there is around Lucky. But we're not here to make an alternative pale lager; we're here to offer something different. We'd rather be crafty than lucky."

Our conversation turned to beer itself, and Tymchuk began by discussing the changes he'd seen in nearly three decades of brewing. "When we started up Wild Rose, we were way out there compared to other breweries. But now there are many fearless young brewers; it's a very exciting time to be brewing. And the brewers are so good; it isn't very often you'll find a bad beer. But," he said, and then paused, "I'm keeping the old torch burning." What was "wild" at Wild Rose in the 1990s isn't as wild anymore.

Cumberland Brewing offers four core beers, all of them classic examples of their styles. The biggest seller is Forest Fog, a 4.3 percent ABV unfiltered American wheat beer that bears a striking resemblance to Velvet Fog, one of the most popular beers Tymchuk had brewed many years earlier at Wild Rose. "It's designed to be our transition beer for new craft drinkers. It's very low in hops; we make the wheat the star." It's also an ale that Cumberland Brewing uses to reciprocate the hugs received from the community. For every litre sold, 25 cents is donated to the Cumberland Community Forest Society, a non-profit organization that raises funds to purchase forest lands in danger of being destroyed.

Just a Little Bitter English Bitter and Red Tape Pale Ale are the brewery's more, but not too, hop-forward beers. The former is a 4.2 percent ABV British-style session ale that is mellow and rounded, with the East Kent Golding and Fuggle hops providing earthy and spicy notes and the Maris Otter malts creating biscuity and nutty flavours. After describing the beer, Tymchuk laughed and said that Just a Little Bitter was initially Cumberland Brewing's "answer for people who wanted something like Lucky." Red Tape Pale Ale (5.5 percent ABV) is named in "honour" of the "beerocracy," the people who present breweries with pages of forms to fill out and lists of regulations to follow. It's an American-style pale ale that is hop-forward, but malt supported. The brewery did not have a regular India pale ale at first but tried out a number of SMASH (single-malt and single-hop) IPAs to see which were most favourably received by the patrons. Finally, "Finally" IPA (6.3 percent ABV) arrived. Mosaic, Citra, and Amarillo hops provide the variety of flavours—tropical fruits, oranges, stone fruits—that often characterize West Coast versions of the style.

Dancing Linebacker Oatmeal Stout (5.2 percent ABV) is the brewery's "darkside" offering. The name was meant to be descriptive, Darren Adam explained: "It's a big fellow, but light on its feet." A full-bodied beer, it's sessionable and easy-drinking. Coffee and chocolate notes are slightly offset by the not-overwhelming bitterness of the Fuggle hops.

After he'd finished describing the beers, I asked Mike Tymchuk whether he still had to face the doubt and skepticism from beer drinkers that craft brewers had confronted a quarter of a century ago. When they were faced with an unfiltered wheat beer, did they object, saying, "If it ain't clear, it ain't beer"? Confronted with a beer so dark they couldn't see through it, did they have to be cautioned, "Don't be afraid of the dark"? And tasting hop-forward beers, did they need to be told, "Bitter is not a four-letter word"? No, he said. It seems that although Cumberland may be a small village, and the downtown buildings may look much as they had in the 1920s when beer parlours first opened and began offering pale, yellow lagers, the people who came to the tasting room at Cumberland Brewing Company have developed educated beer palates and were turning the village into much more than just the "Lucky-est town in British Columbia."

In 2014, when Cumberland Brewing Company had opened its doors, two breweries were in the planning stages in Courtenay, seven kilometres to the east: Forbidden Brewing and Gladstone Brewing. Each would open in 2015, giving the city the first breweries in its history.

Cumberland and Courtenay are very different—the former a small village with locally owned stores, the latter a city of 25,000, the commercial and business centre of the Comox Valley. Cliffe Avenue, the main road leading into Courtenay's downtown area, was lined with fast-food and restaurant chains, franchise motels, and a mall that contained several businesses that could be found in malls across the province.

My first stop was **Forbidden Brewing**, located on the ground floor of the Best Western Westerly Hotel and Convention Centre. It was difficult to locate, mainly because, for reasons I'd learn during my visit, there was no sign outside to indicate its presence. Although the doors were open, the tasting room and growler refill station would not be open for business until later in the day. However, Michael Vincent, one of four co-owners, and Richard Lovat, an assistant brewer, welcomed me inside and showed me around. The tasting room was not unusual, with stools along the bar, high tables, at the end of the long, narrow room, a performance space where jazz musicians played on Friday nights, and local art on the walls. There was a pool table, a table stacked with board games, and a guitar that patrons were free to use hanging on the wall. However, the brewhouse was unusual. Lined up along a wall in a back room were six 57-litre tanks that served as both mash tuns and brew kettles. Each was filled with wort that, when ready for fermentation to begin, would be transferred to one large tank.

A Vancouver Island native who was working in special effects in the Lower Mainland film industry, Vincent had decided it was time to make a change in his life. "I wanted to be my own boss. I met Bob Surgenor, who owned a small brewery in Comox, and when his business folded, I thought it would be great to start a new brewery in the area. That way I could be my own boss. One of the first things I did was to buy these used tanks from a Victoria brew-on-premises business. I put them in storage containers and began looking for partners."

He found four: two homebrewers, Aaron Bible, an archaeologist, and Nicholas Williams, a Grade 1 teacher; Sarah Neufeld, a violinist in a rock band; and Natasha Richardson, Vincent's life partner and a person with bookkeeping and other business skills. He also found a location for his proposed brewery when a friend who worked at the Westerly told him about ground-floor space that was available. He signed what he considered at that time to be a very good lease and chose a name for the new brewery: Forbidden, a reference to Forbidden Plateau, a nearby winter recreation area, and to the idea of beer having been a forbidden pleasure during Prohibition.

Assistant brewer Richard Lovat and co-owner Michael Vincent stand in front of the logo for Forbidden Brewing. Also on the wall are works by local artists. ↑

Although Gladstone Brewing had opened a few blocks up Cliffe Avenue six months earlier, Forbidden quickly became popular when it began business in the middle of July 2015. "We had a full range of people coming by regularly. It was a place to meet, enjoy beer, play board games, and listen to good jazz. I thought a lot about *Cheers*; our place was just like that. Everybody knew each other and liked and respected each other." The beer was good; Forbidden earned a silver medal in the 2015 BC Beer Awards for its Pale Ale and, in 2017, a gold for its Organic Pale Ale.

The popularity of the tasting room and the high quality of the beer created problems. Vincent soon realized that it would be increasingly difficult to make a profit using the nano-scale brewery with its six small tanks. It became imperative that capacity be increased. The difficulties seemed about to be overcome when Vincent announced in mid-January

2018 that the brewery's owners had commissioned the building of a 10-hectolitre brewhouse from Innovative Stainless Solutions, a local company. Forbidden had begun its third full year of operations on a very positive note.

And then, less than three weeks later, troubles began. In early February, the management of the Westerly Hotel announced that the brewery's lease would be revoked. Failure to meet the financial terms of the lease was listed as the primary reason for the action, but such items as having live music (which was permitted under Forbidden's lounge licence) and putting up an outside sign without permission were other reasons given. The electricity was shut off, not only necessitating the closing of the tasting room but also creating the risk of unrefrigerated beer spoiling. The community rallied behind Vincent and his crew, and many people donned T-shirts reading "Unlock Forbidden! Free the Beer!"

By the time of my visit in early April, the issues had been at least temporarily resolved. The electricity was back on, beer was being brewed, and the customers were happy. But one night the sign above the entrance mysteriously disappeared.

In early May the troubles returned. A couple of days after the new brewing equipment had been delivered, the brewery found itself again without power. The electrical system had apparently been disconnected, and the owners of the brewery were denied access to the part of the building that housed the electrical equipment. Vincent acquired a portable generator, the lights came on, and the beer was kept cold. But there wasn't enough juice to even consider brewing on the six old tuns/kettles, let alone the newly delivered system. What had originally seemed to be a very good lease had, to use beer terminology, "gone skunky."

Forbidden offers a range of beers from light to dark. Richard Lovat noted: "Because we have a small system, we can try a lot of different styles." Two of the three top-selling beers, Pilsner and Pale Ale, use organic malts. "It's the way of the future," Vincent explained. "And it's the right thing to do for the planet." The Pilsner (5 percent ABV) is based on the German interpretation of the style. Saaz hops provide a crisp, clean finish, while pilsner and Vienna malts impart a slight sweetness and make the lager a little fuller-bodied than the German prototype. The award-winning Pale Ale (5 percent ABV) seems to be a hybrid of English and West Coast styles. The caramel malts give it a fuller body and taste, while the Cascade hops provide citrus and piney notes. The third of the top three sellers, the IPA (6.5 percent ABV), can be included in a new subcategory of the style, New England IPA. A hazy beer, it uses recently developed hop varietals such as ElDorado ("created" only a decade ago) to contribute what are often described as juicy, fruity notes.

A somewhat unusually high number of Forbidden's core beers are on the dark side. The Black IPA, at 8.5 percent ABV the brewery's strongest beer, is, in Lovat's words, "one of our most unique and well-done beers." He went on to say that everything works together. The Stout (6.7 percent ABV) is roasty, rich, and somewhat sweet, while the Smoked Bock has a different flavour created by the smoked malts. The Scottish Ale is smooth and malty, with virtually no hop presence.

"Exploring the Limits of Honest Beer"—that's the website tag line used to describe the goal for Forbidden Brewing. "We like to be true to style," Vincent remarked, "and still be experimental." This approach is exemplified in the Tropical Saison (5.5 percent ABV). It has the familiar funky notes contributed by the Belgian yeasts, but it also includes fresh coconut and mango—ingredients not available to long-ago Belgian brewers—to create a complex mix of flavours.

As I left Forbidden Brewing, I glanced again at the guitar on the wall and had a silly vision. I imagined Forbidden's brewers, Nicholas Williams and Richard Lovat, just before they headed to the brewhouse to develop a new beer, remembering the goal/mandate that seemed to encourage the gentle pushing of stylistic envelopes. In my mind's eye, they lifted the instrument down and began strumming and singing the words of the popular 1950s Pat Boone song, "Don't Forbid Me."

A five-minute walk north of Forbidden Brewing, **Gladstone Brewing Company** is located in an old building that was once the home of the Seale and Thomson mechanics garage and dealership. The tasting lounge features an automotive decor: vintage mechanics' tools are used as tap handles, the sampler trays are made of old licence plates, and old oil cans, hubcaps, and tool boxes decorate the walls.

I understood the automotive theme, but not the name of the brewery. I couldn't see any connection to the names of local buildings or streets. And so, one of the first things I asked Daniel Sharratt, co-owner with his wife, Alexandra Stephanson, was where the name Gladstone came from. It turned out that, several years ago, Sharratt had lived on Gladstone Avenue in Victoria, and his friends used to call his garage, where he pursued his homebrewing hobby, "the Gladstone Brewery."

"When we got married, we told people that the beer served at our reception came from the Gladstone Brewery," he told me. "We decided to keep the name when we opened up in Courtenay."

Sharratt had come from Ontario, where the craft beer scene was not as advanced as on the West Coast, to pursue graduate studies in economics. He then worked as an economist at the provincial Ministry of Health. And all along, he homebrewed. "I was a high-volume home-brewer," he remarked. "I'd usually brew two or three times a week." By his own admission, he also had an entrepreneurial streak and wanted to have his own business.

His passion for brewing—he was particularly fond of making Belgian-style ales—combined with his entrepreneurial streak, led him to the Comox Valley. "I had a special connection with the area: my grandfather had been stationed at the Comox air force base, my grandparents lived there, and my mother had moved there. Besides, I loved snowboarding, and the snowboarding was great nearby. The area didn't have a brewery at the time, and I thought this would be a good place to open my own business." However, Sharratt's plans were put on hold when Surgenor Brewing opened in Comox in 2009. It went out of business in 2012, and two years later Sharratt leased the space where his brewery now stands. On January 14, 2015, Gladstone Brewing Company (the professional version) opened—in another, much larger garage.

"People around here are very supportive of local businesses. They'd drop by to check us out and try our beer," Sharratt said, making an observation I'd heard from several Vancouver Island brewers. The locals responded very positively: within a week, some of the beer styles had run out, and within three months, plans for expansion were under way. Pizzeria Guerrilla leased space adjacent to the tasting room. Although tourists are always welcome—and there have been a lot of beer tourists and out-of-town beer geeks—Gladstone's focus is on its Comox Valley neighbours. The brewery now cans its beer and distributes it beyond the valley; however, 80 percent of its business is on site, and the locals constitute the main market.

"The community is huge for us," Sharratt said enthusiastically. "The tasting room and patio have become community places. People come to listen to local music, to enjoy a talent show on the patio, and to celebrate our Springtoberfest. It's like a German beer festival, with a Marzen specially brewed for the occasion. We also have a pig roast then." The celebration of things and people local is also carried on a block north at the Cornerstone Café & Taphouse, owned by Sharratt and Stephanson, which offers not only Gladstone beers but also other area beers on tap, displays local artwork, and hosts special events such as a fashion show.

Daniel Sharratt, who used to homebrew in his garage on Gladstone Avenue in Victoria, opened Gladstone Brewing in Courtenay in what used to be an automobile dealership and garage. ➜

"We started off brewing two beers: a Belgian single and an IPA," Sharratt said. "The Belgian was designed to appeal to both craft beer lovers and craft beer newcomers, and we felt we had to have an IPA for the real craft beer aficionados. Then we added a pilsner; this is still a place where there are a lot of lager drinkers." The beers were enthusiastically received not only by locals and visitors but also by judges in major brewing competitions. Just a few months after the brewery opened in

2015, Gladstone Porter won a bronze medal at the Canadian Brewing Awards. The next year, the Czech Dark Lager garnered a gold. The Belgian Single took bronze medals in both 2016 and 2017.

Initially, Daniel Sharratt and John Adair, an award-winning home-brewer who is now a brewer-partner at Sooke Brewing, shared the brewing duties. After Adair departed, Tak Guenette, who had worked at Steamworks and Parallel 49 in Vancouver, took over as the main brewer. Originally from Vancouver Island, he had returned because the pace of mainland life was so great. He didn't have a job lined up; however, Adair's departure provided an opening.

The information sheet given out to visitors to Gladstone Brewing states that the brewery focuses on "Belgian ales, European lagers, and Pacific Northwest–style India pale ales." To those categories could be added English ales and an American crossover ale. One of the flagship beers is the 4.5 percent ABV Belgian Single, which, Sharratt noted, is "a table beer that the monks drank." Fruity and spicy, with the characteristic funkiness generated by the Belgian yeast, it was designed to be approachable and non-threatening for entry-level craft beer drinkers and still interesting and sufficiently complex for craft beer veterans. "We didn't want our first beer to be too far out," Sharratt added. Other Belgian-style offerings have included Belgian Tripel and Brett Saison. The former is an 8.2 percent ABV ale, "the style the monks made to sell," and has spicy, banana, orange, and pear flavours. The latter (7.5 percent ABV) is aged in gin barrels and has juniper and citrus notes, along with a mild oakiness.

Pilsner (5.5 percent ABV, 35 IBUs) and Marzen (5.8 percent ABV, 22 IBUs) are the two major Continental-style lagers brewed by Gladstone. The former, the brewery's top-selling beer, is a Czech-style pilsner. It has a rich, foamy head, biscuity flavours, and a crisp, clean, tangy finish. "If you like Pilsner Urquell, you'll really like this one," Sharratt remarked, referring to the Bohemian lager whose name means "original pilsner." The Marzen is a copper-coloured, full-bodied, dry-finishing beer that tastes a little like freshly baked nut bread. The bitterness of the Magnum hops balances the maltiness. The IPA is "an old-school Pacific Northwest ale." Its 6.6 percent alcohol by volume is in the medium range for the style, as are the 70 IBUs. But it is certainly a bonanza for hop lovers. Words used to describe the aromas and flavours created by the Chinook, Simcoe, Mandarina Bavaria, Summit, and Mosaic hops include piney, earthy, spicy, herbal, fruity, and citrusy. Although Sharratt referred to it as an "old-school" ale, four of the hop varietals have been developed since the beginning of the 21st century; the oldest of the group, Chinook, was first released in 1985. There's a lot of newness in this old-style beer.

Porter is a North American version of a traditional English ale. Based on one of Sharratt's garage brewery recipes, it's more robust and somewhat drier and more bitter that its ancestors. Black, dark crystal, and chocolate malts give coffee and chocolate notes. Cream Ale (5.3 percent ABV, 19 IBUs) is a recently released summer seasonal. Characteristic of the style originally brewed in the later 19th century by

German immigrants who'd come to the United States, it is light-bodied and light in colour. Flaked corn gives a creamy mouthfeel. People with lactose intolerance needn't be worried. No milk products are used; the creaminess refers to texture, not ingredients.

When Gladstone Brewing opened its doors early in the new year of 2015, very few people knew the background of the name. They may still not know; but beer lovers in the Comox Valley and in a widening area of Vancouver Island now know that the name stands for both excellent beers and, when they're in Courtenay, a welcoming tasting room in which to enjoy them.

~~~~~~~~~~

My visit to Gladstone Brewing had originally been planned as the penultimate stop on my Vancouver Island beer journey. However, a day earlier, I had learned from Mike Tymchuk and Darren Adam of Cumberland Brewing that a new brewery would soon be opening in Comox. And so, on the final morning of my travels, I drove over to Comox and visited Jason Walker in the building that had formerly housed a window and door manufacturer and was to become **Land & Sea Brewing** later in the year. It was, ironically, located across Guthrie Road from the building that had been the home of Surgenor Brewing from 2009 to 2012 and was now a party rental store.

Walker had spent most of his adult years doing marketing research and strategy and had worked with Big Rock and Molson breweries. He'd been a fan of Wild Rose Brewery of Calgary and Fort Garry Brewing in Winnipeg when they were among the very few craft breweries on the Prairies. "They introduced me to the flavours of the various beer styles." He had been a resident of the Comox Valley for a decade, had seen the rise and fall of Surgenor, and felt that he wanted to create a Comox craft brewery where the locals could gather. "It would be a celebration of where we live," he said. "The craft industry is growing. It reminds me of Germany where every town has a brewery. Local ale is coming back."

He walked me around the brewery, which at the time was only a large open space with lines on the floor marking where various pieces of equipment would be placed and where the tasting room would be. "Here's the place for the small kitchen we'll have, and here is where the people can sit," he said, laughing. "And this is where the 12-hec brewing system will be." To run it, he had hired Tessa Gabiniewicz, a veteran brewer who'd worked at 33 Acres Brewing in Vancouver and Nelson Brewing. "We'll be specializing in easy-to-drink ales," he told me.

I wished Walker a successful and speedy opening and began the 59-kilometre drive along Highway 19A to Campbell River, home of **Beach Fire Brewing and Nosh House**. As I drew closer to the city of just over 35,000, the largest north of Nanaimo, I caught frequent glimpses of the Strait of Georgia and realized that none of the breweries I'd gone to had been more than three or four kilometres from the salt chuck, a term based on the Chinook trading jargon to refer to the sea. It seemed appropriate that my final stop would be in a place that called itself the "Salmon Capital of the World" and had a brewery whose name suggested a gathering right next to the water. I remembered having read that the city was one of the locations for the 2005 movie *Are We There Yet?* and a short distance from town I was tempted to say aloud to myself, "Almost."

Beach Fire Brewing and Nosh House, which is a 10-minute walk from the water, isn't, as was the case for nearly all the breweries I'd gone to, the first tenant of the building it occupied. Originally a television studio for the local Canadian Television Network affiliate, it had also been a hot tub store, adult toy store (I didn't ask what kind of toys), and a Liberal party campaign headquarters. It looked like none of these now, but like an amalgam of the types of beer-serving establishments co-owners Darrin Finnerty and Laura Gosnell had visited over the years. "We'd been interested in the different ways people had been getting together to enjoy time with each other over beer," Finnerty explained. The bar was not unlike the stand-up bars of English pubs, the long tables with benches were reminiscent of a German beer hall, and a corner with comfortable chairs had the feel of an American cocktail lounge. Along the walls were works of local artists and painted bicycle wheels; the sound baffles hanging from the ceiling were decorated with wave patterns. Perhaps the most interesting feature was a chalkboard food menu hanging from one wall. It was changed frequently during the day as food items were either added or deleted. People wondering what might be available should they decide to visit could check out a picture of the menu on the brewery/restaurant website to see what was currently available.

Finnerty, who has a degree in forestry management from the University of Northern British Columbia, was a homebrewer who had learned the craft through trial and error, listening to podcasts and reading all the books about brewing and beer that he could get his hands on. His friends, fans of his homebrew, had often told him that he should start a brewery. Merecroft Village Pub, a couple of kilometres away, which had existed since the mid-1990s under such names as Cog and Kettle, Fogg and Sudds, and Ripple Rock Brewing, had brewers from other breweries occasionally show up to make beer for them. However, it was essentially a family restaurant located in a shopping centre, and it served a great deal of beer made by Canada's internationally owned megabreweries. "I thought that Campbell River needed a brewpub, a community place where people could gather," Finnerty said. "I realized that if I didn't do it, someone else would, and I'd be kicking myself." He resigned from his job at International Forest Products, which had plants in many countries, to start a very local business, one in which he and co-owner Laura Gosnell had control over the creating and serving of their products.

He decided to name the brewery Beach Fire Brewing and Nosh House. "Campbell River is the only place on Vancouver Island where fires are permitted on the beach," Gosnell told me. "Gathering together around a fire with friends is an important social and community event here. Darren wanted to have a brewpub that would also be a community gathering place." She paused, then chuckled and added: "Without the bonfire, of course!"

Although some people drop by to sip a pint or two while they enjoy board game night, Yoga and a Pint Night, or live music, food has always been central to the experience of being at the brewpub. Its name, after all, is Beach Fire Brewing and Nosh House, the word "nosh" a reference to plates of small snacks designed to be shared. Gosnell oversees the

kitchen. A biology graduate from the University of British Columbia, who'd created a great deal of very artistic pottery, she'd discovered cooking when she was still a child. "I found out that if I did some of the cooking, I wouldn't have to wash the dishes," Gosnell said. "At university, I had jobs cooking at restaurants. I've always loved the creativity of cooking." The menu, which she creates after consultation with the kitchen staff and which changes daily, uses local ingredients as much as possible. "In fact, we have local suppliers coming to us to see if we'd like to take some of their produce. We always think about the food we make in relation to the beer Darrin makes, and we frequently use [the beer] in our recipes." It's not your average pub grub. For my lunch, I enjoyed spaghetti made in-house and clams. Visitors might find such nosh plates to share as beef picadillo tostadas, Buddha Bowl with quinoa and roasted squash, or meals like smoked chipotle veggie burritos.

Laura Gosnell and Darrin Finnerty stand in front of Beach Fire Brewing and Nosh House. The name Beach Fire was chosen to suggest the idea of the brewery becoming a place where the Campbell River community can gather just as it often does around a cheery fire by the seaside. ←

Just as Gosnell enjoys the creativity of working in the kitchen, Finnerty enjoys the making of beer. "I control the beer from the time I start making it in the brewhouse until it arrives in the washroom," he joked. The four core beers are, as he put it, classic examples of traditional styles. "Doing it this way, in an area where most people are just becoming aware of craft beers, gives them a chance to learn what the basic beer styles are." Beach Blonde Ale (5.5 percent ABV, 20 IBUs) is the brewery's entry-level beer. "We like to introduce them to something that is clean and light-bodied and not too hoppy. Then we can move them to a pale ale and then to something darker." The pale, pilsner, wheat, and crystal malts provide Beach Blonde with a complex but not overwhelming mix of flavours, while the Cascade hops contribute counterbalancing piney and citrus notes.

Based on one of Finnerty's homebrewing recipes, High Tide Pale Ale (5.5 percent ABV, 40 IBUs) is an American-style pale ale that is hoppier than many examples of the style, but not as bitter as an IPA. "It's close to an IPA, but it's not one," Finnerty said. He then went on to say that the IPA they had made, which was loaded with different hops, wasn't as popular as the pale ale. The day I visited, Citra hops were used in the pale ale, but Finnerty noted that they would be using a variety of hops to give their patrons the experience of the different flavours that can be created.

Beach Fire's two darker regular beers, Wheel-Bender Stout (4.5 percent ABV, 35 IBUs) and Ember Red Ale (5.1 percent ABV, 15 IBUs), are of Irish and Scottish origin, respectively. The former is an Irish dry stout, a Guinness-like ale that is low in alcohol and light of body, even with the roasty and chocolate flavours of the malt. "It's a recipe that a friend gave me during my homebrewing days." It is also the ale used for what Finnerty calls their "dessert beer," Salted Caramel Stout, into which is incorporated a caramel sauce made by Gosnell. Ember Red Ale is a Scottish ale. Its toasty notes and slight malty sweetness are created by the chocolate and Munich malts. East Kent Golding hops provide earthy notes.

Beach Fire began serving its beers and noshes in November 2016. "After a year and a half, things are still wonderful," Finnerty enthused. "We get more and more regulars, and the place gets busier and busier." While we were talking, one of the large tables modelled after those Finnerty had seen in Germany filled up with people from a nearby office. Some of them enjoyed pints of beer; others shared flights of small sample glasses. Several shared nosh plates. And nobody seemed to worry that there were no hamburgers and fries on the menu or that a pale North American lager from one of the megabrewers wasn't on tap.

My journey of a thousand sips complete, I began the drive back south to Victoria. As I left the parking lot, the sun, which had been making very brief and infrequent cameo appearances for well over a week, shone brightly. Clouds ringed the horizon, but overhead the sky was a wonderful blue. Shrubs bloomed in gardens, and a few buds had burst open on the maples and alders that bordered the highway. It was a wonderful way to end what had been a marvellous trip.

CONCLUSION

THE NEW LOCAL

As I drove south from Campbell River along the Island Highway, I thought about my "journey of a thousand sips," comparing it with my youthful trips to beer parlours and my 2010 tour of Vancouver Island breweries. In 1961, there had been one Vancouver Island brewery, Lucky Lager, which was owned by Labatt Brewing Company, a national company with headquarters in Ontario. In 2010, the Lucky Lager plant had been gone for nearly three decades, but there were breweries in Victoria, Salt Spring Island, Duncan, Nanaimo, Comox, and Campbell River—12 in all. During my current trip, I'd stopped in 18 places and called on 33 breweries. Six more breweries were scheduled to open within the year.

In 1960, when I celebrated my 21st birthday at the Ingraham in Victoria, only something called "beer" (most likely Lucky Lager) was available. Of the just over three dozen specific styles described in one of the appendices for *Beer Quest West* (2011), only eight had three or more examples from Vancouver Island breweries. The most popular styles were brown ale, extra special bitter, IPA, pale ale, and stout. There were only 14 Vancouver Island examples of all lager styles.

In 2018, what are now considered the traditional craft beers, "the old standbys," are still very popular. However, many lesser-known styles have become much more widely available. In 2010, I tasted only one kolsch and one saison that had been brewed on Vancouver Island. By 2018, I had sampled well over six local examples of each style. In addition, such heretofore virtually unknown styles as gose and Berlinerweisse are becoming increasingly popular, as are sour and barrel-aged beers.

Moreover, half of the breweries now offer a pilsner or other light lager. When the craft beer movement had begun, brewers had shied away from making lagers: they were difficult to do well, they were more expensive to make, and they took longer to ferment. In the second decade of the 21st century, brewers have overcome their reluctance (or perhaps trepidation) about making lagers. On an island where Lucky Lager is still popular, breweries have had to be prepared to offer an alternative to drinkers of mainstream pale North American lagers.

What has caused both this tremendous growth in the number of breweries and the rapidly increasing range of styles? One reason is that an increasing number of people are drinking craft beer instead of the mass-produced beers of the large international brewing conglomerates. And these people are developing educated palates: they know the basic characteristics of each style, and they can spot a poorly made version of the style and detect the subtle differences between different breweries' interpretations of a style. They are also interested in discovering newer (usually centuries-old and relatively forgotten) styles.

A second reason for the growth and expansion is that the British Columbia government has developed a set of regulations that make it easier for smaller craft breweries to market their products. Government-owned liquor stores have a price scale that makes it possible for these smaller breweries to compete with the large ones. Perhaps more important, government regulations were changed in 2013 to allow craft breweries to sell their beer on premises. All the breweries I visited had growler stations, where patrons could have their 1.89-litre/64-ounce glass containers filled with fresh beer; frequently they also had coolers filled with cans and bottles for sale. And probably most important, people could now enjoy a beer at the tasting room. In a tasting room, patrons could drink the equivalent of one regular-size

Mike Doehnel stands amidst a field of barley that will be transformed into brewer's malt at his craft malting facility, Doehnel Floor Malting (photo courtesy of Mike Doehnel). ↑

bottle or can of beer per person, either as a single serving or in a few small taster (sample) glasses. If the tasting room had a lounge licence, they could enjoy more than one regular-size serving of beer. Having the opportunity to sell beer these ways provided a source of immediate revenue for small or newly opened breweries.

Perhaps the most significant change I've observed over the years, particularly during the 2010s, has been the development of what could be called "the new local." That beer I had on my 21st birthday may have been brewed at the Lucky Lager plant only a few blocks away from the Ingraham Hotel. But it was local only because of the proximity of the brewery. Lucky Lager had had its origins in the 1930s in San Francisco. A pale American lager produced by General Brewing, it became available in British Columbia when General entered into an agreement to have it brewed by the Coast Breweries consortium, which included the Government Street brewery.

The era of the new local has a resemblance to an era when most beer was purchased and much of it consumed at the place where it was brewed. In that older era, this was partly because without refrigeration and efficient transportation networks, beer could not travel far without spoiling. It was also because the local tavern or pub that made its own beer was a kind of neighbourhood institution, a community gathering place. The new local relates to the "slow food" or "locavore" movement, which developed as a reaction again the fast-food franchise business and the widespread sale of food in places far, far distant from where it was grown, harvested (slaughtered), processed, and packaged. The shorter distance from farm or ranch to table, and the careful cooking of locally sourced ingredients, resulted in better (more healthy, nourishing, and flavourful) meals.

Along the "ale trails" of Vancouver Island, I encountered many aspects of the new local, beginning with the ingredients for making beer. Of course, the water was local, and more than that, as several brewers told me, it was excellent for making beer. Much of the barley for malting is still grown on large farms away from Vancouver Island, usually on the Canadian Prairies, and the larger percentage of hops comes from the Yakima or Willamette Valleys of Washington and Oregon States, respectively. However, there are a small but growing number of Vancouver Island malt houses and hop yards. I visited two during my travels: Doehnel Floor Malting of Saanichton and Cedar Valley Hop Yards just south of Nanaimo. The former is owned by Mike Doehnel, who grew up on a farm on the Saanich Peninsula, was a homebrewer who decided to grow his own barley, and later began a small malting business. His customers have included Spinnakers Gastro Brewpub and Driftwood Brewery.

Cedar Valley Hop Yards is owned by Debbie and Kevin Lamson, who began planting hops in 2012. "Hops grow really well on the 49th parallel," Debbie explained. "The length of the growing season is just right, and so is the weather." They started with 1,200 plants and expanded as the craft beer industry grew. One of Cedar Valley's best customers is Harley Smith, head brewer and co-owner of Longwood Brewery in Nanaimo. His beers use not only the hops grown by the Lamsons but also as many other locally sourced ingredients as possible.

Some or all of the equipment in 23 of 33 Vancouver Island breweries I visited was manufactured in Saanichton. Two childhood friends, Phil Zacharias,

Kevin and Debbie Lamson, owners of Cedar Valley Hop Yards, hold two small hop bines which, by the fall harvest, will have grown to heights of seven metres or more. ↓

a machinist, and Bill Cummings, a welder, both Victoria natives, had helped Vancouver Island Brewery during its start-up in the earlier 1980s and, in 1984, began Specific Mechanical Systems. "They began working out of a garage," Reo Phillips, the company's president, told me when I visited and we were walking through two very large buildings where various pieces of brewing equipment were being manufactured for shipment to breweries around the world. "They were the original employees; now there are over 100 working here." Specific's closest satisfied customer, Category 12 Brewing, is less than a five-minute drive away.

Although the products of several Vancouver Island breweries are available on the BC mainland, with some found in the province's Interior and in provinces to the east, the main distribution area for many is Vancouver Island, and the focus for a number of these is on the brewpub or tasting room that is only steps away from the brewhouse. "If you want our beer, you have to come here," said Cumberland Brewing Company's Darren Adam when I asked about the company's distribution area. Names such as Cumberland Brewing Company, Sooke Oceanside Brewery, and Tofino Brewing link the breweries to specific towns or cities. Some others are named after or name some of their beers after well-known geographical features: Mount Arrowsmith and Forbidden Brewing, and Race Rocks (Lighthouse Brewing) and Shawnigan (Craig Street Brew Pub) ales.

At the tasting rooms/brewpubs, patrons are offered an experience that is centred on, but not limited to, enjoying beer. (Mind you, the beer is very good. At the end of May 2018, I learned that six Island breweries won medals at the Canadian Brewing Awards ceremony: one gold, three silver, and two bronze.) They could enjoy good food prepared on site, available from food trucks parked just outside, or even brought from home. They could participate in board game nights or trivia contests, enjoy beer after a yoga or painting class held in the tasting room, listen to local musicians, or sometimes even display their own skills on karaoke nights. They could sit in an old barber's chair getting a haircut while sipping a beer (holding the glass away from the cascading hair). They could read a book or newspaper or look at local artists' works, hung on the walls.

Most important, they could sit with family and friends, chatting and enjoying each other's company. Aaron Colyn, owner of Twin City Brewing of Port Alberni, spoke of wanting to create a "third place"— not home, not work—where people could gather and socialize over a cold beer. I heard similar statements from other owners: they wanted to provide a place they felt was lacking in their communities. It was a two-way street. The breweries and brewpubs didn't just provide a good space and good beer; they were actively involved in their communities, supporting local charities, local community groups, and amateur sports teams. They embraced their communities and received support from both citizens and civic officials. As Aly Tomlin of Riot Brewing put it, "We give each other big hugs."

I've often wondered whether or not craft brewing was in a boom period that would end in a bust, as had been the case in the 1990s. Most of the people I talked with felt optimistic, noting that Vancouver Island had a craft beer culture that was three and a half decades old and that the percentage of craft beer sold on the Island was higher than in most other places in Canada. "If you make good beer and have a sensible business plan," one brewer commented, "you should do all right. I think the best is yet to come."

I'll drink to that!

DIRECTORY OF VANCOUVER ISLAND BREWERIES AND BREWPUBS

The following directory includes information for Vancouver Island breweries and brewpubs and is based on facts taken from brewery websites and responses to a questionnaire sent to each brewery. Below is an alphabetical directory of breweries and brewpubs that were in operation as of October 2018.

"Core beer list" includes beers available year-round, seasonal releases, and others that are frequently available. (Note that brewers frequently drop beers from their lists and add new ones. For a brewery's most up-to-date list of beers, check its website.)

The word "menu" following "food" signifies that the tasting room or brewpub has a food menu and that patrons are not permitted to bring food into the establishment. "BYOF" means "bring your own food;" patrons are welcome to bring food into or order food to be delivered to the tasting room. Food trucks are frequently parked outside many of the breweries.

The term "tasting room" means that a brewery may serve a maximum 375 millilitres of beer to a person in one day; the maximum size of an individual serving is limited to 125 millilitres. "Tasting room with lounge licence" means that a brewery may serve beer by the glass, bottle, or can. There are no specific limits to the number of glasses, bottles, or cans that can be served to patrons.

Axe & Barrel Brewing Company

2323 Millstream Road, Victoria, BC V9B 3R4

P. 778.433.6746 **W.** axeandbarrel.com

OPENED 2015 (brewery)

OWNERS Ron Cheeke, Diana Kresier

BREW CREW Andrew Tessier, Travis Oickle

BREWERY SIZE 12 hectolitres

TOURS By appointment

CORE BEER LIST Axe Stout, Fruity Mother Pucker Gose (with strawberry and blackberry), King Kolsch, Langford Logger Lager, Speedway Rye Pale Ale, Tessier's Witbier, West Shore India Pale Ale

CANADIAN BREWING AWARDS King Kolsch (silver, 2017)

AVAILABLE IN Draft, growlers, cans

DISTRIBUTION AREA Vancouver Island

ON SITE Tasting room with lounge licence, growler station, and retail store; food—menu; kid friendly—no; dog friendly—yes; wheelchair accessible—yes; events—music nights

Bad Dog Brewing Company

7861 Tugwell Road, Sooke, BC V9Z 0J7

P. 250.642.3621 **W.** baddogbrewing.ca

OPENED 2017

OWNERS John and Rosanne Lyle

BREW CREW John Lyle, Chris Lyle, Paul Lyle

BREWERY SIZE 10 hectolitres

TOURS Yes

CORE BEER LIST Coco Dark Ale, Dizzy Dogs Double IPA, Honey Blonde Ale, Old Red Ale, 642 Session Ale, Tire Biter IPA

AVAILABLE IN Draft, growlers, cans

DISTRIBUTION AREA Vancouver Island

ON SITE Tasting room, growler station, and retail store; food—BYOF; kid friendly—yes; dog friendly—yes; wheelchair accessible—yes

Beach Fire Brewing and Nosh House

594 11th Avenue, Campbell River, BC V9W 4G4

P. 250.914.3473 **W.** beachfirebrewing.ca

OPENED 2016

OWNERS Darrin Finnerty, Laura Gosnell

BREW CREW Darrin Finnerty, Quinton Armstrong

BREWERY SIZE 12 hectolitres

TOURS Yes

CORE BEER LIST Apricot Kettle Sour, Beach Blonde Ale, Ember Red Ale, English Porter, Hefeweizen, High Tide Pale Ale, Honey Ale, IPA, Kettle Sour, Pilsner, Raspberry Ale, Saison, Wheel-Bender Stout, Witbier

AVAILABLE IN Draft, growlers

DISTRIBUTION AREA Campbell River, Comox Valley

ON SITE Tasting room with lounge licence, growler station; food—menu; kid friendly—yes; dog friendly—no; wheelchair accessible—yes; events—live music nights, Yoga and a Pint morning, small-batch beer Tuesdays, board game night, trivia night

Canoe Brewpub

450 Swift Street, Victoria, BC V8W 1S3

P. 250.361.1940 **W.** canoebrewpub.com

OPENED 1998

OWNERS The Truffles Group

BREW CREW Daniel Murphy, Kyle York

BREWERY SIZE 20 hectolitres

TOURS By appointment

CORE BEER LIST Amber Ale, Baltic Porter, Helles, Maibock, Marzen, West Coast Pale Ale, White IPA, Witbier

CANADIAN BREWING AWARDS Beaver Brown (silver, 2012), Bock (gold, 2007; silver, 2014), Lager (silver, 2014), Red Canoe Lager (silver, 2012), River Rock Bitter (bronze, 2012)

AVAILABLE IN Draft, growlers, bottles

DISTRIBUTION AREA Greater Victoria

ON SITE Brewpub with full liquor licence, growler station, and retail sales; food—menu; kid friendly—yes; dog friendly—patio only; wheelchair accessible—yes; events—live music (Thursday through Saturday), Winterbrau Beer Festival (November)

Category 12 Brewing Company

2200 Keating Cross Road, Saanichton, BC V8M 2A6

P. 250.652.9668 **W.** category12beer.com

OPENED 2014

OWNERS Michael and Karen Kuzyk

BREWER Michael Kuzyk

BREWERY SIZE 15 hectolitres

TOURS By appointment

CORE BEER LIST Critical Point Northwest Pale Ale, Disruption Black IPA, Excitation Cacao Nib Espresso Stout, Hiatus Farmhouse Ale, Insubordinate Session IPA, Pivotal ESB, Simplicity Blond, Subversion Imperial IPA, Transmutation Belgian Specialty Ale, 2017 Anomaly Quad, Wild IPA, Wild Saison, Zombie Repellant Ale

CANADIAN BREWING AWARDS Disruption Black IPA (gold, 2015)

AVAILABLE IN Draft, growlers, bottles, cans

DISTRIBUTION AREA Across Canada (except Ontario, Quebec)

ON SITE Tasting room with lounge licence, growler station, and retail sales; food—menu; kid friendly—yes; dog friendly—yes; wheelchair accessible—yes; events—check website

Craig Street Brew Pub

25 Craig Street, Duncan, BC V9L 1V7

P. 250.737.2337 W. csbrewery.ca

OPENED 2006

OWNERS Lance and Liz Steward

BREWER Warren Hulton

BREWERY SIZE 10 hectolitres

TOURS Yes

CORE BEERS Arbutus Pale Ale, Citrus Kolsch, Cowichan Bay Lager, India Session Ale, Mt. Prevost Porter, Shawnigan Irish Ale

AVAILABLE IN Draft, growlers

DISTRIBUTION AREA On site

ON SITE Brewpub with full liquor licence, growler station; food—menu; kid friendly—yes; dog friendly—on patio; wheelchair accessible—yes; events—live music nights

Cumberland Brewing Company

2732 Dunsmuir Avenue, Cumberland, BC V0R 1S0

P. 250.400.2739 W. cumberlandbrewing.com

OPENED 2014

OWNERS Darren Adam, Caroline Tymchuk

BREW CREW Mike Tymchuk, Anders Petersson, Caitlyn Carlisle

BREWERY SIZE 12 hectolitres

TOURS Yes

CORE BEER LIST Dancing Linebacker Oatmeal Stout, "Finally" IPA, Forest Fog American Wheat, Just a Little Bitter English Bitter, Red Tape Pale Ale

AVAILABLE IN Draft, growlers

DISTRIBUTION AREA On site, Comox Valley (limited)

ON SITE Tasting room with lounge licence, growler station; food—menu; kid friendly—yes; dog friendly—no; wheelchair accessible—yes; events—Friday cask nights

Driftwood Brewery

102-450 Hillside Avenue, Victoria, BC V8T 1Y7

P. 250.381.2739 W. driftwoodbeer.com

OPENED 2008

OWNERS Jason Meyer, Kevin Hearsum, Gary Lindsay

BREW CREW Brendon Ross, Jason Wilson, Julie Lavoie, Justin Lockhart, Lucas Renshaw, Alex Marr, Caleb Higgins, Coburn Stubel

BREWERY SIZE 60 hectolitres

TOURS No—production brewery, not open to public

CORE BEER LIST Arcus Pilsner, Belle Royale Kriek Style, Bird of Prey Flanders Red, Clodhopper Dubbel, Crooked Coast Altbier, Cry Me a River Gose, De Auras Wheat Sour, Drawn to Light Abbey Ale, Farmhand Saison, Fat Tug IPA, The Heretic Tripel, Mad Bruin Oud Bruin, Naughty Hildegard ESB, New Growth Canadian Pale Ale, Old Cellar Dweller Barley Wine, Son of the Morning Strong Golden Ale, White Bark Witbier

CANADIAN BREWING AWARDS Bird of Prey Flanders Red (silver, 2012), Fat Tug IPA (gold, 2011), Old Cellar Dweller Barley Wine (silver, 2013), Russian Imperial Stout (silver, 2011; bronze, 2012)

AVAILABLE IN Draft, growlers, bottles

DISTRIBUTION AREA Across Canada (except Quebec, Northwest Territories, New Brunswick)

ON SITE Tasting room, growler station, and retail sales; kid friendly—no; dog friendly—no; wheelchair accessible—no

Forbidden Brewing Company

1590 Cliffe Avenue, Suite A, Courtenay, BC V9N 2K4

P. 250.702.7975 **W.** forbiddenbrewing.com

OPENED 2015

OWNERS Michael Vincent, Nicholas Williams, Sarah Neufeld, Aaron Bible, Natasha Richardson

BREW CREW Nicholas Williams, Richard Lovat

BREWERY SIZE 10 hectolitres

TOURS By appointment

CORE BEER LIST Black IPA, Blonde Ale, IPA, Organic Pale Ale, Pilsner, Saison, Stout

AVAILABLE IN Draft, growlers

DISTRIBUTION AREA On site only

ON SITE Tasting room with lounge licence, growler station; food—BYOF; kid friendly—yes; dog friendly—yes; wheelchair accessible—yes; events—Friday night jazz and Sunday afternoon drop-in jazz

4 Mile Brewpub

199 Island Highway, Victoria, BC V9B 1G1

P. 250.479.2514 **W.** fourmilehouse.com

OPENED 2014 (brewpub)

OWNERS Graham and Wendy Haymes

BREW CREW Steve Gray, Richard Edwards

BREWERY SIZE 10 hectolitres

TOURS By appointment

CORE BEER LIST Blackberry Session Ale, Brothel Brown Ale, East Coast IPA, Golden Ale, Grapefruit IPA, Hazy Citra Pale Ale, Imperial IPA, Lager, Mosaic Session IPA, Pilsner, Tangerine Dream American Wheat Ale, West Coast IPA, Winter IPA

AVAILABLE IN Draft, growlers, bottles

DISTRIBUTION AREA British Columbia, Alberta, Saskatchewan, Manitoba

ON SITE Brewpub with full bar, growler station, and retail store; food—menu; kid friendly—yes; dog friendly—no; wheelchair accessible—yes

Gladstone Brewing Company

244 4th Street, Courtenay, BC V9N 1G6

P. 250.871.1111 **w.** gladstonebrewing.ca

OPENED 2015

OWNERS Daniel Sharratt, Alexandra Stephanson

BREW CREW Tak Guenette, Levon Olson, Ryan Staffler

BREWERY SIZE 18 hectolitres

TOURS No

CORE BEER LIST Belgian Single, Cream Ale, Hazy Pale Ale, IPA, Kolsch, Pilsner, Porter, Red Ale, Saison

CANADIAN BREWING AWARDS Belgian Single (bronze, 2016, 2017), Czech Dark Lager (gold, 2017), Porter (bronze, 2015)

AVAILABLE IN Draft, growlers, bottles, cans

DISTRIBUTION AREA Vancouver Island

ON SITE Tasting room with lounge licence, growler station, and retail sales; food—menu; kid friendly—yes; dog friendly—patio only; wheelchair accessible—yes; events—live music nights, Wednesday night board games

Howl Brewing Company

1780 Mills Road, North Saanich, BC V8L 5S9

P. 778.977.4695

OPENED 2018

OWNERS Dan Van Netten, Alayna Briemon

BREW CREW Dan Van Netten, Ben Van Netten

BREWERY SIZE 6 hectolitres

TOURS Yes

CORE BEER LIST Blackberry Wheat, Deep Cove Pale Ale, Land's End IPA, Old Tavern ESB, Strawberry Ale

AVAILABLE IN Draft, growlers

DISTRIBUTION AREA Victoria, Saanich Peninsula

ON SITE Tasting room and growler station; food—BYOF; kid friendly—yes; dog friendly—on patio; events—food events with next-door restaurant

Hoyne Brewing Company

101-2740 Bridge Street, Victoria, BC V8T 5C5

P. 250.590.5758 W. hoynebrewing.ca

OPENED 2011

OWNERS Sean Hoyne, Chantal O'Brien

BREW CREW Sean Hoyne, Chris McCrodan, Dave MacNaughton, Dylan Hoyne, Jay Bell

BREWERY SIZE 35 hectolitres

TOURS By appointment

CORE BEER LIST Appleton ESB, Dark Matter, Devil's Dream IPA, Down Easy Pale Ale, Entre Nous Belgian Cherry Witbier, Gratitude Winter Warmer, Helios Dortmunder Golden Lager, Hoyner Pilsner, Vienna Lager, Voltage Espresso Stout, Wolf Vine Wet Hopped Pale Ale

CANADIAN BREWING AWARDS Big Bock (bronze, 2014), Dark Matter (bronze, 2016), Hoyner Pilsner (bronze, 2014)

AVAILABLE IN Draft, growlers, bottles

DISTRIBUTION AREA British Columbia, Alberta

ONSITE Tasting room, growler station, and retail sales; kid friendly—yes; dog friendly—yes; wheelchair accessible—no

Lighthouse Brewing Company

2-836 Devonshire Road, Victoria, BC V9A 4T4
P. 250.383.6500 **W.** lighthousebrewing.com
OPENED 1998
OWNER David Thomas
BREW CREW Darrin Gano, Lisa Drapaka
BREWERY SIZE 50 hectolitres
TOURS By appointment

CORE BEER LIST Bowline Pilsner, Citrus Shore Session Ale, Company Lager, Groundswell Fresh Hop IPA, Keepers Stout, Nightwatch Coffee Lager, Numbskull Ahtanum Imperial IPA, Race Rocks Ale, Ryujin Belgian Tripel with Plums, Seaport Vanilla Stout, Shipwreck IPA, Tasman Pale Ale

CANADIAN BREWING AWARDS Keepers Stout (bronze, 2007, 2013; silver, 2009), Lighthouse Lager (gold, 2008), Navigator Doppelbock (silver, 2011), Overboard Imperial Pilsner (bronze, 2011), Race Rocks Ale (bronze, 2012), Seaport Vanilla Stout (silver, 2018)

AVAILABLE IN Draft, growlers, bottles, cans

DISTRIBUTION AREA British Columbia, Alberta, Saskatchewan (occasionally), Manitoba

ON SITE Tasting room, growler station, and retail sales; kid friendly—yes; dog friendly—yes; wheelchair accessible—no

Longwood Brew Pub

5775 Turner Road, Nanaimo, BC V9T 6L8

P. 250.729.8225 **W.** longwoodbrewpub.com

OPENED 2000

OWNERS John McPhail, Mike Campbell

BREWER Graham Payne

BREWERY SIZE 10 hectolitres

TOURS By appointment

CORE BEER LIST Berried Alive Raspberry Ale, The Big One IPA, Czech Pilsner, Extra Special Bitter, Irish Red Ale, Longwood Ale (blonde), Steam Punk Dunkelweizen, Stoutnik Russian Imperial Stout, The Big One

AVAILABLE IN Draft, growlers, kegs

DISTRIBUTION AREA Nanaimo area

ON SITE Brewpub with full bar, growler station, and retail sales; food—menu; kid friendly—yes; dog friendly—no; wheelchair accessible—yes; events—live music

Longwood Brewery

101A-2046 Boxwood Road, Nanaimo, BC V9S 5W7

P. 250.591.2739 **W.** longwoodbeer.com

OPENED 2013

OWNERS Harley Smith, Tracy McLean

BREW CREW Harley Smith, Peter Kis-Toth, Mike Ephier

BREWERY SIZE 25 hectolitres

TOURS By appointment

CORE BEER LIST Beetnik Root Stout, Berried Alive Raspberry Ale, The Big One IPA, Cake Chocolate Raspberry Stout, Full Patch Pumpkin Saison Ale, Island Time Lager, Quinceotica Harvest Lager, Steam Punk Dunkelweizen, Stoutnik Russian Imperial Stout, The Big One, Winter's Own Weizenbock

AVAILABLE IN Draft, growlers, bottles, cans

DISTRIBUTION AREA British Columbia

ON SITE Tasting room, growler station, and retail sales; kid friendly—yes; dog friendly—yes; wheelchair accessible—yes; events—annual Longwoodstock concert

Love Shack Libations

1-4134 Island Highway West, Qualicum Beach, BC V9K 2B2

P. 250.228.2477 **W.** loveshacklibations.com

OPENED 2017

OWNERS Dave and Rachel Paul

BREWER Dave Paul

BREWERY SIZE 1 hectolitre

TOURS Yes

CORE BEER LIST Crafty Cream Ale, DPA Dark Pale Ale, Killer Kolsch, Precious Porter, RPA Rye Pale Ale

AVAILABLE IN Bottles

DISTRIBUTION AREA Parksville-Qualicum area

ON SITE Tasting room, retail sales; food—snacks and BYOF; kid friendly—yes; dog friendly—no; wheelchair accessible—yes

Moon Under Water Brewery and Pub

350B Bay Street, Victoria, BC V8T 1P7

P. 250.380.0706 **W.** moonunderwater.ca

OPENED 2012

OWNERS Clay Potter, Anne Farmer, Steve Ash

BREW CREW Clay Potter, Jeff Koehl, Patrick Sand

BREWERY SIZE 10 hectolitres

TOURS By appointment

CORE BEER LIST Berliner-Style Weisse, Creepy Uncle Dunkel Dark Lager, Dark Side of the Moon Oatmeal Session Stout, Farmhouse Gruit, Hip as Funk Farmhouse IPA, Light Side of the Moon Session Lager, Potts Pils, This is Hefeweizen, Tranquility California IPA

CANADIAN BREWING AWARDS Creepy Uncle Dunkel (silver, 2015, 2016), Farmhouse Gruit (gold, 2018), Potts Pils (silver, 2014, 2015; bronze, 2016; gold, 2017), This is Hefeweizen (bronze, 2014)

AVAILABLE IN Draft, growlers, bottles, cans

DISTRIBUTION AREA British Columbia

ON SITE Brewpub and tasting room with lounge licence, growler station, and retail sales; food—menu; kid friendly—tasting room only; dog friendly—Penny Room and tasting room only; wheelchair accessible—yes; events—music bingo nights, wing and cask Wednesdays

Mount Arrowsmith Brewing Company

109-425 East Stanford Avenue East, Parksville, BC V9P 2N4

P. 250.951.0125 **W.** arrowsmithbrewing.com

OPENED 2017

OWNERS Dan Farrington, Matt Hill, Rob Hill, Andrew Hill, Mike Hill, Dave Woodward

BREW CREW Dave Woodward, Adam Sparky

BREWERY SIZE 20 hectolitres

TOURS On request

CORE BEER LIST Arrowsmith Blonde, Comfortably Chum Hefeweizen, Harvest Fresh IPA, Jagged Face IPA, Low Pressure Porter, Salish Sea Pale Ale, Sea Run Saison, Spring Tide Belgian India Session Ale

AVAILABLE IN Draft, growlers, bottles

DISTRIBUTION AREA Vancouver Island, Vancouver

ON SITE Tasting room with lounge licence, growler station, and retail sales; food—menu; kid friendly—yes; dog friendly—yes; wheelchair accessible—yes; events—live music nights, "Piping of the Cask"

Phillips Brewing and Malting Company

2010 Government Street, Victoria, BC V8T 4P1

P. 250.380.1912 **W.** phillipsbeer.com

OPENED 2001

OWNER Matt Phillips

BREW CREW Todd Fowler, Andy Innes, Alex Leckie, Jono Moore, Tristan Wood, Jackson Sinclair

BREWERY SIZE 40 hectolitres and 120 hectolitres

TOURS Yes—see website

CORE BEER LIST Amnesiac Double IPA, Analogue 78 Kolsch, Blue Buck Ale, Bottle Rocket ISA, Electric Unicorn White IPA, Ginger Beer Ale, Hop Circle IPA, Levidrome Imperial Pilsner, Longboat Chocolate Porter, Pilsner, Raspberry Wheat, Short Wave Pale Ale, 6IX Double Dry Hopped IPA, Slipstream Cream Ale

CANADIAN BREWING AWARDS Amnesiac Double IPA (bronze, 2008, 2009, 2012), Black Toque Cascadian Dark (silver, 2009), Blue Buck Ale (silver, 2012), Chocolate Porter (gold, 2008, 2009), Coffee Stout (bronze, 2012), Electric Unicorn White IPA (silver, 2017), Hammer

Imperial Stout (bronze, 2013), Raspberry Wheat (silver, 2007),
Scotch Fog (silver, 2007, 2009), Surly Blonde (bronze, 2007, 2008)

AVAILABLE IN Draft, growlers, bottles, cans

DISTRIBUTION AREA British Columbia, Alberta, Ontario

ON SITE Tasting room with lounge licence, growler station, and
retail sales; food—snacks and BYOF; kid friendly—yes; dog friendly—
no; wheelchair accessible—yes; events—see website

Red Arrow Brewing Company

5255 Chaster Road, Duncan, BC V9L 5J2

P. 250.597.0037 **W.** redarrowbeer.ca

OPENED 2015

OWNERS Lance and Liz Steward, Chris Gress

BREWER Chris Gress

BREWERY 20 hectolitres

TOURS Yes

CORE BEER LIST Fresh Hop Co-op Sunset Empire New England
Style IPA, Heritage River Hefeweizen, Invasion of the Blackberry
Lager, Kustom Kolsch, Midnite Umber Ale, Old Style Lager,
1000 Light Years from Home Chocolate Milk Stout, Piggy Pale Ale,
Sweet Leaf IPA

CANADIAN BREWING AWARDS Midnite Umber Ale (bronze, 2016),
Piggy Pale Ale (bronze, 2016)

AVAILABLE IN Draft, growlers, bottles

DISTRIBUTION AREA British Columbia, Alberta

ON SITE Tasting room, growler station, and retail sales; food—BYOF;
kid friendly—yes; dog friendly—yes; wheelchair accessible—yes;
events—special birthday party, car show and shine

Riot Brewing Company

101A-3055 Oak Street, Chemainus, BC VOR 1K1

P. 250.324.7468 **W.** riotbrewing.com

OPENED 2016

OWNERS Aly Tomlin, Ralf Rosenke, Morgan Moreira

BREW CREW Fabian Specht, Ryan Jones, Jesse Grass

BREWERY SIZE 17 hectolitres

TOURS By appointment

CORE BEER LIST Currant-ly Unavailable Black Current Blonde, Good Vibrations Classical Pilsner, Junk Punch IPA, Life Partners Pale Ale, Lipslide Lager, Sorry We Took So Long Saison, Vortex Robust Porter, Working Class Hero Dark Mild

CANADIAN BREWING AWARDS Good Vibrations Classical Pilsner (silver, 2017), Vortex Robust Porter (silver, 2018)

AVAILABLE IN Draft, growlers, bottles, cans

DISTRIBUTION AREA Vancouver Island, BC Lower Mainland, Okanagan

ON SITE Tasting room with lounge licence, growler station, and retail sales; food—BYOF; kid friendly—yes; dog friendly—yes; wheelchair accessible—yes; events—live music nights, karaoke nights, open-mike night, magic night, comedy night, painting nights, yoga nights

Salt Spring Island Ales

270 Furness Road, Salt Spring Island, BC V8K 1Z7

P. 844.388.7742 **W.** saltspringislandales.com

OPENED 1998

OWNERS Michael Forbes, Ian Laing

BREW CREW Heather Kilbourne, Tim Rennie

BREWERY SIZE 10 hectolitres

TOURS No

CORE BEERS Belgian Quad, British IPA, Dry Porter, Earl Grey India Pale Ale, Extra Special Bitter, Golden Ale, Hazy IPA, Heather Ale, Hibiscus Hefe, Mexican Lager, Nettle Ale, Spring Fever Gruit

CANADIAN BREWING AWARDS Dry Porter (silver, 2014), Golden Ale (gold, 2004, 2009), Odd Fellows IPA (silver, 2004)

AVAILABLE IN Draft, growlers, bottles, cans

DISTRIBUTION AREA British Columbia

ON SITE Tasting room, growler station, and retail sales; food—BYOF; kid friendly—yes; dog friendly—picnic area; wheelchair accessible—no

Small Block Brewing Company

203-5301 Chaster Road, Duncan, BC V9L 6T7

P. 250.597.0045 **W.** smallblockbrewery.com

OPENED 2018

OWNERS Aaron and Cate Scally

BREWER Zach Blake

BREWERY SIZE 12 hectolitres

TOURS Yes

CORE BEER LIST Dagmar ISA, Hornet Blonde Ale, Malrdhat Best Bitter, Miss Lead Oatmeal Stout, Nail Head Canadian Pale Ale, Test and Tune Hazy IPA

AVAILABLE IN Draft, growlers, cans

DISTRIBUTION AREA Vancouver Island

ON SITE Tasting room with lounge licence, growler station, and retail sales; food—snacks and BYOF; kid friendly—yes; dog friendly— no; wheelchair accessible—yes; events—acoustic jam session nights, game nights, cask Fridays

Sooke Brewing Company

2057 Otter Point Road, Sooke, BC V9Z 1H7

P. 250.642.0106 **W.** sookebrewing.com

OPENED 2017

OWNERS Carl Scott, Yari Nielsen, Anton Rabien, Trevor Wilson, John Adair

BREWER John Adair

BREWERY SIZE 15 hectolitres

TOURS By appointment

CORE BEER LIST Belgian Blonde, IPA, and rotating beers within general categories, e.g., lager, hoppy, dark, Belgian style, etc., including Oatmeal Stout, Vienna Lager

CANADIAN BREWING AWARDS Gin Bourbon Barrel Aged Saison (bronze, 2018)

AVAILABLE IN Draft, growlers, crowlers

DISTRIBUTION AREA Lower Vancouver Island

ON SITE Tasting room with lounge licence, growler station; food—BYOF; kid friendly—yes; dog friendly—no; wheelchair accessible—yes; events—board game nights, trivia nights

Sooke Oceanside Brewery

1-5529 Sooke Road, Sooke, BC V9Z 0C7

P. 778.352.2739 **W.** sookeoceansidebrewery.com

OPENED 2016

OWNERS Ryan Orr, Karri Jensen

BREWER Garritt Lalonde

BREWERY SIZE 7 hectolitres

TOURS By appointment

CORE BEER LIST BoneYard IPA, Bonfire Blonde, Leechtown Lager, Reena O'Reilly Dry Irish Stout, Renfrew Red, Saseenos

India Session Ale, Springboard IPA, Stiff Jab Pale Ale, Stuck in the Mud Porter

CANADIAN BREWING AWARDS Baltic Porter (bronze, 2018)

AVAILABLE IN Draft, growlers, bottles

DISTRIBUTION AREA Vancouver Island

ON SITE Tasting room, growler station, and retail sales; food—BYOF; kid friendly—yes; dog friendly—yes; wheelchair accessible—yes; events—Deconstruction Cask Night

Spinnakers Gastro Brewpub

308 Catherine Street, Victoria, BC V9A 3S8

P. 250.386.2739 **W.** spinnakers.com

OPENED 1984

OWNER Paul Hadfield

BREW CREW Kala Hadfield, Matt West-Patrick, Matt Stanley, Tommie Grant, Lieve Peeters, Andy Westby, Alex Frost

BREWERY SIZE 8 hectolitres

TOURS By appointment

CORE BEER LIST Blue Bridge Double Pale Ale, Cascadia Dark Ale, English Style India Pale Ale, Estate Sooke Bitter, Fig Deal Barley Wine, Gose Reposado, Jameson's Scottish Ale, Jolly Hopper Imperial IPA, Juice Monkey IPA, Lager, Mitchell's ESB, Northwest Ale (American pale ale), Original Pale Ale, Titanic Stout, Tour de Victoria Kolsch

AVAILABLE IN Draft, growlers, bottles, cans

DISTRIBUTION AREA British Columbia

ON SITE Brewpub with full bar, growler station, and retail sales; food—menu; kid friendly—yes; dog friendly—no; wheelchair accessible—yes; events—live music, beer release parties

Swans Brewery, Pub, and Hotel

506 Pandora Avenue, Victoria, BC V8W 1N6

P. 250.361.3310 W. swanshotel.com

OPENED 1989

OWNER University of Victoria Properties

BREWER Chris Lukie

BREWERY SIZE 20 hectolitres

TOURS By appointment

CORE BEER LIST Biere de Garde, Export Stout, Flammenbeer, Guilty Pleasure Raspberry Blonde Ale, Helles Lager, Island Bock, Muy Hoppy IPA, Pepper Blonde, Pitch Black Chamomile Black Pilsner, Regal Standard Scotch Ale, Rye PA, Thomas Uphill Amber, Venerator Doppelbock, YYJ Pilsner

Canadian Brewing Awards (since 2007 only; from 2003 to 2006, six golds, six silvers, two bronzes):Appleton Brown (silver, 2008), Arctic Ale (silver, 2012; bronze, 2013, 2014), Coconut Porter (gold, 2010), Extra IPA (bronze, 2012), Hefeweizen (gold, 2008), Legacy Ale (gold, 2007, 2013; bronze, 2009), Oatmeal Stout (gold, 2007), Pandora Pale Ale (bronze, 2011), Scotch Ale (silver, 2007, 2011; gold, 2012), Swans ESB (bronze, 2008), Tessier's Witbier (gold, 2008)

AVAILABLE IN Draft, growlers, bottles

DISTRIBUTION AREA Vancouver Island

ON SITE Brewpub with full bar, growler station, and retail sales (at adjacent liquor store); food—menu; kid friendly—yes; dog friendly—no; wheelchair accessible—yes

Tofino Brewing Company

691 Industrial Way, Tofino, BC V0R 2Z0

P. 250.725.2899 W. tofinobrewingco.com

OPENED 2011

OWNERS Bryan O'Malley, Chris Neufeld, Dave McConnell

BREW CREW Bryan O'Malley, Kieran Campbell, Andy Brillinger

BREWERY SIZE 30 hectolitres

TOURS Yes

CORE BEER LIST Blonde Ale, Cosmic Wave Double IPA, Dark Lager, Dawn Patrol Coffee Porter, Hoppin' Cretin IPA, Kelp Stout, Spruce Tree Ale, Tofino Lager, Tuff Session Ale

AVAILABLE IN Draft, growlers, bottles, cans

DISTRIBUTION AREA British Columbia, Alberta

ON SITE Tasting room with lounge licence, growler station, and retail sales; food—snacks and BYOF; kid friendly—yes; dog friendly—no; wheelchair accessible—yes; events—Trivial Pursuit Thursdays, cask nights

Twin City Brewing Company

4503 Margaret Street, Port Alberni, BC V9Y 6G8

P. 778.419.2739 **W.** twincitybrewing.ca

OPENED 2017

OWNER Aaron Colyn

BREW CREW Aaron Colyn, Martin Vliegenthart, Shinahkoh Couture

BREWERY SIZE 12 hectolitres

TOURS Yes

CORE BEER LIST Poindexter with Centennial APA, Porter Alberni Dry Porter, Run of the Mill IPA, Sparkling Leotard Grapefruit Radler, Swedish Gymnast Blonde Ale, Tickity Boo British Pale Ale, Vanishing Act Pineapple Coconut Sour

AVAILABLE IN Draft, growlers

DISTRIBUTION AREA Alberni Valley, central and southern Vancouver Island

ON SITE Brewpub, growler station; food—menu; kid friendly—yes; dog friendly—no; wheelchair accessible—yes

Vancouver Island Brewing Company

2330 Government Street, Victoria, BC V8T 5G5

P. 250.361.0007 W. vibrewing.com

OPENED 1984

OWNER Bob MacDonald

BREW CREW Danny Seeton, Ralf Pittroff

BREWERY SIZE 120 hectolitres

TOURS Yes—see website

CORE BEER LIST Broken Islands Hazy IPA, Dominion Dark Lager, Faller Northwest Pale Ale, Grapefruit Agave Gose, Hermannator Ice Bock, Islander Lager, Juan de Fuca Cerveza, Piper's Pale Ale, Twisted Stalk Blackberry Helles, Ukidama Lychee Saison, Victoria Lager

CANADIAN BREWING AWARDS Beachcomber Summer Ale (silver, 2012), Dominion Dark Lager (silver, 2018), Hermannator Ice Bock (gold, 2011; silver, 2012), Hermann's Dark Lager (silver, 2011, 2013; gold, 2012,2015), Island Lager (bronze, 2010), Piper's Pale Ale (gold, 2007), Sea Dog Amber (gold, 2011; bronze, 2014), Vancouver Island Lager (gold, 2012, 2014, 2015)

AVAILABLE IN Draft, growlers, bottles, cans

DISTRIBUTION British Columbia, Alberta, Manitoba

ON SITE Tasting room, growler station, and retail sales; kid friendly—yes; dog friendly—yes; wheelchair accessible—yes

Victoria Caledonian Distillery & Twa Dogs Brewery

761 Enterprise Crescent, Victoria, BC V8Z 6P7

P. 778.401.0410 W. victoriacaledonian.com

OPENED 2016

OWNER Graeme Macaloney

BREW CREW Dean McLeod, Nicole MacLean

BREWERY SIZE 50 hectolitres

TOURS Daily—see website

CORE BEER LIST (LISTED AS TWA DOGS) Chili Chocolate Milk Stout, Cloud Chamber SMASH Double IPA, Drouthy Neibor IPA, Holy Willie's Robust Porter, Jolly Beggar's Pale Ale, Keekin' Glass Pilsner, Melodie Raspberry Kolsch, Mistress of My Soul Saison, Parting Kiss Bourbon Barrel Ale, Seas Between Us Red IPA, Shun the Light Scotch Ale, Silver Flood Belgian Wit

AVAILABLE IN Draft, growlers, bottles, cans

DISTRIBUTION AREA British Columbia, Alberta

ON SITE Tasting room with lounge licence, growler station, and retail sales; food—BYOF; kid friendly—yes; dog friendly—yes; wheelchair accessible—yes; events—annual Burns Dinner, community events, bands, birthday parties

White Sails Brewing Company

125 Comox Road, Nanaimo BC V9R 3H9

P. 250.754.2337 W. whitesailsbrewing.com

OPENED 2015

OWNERS Brad McCarthy, Monty McKay

BREW CREW Tyler Papp, Mike Nemeth

BREWERY SIZE 15 hectolitres

TOURS By appointment

CORE BEER LIST Departure Bay Session Wheat Ale, Fresh Hop Harvest Ale, Gallows Point Chocolate Porter, Mount Benson IPA, Old City SMASH, Snake Island Cascadian Dark Ale, Yellow Point Pale Ale

AVAILABLE IN Draft, growlers, bottles

DISTRIBUTION AREA Vancouver Island, Greater Vancouver

ON SITE Tasting room with lounge licence, growler station, and retail sales; food—snack menu and BYOF; kid friendly—yes; dog friendly—no; wheelchair accessible—yes; events—Friday live music and cask night

Wolf Brewing Company

940 Old Victoria Road, Nanaimo, BC V9R 6Z8

P. 250.716.2739 **W.** wolfbrewingcompany.com

OPENED 2011 (originally opened in 2000 as Fat Cat Brewery, under different owners)

OWNERS Jennifer and Dean Lewis

BREWER Kevin Ward

BREWERY SIZE 25 hectolitres

TOURS Yes

CORE BEER LIST Belgian Tripel, Black and Tan, Cerberus Imperial IPA, Dirty Harry California Common, English 3 Grain Bitter, Golden Honey Ale, India Pale Ale, Jinglepot Milk Stout, Pilsner, Porter, Wee Heavy Scotch Ale

AVAILABLE IN Draft, growlers, bottles

DISTRIBUTION AREA Vancouver Island, Powell River

ON SITE Tasting room with lounge licence, growler station, and retail sales; food—menu; kid friendly—yes; dog friendly—yes; wheelchair accessible—yes

~~~~~~~~

GLOSSARY OF BREWING TERMS

This short list is designed to give brief definitions of some basic terms relating to beer and brewing. More terms and fuller definitions can be found in Dan Rabin and Carl Forget's *Dictionary of Beer and Brewing*, second edition (Boulder, CO: Brewers Publications, 1998), and *The Oxford Companion to Beer*, edited by Garrett Oliver (New York: Oxford University Press, 2011). Descriptions of specific beer styles can be found in Appendix 3.

ABV Abbreviation for alcohol by volume.

ABW Abbreviation for alcohol by weight.

additive An ingredient such as fruit or spices added to the wort during or after the boiling process to add flavours.

adjunct Corn, rice, or some unmalted cereal grains that are sources of fermentable sugar and can be substituted for malted grain (usually barley) in the brewing process. Beers brewed with adjuncts are usually paler in colour and lighter in body. Beer purists complain that megabrewers use adjuncts to cut costs and that the finished products lack taste.

aftertaste Taste and feel on the tongue after swallowing a mouthful of beer.

alcohol by volume (ABV) Standard mainstream lagers are usually around 5 percent ABV or 4 percent alcohol by weight. Microbrewers often create beers that have higher ABV percentages, although these do not often exceed 10 percent. Occasionally, brewers have created strong (sometimes called extreme or big) beers that have even higher ABV percentages.

alcohol by weight (ABW) Because alcohol weighs less than water, ABW percentages are lower than ABV percentages by approximately 20 percent.

ale One of the two main categories of beer (the other is lager). Ales are created with top-fermenting yeast (yeast that rises to the top of the wort during the fermentation process). They are fermented at temperatures of between 16 and 20 degrees Celsius and are frequently darker, fuller-bodied, and more robust in flavour than lagers.

all-grain beer Beer brewed using only malted grains. No malt extracts (syrup made from malt) or adjuncts (such as corn or rice) are used.

barley The cereal grain that, when malted and mashed to produce fermentable sugars, is one of the main ingredients of beer. The grain comes in two- and six-row varieties, the former being preferred for its higher quality.

barrel The standard American measurement by volume for beer, a barrel contains just over 117 litres or 31 gallons of beer—that's 55 six-packs.

barrel-aged Beer that is aged in wooden barrels that previously held such alcoholic beverages as port wine, bourbon, or rum takes on some of the flavours of those liquors, in addition to the flavours of the type of wood with which the barrels are made. Some brewers put barrel staves in conditioning tanks to add flavour.

beer An alcoholic drink made with the fermented sugars from malted grains, usually barley, and flavoured with hops. In Spain, say *"cerveza,"* in France *"bière,"* in Italy *"birra,"* and in Germany and Holland *"bier,"* and you'll derive more enjoyment from your European travels.

body Sometimes referred to as mouthfeel, it is the tactile sensation— such as thickness or thinness of beer—in the mouth.

bomber A 650 millilitre bottle.

boutique brewery Synonym for craft brewery.

Brettanomyces A strain of yeast often used in traditional Belgian styles, such as lambics and saisons, to give the finished beer "funky" tastes and sourness. Frequently referred to as "brett."

brewpub A pub that brews its own beer mainly for consumption on the premises, although the beers are sometimes available for takeout in kegs, growlers, bottles, or cans.

bright beer Beer that, after primary fermentation and filtration and before packaging, is placed in a large tank for clarification, carbonation, and further maturation.

budget beer Low-priced beer, sometimes referred to by megabreweries as "value-priced" beer and by beer purists as "lawnmower" beer. Frequently, budget beers are brewed with large quantities of less expensive adjuncts (such as corn and rice) replacing malted barley. Many devoted craft beer drinkers drank budget beers as poor college students.

Campaign for Real Ale (CAMRA) A consumer organization that was started in England in 1971 to protest the invasion of English pubs by megabrewers supplying mass-produced pale lagers. The organization fought for the preservation of "real ale"—cask-conditioned, non-pasteurized beer. CAMRA has branches in the United States and Canada and is credited with encouraging the Canadian craft brewing movement that began in the 1980s.

carbonation The dissolving of carbon dioxide, a by-product of the fermentation process, into beer, creating bubbling and foaming when a bottle is poured or a keg tapped. Beers such as pale lagers, designed to be served at lower temperatures, are more carbonated than those served at higher temperatures. Many drinkers of North American pale lagers are surprised at how relatively "flat" some British ales seem.

cask ale Beer that undergoes conditioning and secondary fermentation in the vessel (usually a small keg) from which it is served. Frequently, craft breweries or brewpubs hold cask nights that feature small batches of freshly brewed cask ale.

collaboration beer A beer brewed together by two or more breweries.

conditioning A secondary fermentation in which yeast is added after beer has been transferred from fermenting tanks to kegs, casks, or bottles.

contract brewery A company without brewing facilities that hires another brewery to produce its recipes, but then markets and sells the product itself. This arrangement allows the former to avoid the expense of purchasing equipment and the latter to operate at greater capacity. The term is sometimes used to refer to the brewery that makes the product under contract for another company.

coolship A large, flat-bottomed, shallow, uncovered tank filled with wort on which wild, airborne yeast acts.

cottage brewery Synonym for a small craft brewery.

craft brewery A brewery producing small batches of all-malt (containing no adjuncts) beer.

crossover beer A beer that is sufficiently similar to mainstream beers to give inexperienced drinkers an introduction to craft beers. Some brewers refer to these as "training wheels" beers. Blonde and golden ales are popular crossover beers.

crowler A 946-millilitre (32-ounce) can that is individually filled with beer and sealed at a brewpub or tasting room.

draft beer A beer, often unpasteurized, that is served directly from a keg or cask. The term "bottled (or canned) draft beer" used by some brewers is an oxymoron.

drinkability A term frequently used in the advertising of megabrewers to describe a beverage that tastes good, has a smooth texture, is easy to swallow, is non-threatening, and makes the drinker want another.

dry beer A beer brewed with yeasts that create a higher alcohol content and which, because there is less sugar in the finished product, is not very sweet and has very little aftertaste.

dry hopping Adding hops late in the brewing process to enhance flavour and aroma without increasing bitterness.

ester A compound formed during fermentation that gives fruity aromas and tastes to beer.

extract A syrupy or sometimes powdered concentration of wort that homebrewers often use instead of malted grains.

fermentation The action of yeast on the sugar in wort, producing carbon dioxide and alcohol. Bottom-fermenting yeasts are used for brewing lagers, top-fermenting yeasts for ales.

fire brewing Process of using direct fire instead of steam or hot water to boil the wort.

firkin A 40.9-litre container. Drinkers consuming products drawn from these containers have been heard to exclaim, "This firkin beer is firkin good."

foam The gathering of bubbles of carbon dioxide at the top of a glass or mug of beer. Aficionados judge the quality of foam by its colour, thickness, and retention period. Sometimes referred to as "suds."

gluten-free beer Beer made without barley or wheat, both of which contain ingredients that can cause people with gluten intolerance to have serious adverse reactions. Rice, sorghum, and corn, which are sources of fermentable sugars, are frequently used as substitutes for barley and wheat.

green beer Freshly fermented, unconditioned beer. Also, what some people drink too much of on March 17.

growler A 1.89 litre (64 ounce) refillable glass bottle used as a beer container by many brewpubs that sell their beer for customers to take off premises.

head The foam collected at the top of a glass or mug of beer. Also, a part of the anatomy that hurts the morning after a night of excessive imbibing.

hectolitre One hundred litres, a standard measurement in Canada of brewing production or of the capacity of a brewing system. A hectolitre is the equivalent of just under 50 six-packs of beer.

hop The cone-shaped flower of a climbing vine related to cannabis that is used to provide bitterness and a variety of aromas and tastes to beer. Before the development of refrigeration, hops were added as a preservative for ales shipped from England to India. Many varietals of hops used in brewing have been developed in the last 50 years. One of the most important, Cascade, is often an ingredient in India pale ales, the most popular style of the craft brewing "revolution" of the last four decades.

IBU Abbreviation for International Bitterness Unit.

ice beer A beer conditioned at temperatures sufficiently low to cause water to form ice crystals, which are then removed to give the beer a higher alcohol content.

imperial A term often applied to beers with high alcohol content (usually above 7 percent ABV).

International Bitterness Unit (IBU) Unit of measurement, in parts per million, of the level of bitterness contributed to beer by hop compounds. The higher the number of units, the greater the bitterness. The bitterness counteracts sweetness contributed by the malt. Pale North American lagers are low in IBUs (15 or lower), while India pale ales are high (often 60 IBUs or more). The term International Bittering Units is sometimes used.

krausening The process of introducing a small amount of fermenting wort into fully fermented beer to cause secondary fermentation and natural carbonation.

lace Patterns of foam created on the inside of a glass as the beer level goes down. Beer aficionados consider lacing to be one of the important visual qualities of beer.

lager From the German word *lagern*, "to store," lager refers to beers that are brewed with bottom-fermenting yeasts and then stored for conditioning for longer periods and at lower temperatures than ales, usually around nine degrees Celsius. Developed in Germany, lager beers became more widely brewed with the development of refrigeration. Now the most consumed type of beer around the world, lagers are the main products of the international megabrewers. Until recently, many craft brewers did not include lagers in their portfolios as the length of the fermentation period tied up tanks for too long.

light beer A beer that is low in calories and alcohol content, usually 4 percent ABV. Many brewers label these products with the spelling "lite."

light struck Term applied to beer that has developed an unpleasant, "skunky" taste as a result of exposure to sunlight. In TV ads, beers in clear bottles placed on chairs on the beach look wonderful, but the contents would most certainly be light struck and taste dreadful.

liquor A term used by brewers to refer to the water used in making beer. Because the mineral content of water influences the taste of beer, it is important to have the appropriate liquor for the beer style being brewed.

malt Grain (usually barley) that is soaked in water until germination begins and then heat-dried to convert the starches in it into soluble, fermentable sugars. The length and temperature of the procedure produces different colours of malt that create different flavours and colours in beer.

malt extract A syrup or powder obtained from the wort. It is sometimes used instead of malt in the brewing process.

mash tun An insulated brewing vessel in which the malted grains and water are mixed and heated.

mashing The process of steeping ground malt in hot water to produce wort, a liquid containing soluble sugars that are converted into alcohol during the fermentation process.

microbrewery A small brewery with a small annual production, most of which is sold off-premises in kegs, bottles, or cans. The term was a general synonym in the earlier years for all craft breweries, some of which are now very large.

mouthfeel Texture of beer experienced in the mouth. Beers may be light-to full-bodied and lightly to heavily carbonated.

nanobrewery A brewery using small brewing equipment, usually of one- or two-barrel capacity, and producing a limited volume of beer annually. Some restaurants have purchased nanobrewing systems so that they can make and serve their own beers.

nitrogen A gas that, when used instead of carbon dioxide to dispense draft beer, gives the beer a creamy texture. "Nitro beers," in which the beer from a tap or in cans or bottles has been infused with nitrogen, have a smooth, creamy mouthfeel. Nitro beers became popular during the middle of the 2010s.

nose The aroma of freshly poured beer. Also, a part of the face that may turn red when a person consumes far too much beer at one time.

open fermentation Putting boiled wort into large open containers so that it can attract wild, airborne yeasts to begin fermentation.

organic beer Beer made from all or nearly all ingredients that have been certified as organically grown.

pasteurization The brief exposure of beer to high heat to kill micro-organisms and to extend bottled or canned beer's shelf life. Many microbreweries do not pasteurize their brews, contending that the process adversely affects taste.

pitching Adding yeast to cooled wort in fermentation tanks to begin the process of fermentation.

publican A pub or tavern's owner or manager.

real ale Unpasteurized, cask-conditioned beer served on draft.

Reinheitsgebot The Bavarian Purity Law, enacted in 1516, which mandated that only barley malt (and, later, other malts), hops, water, and (after it had been identified) yeast could be used to brew beer. Although the German government repealed the law in 1987, many craft breweries advertise their adherence to the philosophy of the law.

rice A grain that, because it contains a very high percentage of starch that can be converted into fermentable sugar, is often used as an "adjunct" or substitute for more expensive barley or wheat malts.

saccharification The process of turning malt starches into fermentable sugars.

scurvy grass ale According to the *Dictionary of Beer and Brewing*, this was a combination of watercress and ale believed to stave off scurvy. So, if you're planning a solo boat trip across the ocean . . .

seasonal beer A beer that is released for a specific season, for example, pumpkin beer in the autumn and bock beer in the spring.

session beer Because of their low alcoholic levels and smooth mouthfeel, several session beers can be consumed during an evening (a session) at a pub or tavern. Recently, many craft breweries have begun to make session IPAs.

sessionable term used to refer to beers that are of sufficiently low alcoholic content that a few can be enjoyed "safely" during a "session"

shelf life The length of time that canned or bottled beer can be kept before beginning to spoil. For most craft beers, this is usually around three months. High-alcohol beer styles such as barley wine may be kept (aged) for considerably longer periods.

SMASH Acronym for beer brewed with a single malt and a single hop. Brewers enjoy making these beers to explore different flavours created by the combination of specific varieties/types of the two ingredients.

sour beer Ales that are given a sourness through the introduction of such bacteria as *Lactobacillus* or *Pediococcus*. Among the better-known styles of sour beers are Berliner weisse, gose, and lambic.

sparging Hot-water rinsing of mash after the initial separation of mash and wort. The process removes fermentable sugars still remaining in the mash.

special-edition beers Usually limited, small batches of unusual or experimental styles of beer.

style A group of beers that share many of the same characteristics of appearance, aroma, taste, and alcohol content. (See Appendix 3 for discussions of specific styles and the names of some Vancouver Island breweries' examples.)

tulipai The *Dictionary of Beer and Brewing* defines the term as "yellow water" and as a synonym for "tiswin," a beer once brewed by the Apaches. Perhaps it could be used as an alternate word for an impolite term some people use in describing adjunct-laden pale North American lagers.

value-priced beer Term used by breweries (usually megabreweries) for beers that are priced lower than the other beers they produce.

Frequently, value-priced beers use a high proportion of adjuncts. *See* budget beer.

wet hopping The addition of freshly picked hops during the fermentation process to add flavours and aromas to the beer. Wet-hopped beer is available in the fall, shortly after the hop harvest.

wort Pronounced "wert" it is the sugar solution created during the mashing process. The solution is boiled with hops, then cooled. Yeast then turns the sugar into alcohol and carbon dioxide.

yeast The unicellular, microscopic organism that converts sugars in the wort into alcohol and carbon dioxide. Before it was identified, it was considered miraculous and called "Godisgood."

zymology The scientific study of the processes of fermentation.

~~~~~~~~~~~

A GUIDE TO BEER STYLES

The following guide to beer styles is divided into three sections: lagers, ales, and specialty beers. Following the description of each style are examples that breweries on Vancouver Island have made over the last two or three years. Because breweries stop producing some beers and add others, some of the examples may no longer available. In putting together the style descriptions, I have drawn on Randy Mosher's *Tasting Beer: An Insider's Guide to the World's Greatest Drink* (North Adams, MA: Storey Publishing, 2009), Garrett Oliver's *The Brewmaster's Table* (New York: HarperCollins, 2003), *The Oxford Companion to Beer*, edited by Garrett Oliver (New York: Oxford University Press, 2011), and the second edition of Dan Rabin and Carl Forget's *Dictionary of Beer and Brewing* (Boulder, CO: Brewers Publications, 1998).

LAGERS

Lagers use bottom-fermenting yeast, are generally more highly carbonated, and are lighter-bodied than most ales. With the development of refrigeration in the later part of the 19th century, lagers, which must be brewed and stored at lower temperatures, have become very popular in the United States, where brewers from Germany, the birthplace of most lagers, created versions of the beers of their homeland and established very large breweries and extensive distribution networks. Varieties of North American pale lagers are the most widely consumed beers in the world.

bock A German-style beer with much fuller and more robust flavours than most other lagers. Lightly hopped, bocks are dark in colour—from copper to a deep brown—and medium to full in body. Doppelbock is stronger in alcoholic content, fuller-bodied, and darker than bock. It often has chocolate and coffee notes.

Swans Island Bock • Swans Venerator Doppelbock • Vancouver Island Hermannator Ice Bock

California common Also called steam beer because of the hissing sound made when a keg is tapped. Developed in California in the 19th century, this beer is amber-coloured and medium-bodied and is fairly highly hopped. Anchor Brewing Company of California has copyrighted the term "steam beer."

Wolf Dirty Harry California Common

Dortmunder export Pale gold in colour, with a medium hop bitterness and a crisp finish. The malts contribute biscuit flavours to this medium-bodied beer.

Hoyne Helios Dortmunder Golden Lager • Vancouver Island Victoria Lager

dunkel Light to dark brown in colour, this is a full-bodied lager with rich, malty flavours.

Moon Under Water Creepy Uncle Dunkel Dark Lager

helles From the German word meaning "bright," this medium-bodied beer balances malt and hop flavours. Light straw to golden in colour, it often features toasty malt flavours.

Canoe Helles • Craig Street Cowichan Bay Lager • Riot Lipslide Lager • Swans Helles Lager

maibock A golden-coloured bock beer available in the later spring (May). It is distinguished by its sweet, malty notes and relatively light body.

⁂ *Canoe Maibock*

marzen/Oktoberfest Brewed in late spring and served in the fall, this is a medium-to-full-bodied, very malty, copper-coloured beer with a crisp hop bitterness.

⁂ *Canoe Marzen • Gladstone Marzen*

Mexican lager A variation on the Vienna lager style, Mexican lagers often use flaked maize to add hints of corn flavour to the grainy taste.

⁂ *Salt Spring Island Mexican Lager • Vancouver Island Juan de Fuca Cerveza*

North American lager Pale in colour, very light in body, and highly carbonated, with minimal hop and malt flavours.

⁂ *Lighthouse Company Lager • Longwood Island Time Lager • Moon Under Water Light Side of the Moon Session Lager • Red Arrow Old Style Lager • Sooke Oceanside Leechtown Lager • Spinnakers Lager*

Oktoberfest *See* marzen.

pilsner Bohemian (Czech) pilsner is a light-bodied and clear beer, light straw to golden in colour, with a crispness imparted by the hops. It was originally brewed in Pilsen, where the soft water enhanced the crisp cleanness of the beer. German pilsner is a light-to-medium-bodied lager, straw to gold in colour, with spicy hop notes and a slight malt sweetness. It is fuller in body and maltier than Czech pilsner.

⁂ *Axe & Barrel Langford Logger • Beach Fire Pilsner • Driftwood Arcus Pilsner • Forbidden Pilsner • 4 Mile Pilsner • Gladstone Pilsner • Hoyne Hoyner Pilsner • Lighthouse Bowline Pilsner • Longwood Czech Pilsner • Moon Under Water Potts Pils • Phillips Levidrome Imperial Pilsner • Phillips Pilsner • Riot Good Vibrations Classical Pilsner • Tofino Lager • Twa Dogs Keekin' Glass Pilsner • Vancouver Island Islander Lager • Wolf Pilsner*

rauchbier From the German word for "smoke," a dark-coloured lager using malt roasted over open fires to impart a smoky flavour.

⁂ *Swans Flammenbeer*

schwarzbier From the German word for "black," a very dark-coloured, light-to-medium-bodied beer. The roasted barley malts impart chocolatey flavours that are balanced with a low to medium hop bitterness.

} *Gladstone Czech Dark Lager* • *Swans Pitch Black Chamomile Black Pilsner* • *Tofino DarkLager* • *Vancouver Island Dominion Dark Lager*

steam beer *See* California common.

Vienna lager Medium-bodied and reddish brown to copper, this lager has a malt sweetness balanced with a clean, crisp, but not too strong, hop bitterness. Mexican lagers are often a variation of the Vienna lager style.

} *Hoyne Vienna Lager* • *Sooke Brewing Vienna Lager*

weizenbock A dark, malty wheat beer with a fairly high alcoholic content.

} *Longwood Winter's Own Weizenbock* • *Moon Under Water Victorious Weizenbock*

ALES

Using top-fermenting yeast, ales do not require the cooler temperatures for fermenting and conditioning that lagers do, and the brewing cycles are much shorter. Generally speaking, ales are fuller-bodied, darker in colour, and richer and more robust in flavour. When the craft brewing movement began in the late 1970s and early 1980s, most craft brewers produced ales, offering beers that were very different in taste from lagers made by the megabrewers.

altbier From the German word meaning "old" (traditional), this ale is copper to brown in colour and has toasted malty flavours balanced by hop notes that help to create a clean, crisp finish.

} *Driftwood Crooked Coast Altbier*

amber ale Copper to light brown in colour, this beer has been called a "darker, fuller-bodied pale ale." It maintains a balance between caramel malt notes and citrusy hop flavours.

} *Canoe Amber Ale* • *Lighthouse Race Rocks Ale* • *Phillips Blue Buck Ale* • *Red Arrow Midnite Umber Ale* • *Swans Thomas Uphill Amber*

American blonde/golden ale Lightly to moderately hopped and straw to golden in colour, this blonde beverage is a light-bodied and crisp beer often offered as a "crossover" beer to newcomers to craft beer.

Beach Fire Beach Blonde Ale • Forbidden Blonde Ale • 4 Mile Golden Ale • Longwood Ale • Mount Arrowsmith Blonde • Small Block Hornet Blonde Ale • Sooke Oceanside Bonfire Blonde Ale • Tofino Blonde Ale • Twin City Swedish Gymnast Blonde Ale

American dark ale Also known as Cascadian dark ale or black IPA. This recently developed American style is dark brown to black in colour and combines roasty malt flavours with a strong hop presence.

Category 12 Disruption Black IPA • Forbidden Black IPA • Love Shack DPA Dark Pale Ale • Spinnakers Cascadia Dark Ale • White Sails Snake Island Cascadian Dark Ale

American wheat ale An American version of hefeweizen that is frequently filtered.

Cumberland Forest Fog American Wheat Ale • White Sails Departure Bay Session Wheat Ale

barley wine High in alcoholic content (usually over 10 percent ABV), this has been called a "sipping beer." It is full-bodied and dark brown in colour and has complex malt flavours that include caramel, toasty, and fruity notes.

Driftwood Old Cellar Dweller Barley Wine • Spinnakers Fig Deal Barley Wine

Belgian blonde/golden ale Light to medium in body and gold to deep amber in colour, this ale has a malty sweetness, spicy notes, and moderate hoppiness.

Category 12 Simplicity Blond • Driftwood Son of the Morning Strong Golden Ale • Moon Under Water Shatterbier Golden Ale • Salt Spring Island Golden Ale • Sooke Brewing Belgian Blonde Ale

Belgian dubbel A Belgian ale noted for its rich malty flavours and spicy notes. Dark amber to brown, it is lightly hopped. Generally sweet to the taste, with a light to moderate bitterness, it has a dry finish.

Driftwood Clodhopper Dubbel

Belgian India pale ale *See* India pale ale.

Belgian quad High in alcoholic content (usually over 10 percent ABV), this dark-coloured ale is sweet and malty, with spicy notes.

⎰ *Category 12 2017 Anomaly Quad* • *Salt Spring Island Belgian Quad*

Belgian single ale Often called the Belgian "session ale," this easy-drinking, low-alcohol beer is hoppier than most Belgian beers but has the "funky" yeast flavours characteristic of many of that country's ales.

⎰ *Gladstone Belgian Single*

Belgian tripel Although lighter in body than dubbel, this Belgian ale is stronger in alcoholic content (7–10 percent ABV). Bright yellow to gold, it has spicy and fruity notes and a sweetness that is balanced by a moderate hop bitterness.

⎰ *Driftwood The Heretic Tripel* • *Wolf Belgian Tripel*

Berliner weisse A crisp, low-alcohol (usually under 5 percent ABV) wheat beer, with tart, sour, and citrusy notes.

⎰ *Moon Under Water Berliner-Style Weisse*

bière de garde Meaning "beer to keep," this traditional French ale is a smooth, rich, malt-forward beer, with just enough hops to provide some balance to the malt sweetness. It is, as the name suggests, aged for many months (or more).

⎰ *Swans Biere de Garde*

bitter The beer that is most often associated with an evening at an English pub, it has a balance between malt sweetness and hop bitterness, with earthy, nutty, and grainy flavours. Light-bodied and gold to copper in colour, it is low in carbonation and in alcoholic content (often under 5 percent ABV). Extra special bitter, or ESB, is fuller-bodied and higher in alcoholic content than bitter. Although it has more bitterness than regular bitter, rich malty flavours dominate. Dark gold to copper in colour, it is low in carbonation.

⎰ *Category 12 Pivotal ESB* • *Cumberland Just a Little Bitter English Bitter* •
Driftwood Naughty Hildegard ESB • *Howl Old Tavern ESB* • *Hoyne Appleton*
ESB • *Longwood Extra Special Bitter* • *Salt Spring Island Extra Special*

Bitter • Small Block Malrdhat Best Bitter • Spinnakers Mitchell's ESB • Wolf English 3 Grain Bitter

brown ale Noted for its rich malt flavours, including nutty, toffee, and chocolate notes, this medium-bodied beer is generally sweet, although moderate hopping prevents the sweetness from becoming cloying.

4 Mile Brothel Brown Ale

Cascadian dark ale *See* American dark ale.

cream ale Straw to pale gold in colour, this light-bodied ale is high in carbonation but low in hop bitterness and has a malty sweetness.

Gladstone Cream Ale • Love Shack Crafty Cream Ale • Phillips Slipstream Cream Ale

dark mild A popular English session beer that is light to medium in body and gold to dark brown in colour. Fairly low in alcohol (usually under 5 percent ABV) and in carbonation, it has almost no hop presence. Chocolate and caramel malt flavours dominate.

Riot Working Class Hero Dark Mild

dunkelweizen A wheat beer that uses dark malts and is sweeter than hefeweizen.

Longwood Steam Punk Dunkelweizen

extra special bitter (ESB) *See* bitter.

Flanders oud bruin This centuries-old Belgian style is light to medium in body and deep copper to brown in colour. It is both sweet and spicy. The use of burnt sugar contributes to the sweetness, while the yeasts and such additives as pepper provide spicy notes.

Driftwood Mad Bruin Oud Bruin

Flanders red A Belgian-style beer that is light-bodied and red in colour. Often barrel-aged for over a year, it is sour and tart and has fruity notes.

Driftwood Bird of Prey Flanders Red

golden ale *See* American blonde/golden ale.

gose Pronounced gos-uh, this low-alcohol German wheat beer is crisp and tart, with salty notes.

Axe & Barrel Fruity Mother Pucker Gose · Driftwood Cry Me a River Gose · Spinnakers Gose Reposado

gruit A thousand-year-old style from western Europe that uses herbs and spices instead of hops for bittering and flavour. Ingredients have included mugwort, bergamot, spruce tips, heather, and wormwood. The modern revival of gruit is celebrated by Gruit Day, observed annually in early February.

Moon Under Water Farmhouse Gruit · Salt Spring Island Spring Fever Gruit

hefeweizen From the German words for "yeast" and "wheat," this pale-to-amber-coloured ale has been called "liquid bread." Generally close to 50 percent of the malt used is wheat. Highly carbonated, it has virtually no hop character but does have banana and clove notes. Because it is unfiltered, it has a hazy appearance.

Beach Fire Hefeweizen · Moon Under Water This is Hefeweizen · Mount Arrowsmith Comfortably Chum Hefeweizen · Red Arrow Heritage River Hefeweizen

India pale ale (IPA) Pale gold to amber, this ale is more heavily hopped than are pale ales. In English IPAs, the hop influence is moderated somewhat by the malts, which add bready, caramel notes. American IPAs are much more aggressively hopped, increasing the bitterness and also adding citrusy and floral notes. Double or imperial IPAs are fuller-bodied, intensely hoppy, and higher in alcoholic content. Session IPAs (ISAs), a newer version of the style, are lower in alcoholic strength (usually below 5 percent). The recently developed East Coast IPA style has become increasingly popular. These IPAs are hazy, have a smooth mouthfeel and little bitterness. Tropical fruit and floral tastes are prevalent. In another recent development, brewers are creating IPAs using a single hop variety, thereby emphasizing the characteristic flavours of that variety. Rye IPA replaces some of the barley malt with malted rye, which adds spicy and tangy notes.

Axe & Barrel West Shore IPA · Bad Dog Dizzy Dogs Double IPA · Bad Dog Tire Biter IPA · Beach Fire IPA · Canoe White IPA · Category 12 Insubordinate Session

IPA • Category 12 Subversion Imperial IPA • Category 12 Wild IPA • Craig Street India Session Ale • Cumberland "Finally" IPA • Driftwood Fat Tug IPA • Forbidden IPA • 4 Mile East Coast IPA • 4 Mile Imperial IPA • 4 Mile Mosaic Session IPA • 4 Mile West Coast IPA • Gladstone IPA • Howl Land's End IPA • Hoyne Devil's Dream IPA • Lighthouse Citrus Shore Session Ale • Lighthouse Groundswell Fresh Hop IPA • Lighthouse Numbskull Ahtanum Imperial IPA • Lighthouse Shipwreck IPA • Longwood The Big One IPA • Love Shack RPA Rye Pale Ale • Moon Under Water Hip as Funk Farmhouse IPA • Moon Under Water Tranquility IPA • Mount Arrowsmith Harvest Fresh IPA • Mount Arrowsmith Jagged Face IPA • Mount Arrowsmith Spring Tide Belgian India Session Ale • Phillips Amnesiac Double IPA • Phillips Bottle Rocket ISA • Phillips Electric Unicorn White IPA • Phillips Hop Circle IPA • Phillips 6IX Double Dry Hopped IPA • Red Arrow Fresh Hop Co-op Sunset Empire New England Style IPA • Red Arrow Sweet Leaf IPA • Riot Junk Punch IPA • Salt Spring Island British IPA • Salt Spring Island Earl Grey IPA • Salt Spring Island Hazy IPA • Small Block Dagmar India Session Ale • Small Block Test and Tune Hazy IPA • Sooke Brewing IPA • Sooke Oceanside Bone Yard IPA • Sooke Oceanside Saseenos India Session Ale • Sooke Oceanside Springboard IPA • Spinnakers English Style IPA • Spinnakers Jolly Hopper Imperial IPA • Spinnakers Juice Monkey IPA • Swans Muy Hoppy IPA • Swans Rye PA • Tofino Cosmic Wave Double IPA • Tofino Hoppin' Cretin IPA • Twa Dogs Cloud Chamber SMASH Double IPA • Twa Dogs Drouthy Neibor IPA • Twa Dogs Seas Between Us Red IPA • Twin City Run of the Mill IPA • Vancouver Island Broken Islands Hazy IPA • White Sails Mount Benson IPA • Wolf Cerberus Imperial IPA • Wolf IPA

kolsch Originally brewed in Cologne, Germany, this beer has been jokingly referred to as "the ale that wishes it were a lager," because of its light body, pale colour, and high carbonation. It balances gentle hop and malt flavours and has a crisp mouthfeel and a dry finish.

Axe & Barrel King Kolsch • Gladstone Kolsch • Love Shaok Killer Kolsch • Phillips Analogue 78 Kolsch • Red Arrow Kustom Kolsch • Spinnakers Tour de Victoria Kolsch

lambic This 400-year-old Belgian-style ale is unusual in that its fermentation process is natural or spontaneous, using wild yeast that is floating in the air. It has been described as fruity, earthy, sour or tart, and very dry. Gold to amber in colour, it is light-bodied and low in carbonation. Unmalted wheat is used in the brewing process. Sometimes brewers will blend old (aged) lambic with young lambic to create a beer called gueuze, a dry, fruity, effervescent beer. In fruit lambics, whole fruits are added after the start of fermentation, and the resulting mixture aged in oak or chestnut barrels. Kriek uses cherries; framboise, raspberries; pêche, peaches; and cassis, black currants.

Driftwood Belle Royale Kriek Style

pale ale This gold to amber ale, which was much paler than the popular brown ales and porters of the late 18th century, balances nutty, caramel malt notes with a noticeable hop bitterness. English-style pale ale is earthier in flavour as contrasted to West Coast–style American pale ale, which has fuller hop bitterness, flavour, and aroma. Both are crisp and have a dry finish. Belgian pale ale is less bitter than the other two and is lighter-bodied with some malty sweetness. Many brewers are now creating single-hop pale ales to highlight the unique characteristics of specific varieties of hops.

Axe & Barrel Speedway Rye Pale Ale • Beach Fire High Tide Pale Ale • Canoe West Coast Pale Ale • Category 12 Critical Point Northwest Pale Ale • Craig Street Arbutus Pale Ale • Cumberland Red Tape Pale Ale • Driftwood New Growth Canadian Pale Ale • Forbidden Organic Pale Ale • 4 Mile Hazy Citra Pale Ale • Gladstone Hazy Pale Ale • Howl Deep Cove Pale Ale • Hoyne Down Easy Pale Ale • Hoyne Wolf Vine Wet Hopped Pale Ale • Lighthouse Tasman Pale Ale • Mount Arrowsmith Salish Sea Pale Ale • Phillips Short Wave Pale Ale • Red Arrow Piggy Pale Ale • Riot Life Partners Pale Ale • Small Block Nail Head Canadian Pale Ale • Sooke Oceanside Stiff Jab Pale Ale • Spinnakers Blue Bridge Double Pale Ale • Spinnakers Northwest Ale • Spinnakers Original Pale Ale • Tofino Tuff Session Ale • Twa Dogs Jolly Beggar's Pale Ale • Twin City Tickity Boo British Pale Ale • Twin City Poindexter with Centennial APA • Vancouver Island Faller Northwest Pale Ale • Vancouver Island Piper's Pale Ale • White Sails Yellow Point Pale Ale

porter Named after the late 18th-century London workers for whom it was originally brewed, this brown-to-black-coloured and full-bodied ale uses several malts to create a complex variety of flavours. Relatively low in alcohol, it is moderately bitter. Baltic porters have higher alcoholic content.

Beach Fire English Porter • Canoe Baltic Porter • Craig Street Mt. Prevost Porter • Gladstone Porter • Love Shack Precious Porter • Mount Arrowsmith Low Pressure Porter • Riot Vortex Robust Porter • Salt Spring Island Dry Porter • Sooke Oceanside Stuck in the Mud Porter • Twa Dogs Holy Willie's Robust Porter • Twin City Porter Alberni Dry Porter • Wolf Porter

red ale This light to highly hopped, medium-bodied beer is amber to copper in colour, with toasted malt notes and a caramel sweetness.

Bad Dog Old Red Ale • Craig Street Shawnigan Irish Ale • Gladstone Red Ale • Longwood Irish Red Ale • Sooke Oceanside Renfrew Red Ale

saison/farmhouse ale Designed as a beer with which farm workers could quench their thirst during hot summer days in the fields, this

Belgian-style ale is gold to amber in colour, light to medium in body, and highly carbonated. It is spicy (often white pepper is used), moderately bitter, fruity, and sour or tart.

> Beach Fire Saison • Category 12 Hiatus Farmhouse Ale • Category 12 Wild Saison • Driftwood Farmhand Saison • Forbidden Saison • Gladstone Saison • Mount Arrowsmith Sea Run Saison • Riot Sorry We Took So Long Saison • Twa Dogs Mistress of My Soul Saison

Scotch ale/wee heavy This strong, dark, creamy, full-bodied ale is mahogany in colour. It has caramel flavours and sometimes, because of the malts used, smoky notes.

> Swans Regal Standard Scotch Ale • Twa Dogs Shun the Light Scotch Ale • Wolf Wee Heavy Scotch Ale

Scottish ale Designated as light, heavy, or export depending on the alcoholic content, this ale is usually not as strong as Scotch ale. Malt flavours dominate over hops.

> Beach Fire Ember Red Ale • Forbidden Scottish Ale • Spinnakers Jameson's Scottish Ale

stout Dark brown to opaque black, it is noted for the roasted flavours imparted by the malted and unmalted barley. English stout is a somewhat sweet ale with caramel and chocolate flavours, which are balanced by the hop bitterness. Irish stout is drier than English versions and often has coffee and chocolate flavours. Designed to be a session beer, it is slightly lighter in body than the English version. Oatmeal stout, in which unmalted oatmeal is added in the brewing process, is very smooth in texture. Russian (imperial stout) usually has an alcoholic content above 10 percent ABV. It not only is more bitter than other stouts, but also has much fuller malt flavours.

> Axe & Barrel Axe Stout • Beach Fire Wheel-Bender Stout • Cumberland Dancing Linebacker Oatmeal Stout • Forbidden Stout • Hoyne Dark Matter • Lighthouse Keepers Stout • Longwood Stoutnik Russian Imperial Stout • Moon Under Water Dark Side of the Moon Oatmeal Session Stout • Small Block Miss Lead Oatmeal Stout • Sooke Brewing Oatmeal Stout • Sooke Oceanside Reena O'Reilly Dry Irish Stout • Spinnakers Titanic Stout • Swans Export Stout • Wolf Jinglepot Milk Stout

witbier From the Belgian word for "white," this unfiltered wheat beer is pale and cloudy in appearance. Highly carbonated and crisp, it is light to medium in body and is often flavoured with coriander and orange peel.

> *Axe & Barrel Tessier's Witbier • Beach Fire Witbier • Canoe Witbier • Driftwood White Bark Witbier • Twa Dogs Silver Flood Belgian Wit*

SPECIALTY BEERS

In addition to creating a great variety of beer styles through their different uses of the four basic ingredients (malts, hops, yeast, and water), brewers often use such additives as fruits, vegetables, herbs, spices, honey, chocolate, and coffee to introduce nuances of flavour. (In the following list, where the name of a beer does not indicate what additive is used, the additive is named in parentheses.)

Fruit beers (Note that Belgian fruit lambics are not included in this list.)

> *Beach Fire Apricot Kettle Sour • Beach Fire Raspberry Ale • Category 12 Wild Saison (loganberries) • 4 Mile Grapefruit IPA • 4 Mile Tangerine Dream American Wheat Ale • Howl Blackberry Wheat Ale • Howl Strawberry Wheat Ale • Hoyne Entre Nous Belgian Cherry Witbier • Lighthouse Ryujin Belgian Tripel with Plums • Longwood Berried Alive Framboise (raspberry) • Longwood Cake Chocolate Raspberry Stout • Longwood Full Patch Pumpkin Saison Ale • Longwood Quinceotica Harvest Lager (quince) • Phillips Citricity Grapefruit Zest IPA • Phillips Raspberry Wheat • Red Arrow Invasion of the Blackberry Lager • Riot Currant-ly Unavailable Black Current Blonde • Swans Guilty Pleasure Raspberry Blonde Ale • Twa Dogs Melodie Raspberry Kolsch • Twin City Peach Mango Smoothie IPA • Twin City Strawberry Hibiscus Sour • Twin City Vanishing Act Pineapple Coconut Sour • Vancouver Island Twisted Stalk Blackberry Helles • Vancouver Island Ukidama Lychee Saison*

Vegetable/herb and spice beers

> *Lighthouse Seaport Vanilla Stout • Longwood Beetnik Root Stout • Phillips Ginger Beer Ale • Salt Spring Island Heather Ale • Salt Spring Island Hibiscus Hefe • Salt Spring Island Nettle Ale • Swans Pepper Blonde • Tofino Kelp Stout • Tofino Spruce Tree Ale • Twa Dogs Chili Chocolate Milk Stout*

Honey beers

> *Bad Dog Honey Blonde Ale • Beach Fire Honey Ale • Longwood Honey Hop Pale Ale • Wolf Golden Honey Ale*

Chocolate and coffee beers (Note that while some malts can impart coffee and chocolate notes to a beer, only those beers that use coffee and chocolate are included in this list.)

Category 12 Excitation Cacao Nib Espresso Stout • Hoyne Voltage Espresso Stout • Lighthouse Nightwatch Coffee Lager • Phillips Longboat Chocolate Porter • Red Arrow 1000 Light Years from Home Chocolate Milk Stout • Tofino Dawn Patrol Coffee Porter • White Sails Gallows Point Chocolate Porter

FROM GRAIN TO GLASS: BREWING, PACKAGING, AND DRINKING BEER

THE BIG FOUR: BASIC INGREDIENTS

Water, malted grain, hops, and yeast—for centuries, these ingredients have been used to brew beer. Because there are different types of each ingredient and the four can be combined in a variety of ways, they can be used to create dozens of different styles of beer.

Throughout the 20th century, beer advertising frequently emphasized water to stress the purity and the crisp, clean flavour of the beer. For example, Olympia Brewing proclaimed, "It's the water," and made much of the artesian wells that lay beneath the facility in Tumwater, Washington. Of course, water is important—it makes up at least 90 percent of a glass or bottle of beer. Brewers call it "liquor," and five litres of it are required for each litre of beer produced. In addition to the water content of the product, water is used in the brewing process and in the vigorous cleaning of equipment.

The relative hardness or softness of water influences the taste of the beverage, and before the 20th century, certain styles emerged because of the composition of the water close to a brewery. The hard water of England's Burton-on-Trent contributed to the distinctive taste of the pale ales brewed there; the soft water in Pilsen, Czech Republic (then called Bohemia), was an important element of its acclaimed lagers. Now, scientific techniques enable brewers to alter tap water so that it possesses the qualities needed for whatever style they may be brewing. The process is called "building water."

Centuries ago, beer was certainly safer to drink than the water that went into its production. In some ways, that may still be true. Air and ground pollution contaminate the lakes and streams that are the sources of water. Moreover, the supposedly pristine waters of lakes, streams, and natural wells may have absorbed chemicals that, while not harmful, could, unless removed, adversely affect the taste of the beer brewed.

Malt supplies the fermentable sugars that become the alcohol in beer. It is made when kernels of grain (usually barley, but sometimes wheat or rye) are steeped in water until they germinate; they are then dried and roasted in kilns. During the process, insoluble starches are converted into the soluble starches and sugars essential to the brewing process. By using different strains of grain, and kilning at different and varying temperatures, different kinds of malt are produced, each one helping to create a style of beer with a distinctive colour, flavour, and aroma. For example, Vienna malt, which is gold in colour, adds nutty, toasty notes to beer. Chocolate malts can create a flavour that seems slightly burnt. And amber malts evoke the flavours of toffee and bread. Some very large brewing companies replace a portion of the malts with such less expensive adjuncts as corn and rice, which also contain fermentable sugars.

Hops, the cone-shaped "flowers" of a plant related to cannabis, have lupulin glands that contain alpha acids. These alpha acids produce a bitterness that balances the sweeter malt tastes in beer, often create citrusy or floral aromas and flavours, and act as preservatives. In fact, when the British shipped beer to colonial officials in India, they used heavy doses of hops to help it survive the long sea journey. With over

100 varieties of hops available, it is not surprising that the various hop extracts, powders, pellets, and whole flowers used in brewers' recipes (usually at a ratio of 1 part to over 30 parts of malt) have been called the spices of brewing. What are often referred to as the "C hops"—Cascade, Centennial, and Chinook—have been regularly used by craft brewers in their very popular India pale ales. The "noble hops"—Hallertau, Saaz, and Tettnang, to name three—are used by brewers to create the crisp and delicate bitterness that characterize German- and Bohemian-style pilsners. Most beer recipes call for the use of hop pellets. However, in recent years, freshly harvested hops are very quickly transported to a nearby brewery and used to create beers that are often called "fresh-hopped" or "wet-hopped."

Some modern brewers complement or replace a portion of the hops in a recipe with herbs that, before the widespread use of hops in the latter Middle Ages, were used to contribute bitterness and flavour to beer. Some of the bittering and aroma ingredients being used include spruce tips, nettles, and clary sage.

Yeasts, one-celled micro-organisms, are essential to the brewing of beer. Without them there would be no beer, just a flat, malt-flavoured, non-alcoholic beverage. Yeasts feed on the fermentable sugars derived from malt or adjuncts and produce alcohol and carbon dioxide as "waste materials." Medieval monks, who brewed what was to them liquid sustenance, referred to yeast as "Godisgood." Early brewers often depended on airborne, invisible strains of this divine gift to alight on their liquid and work its heavenly miracles. Some modern breweries place wort in a large open vessel called a coolship where it is exposed to airborne yeasts.

Yeast was first specifically identified in the 17th century, and in the 19th century, the research of French scientist Louis Pasteur made possible the isolation and development of over 100 strains that are used in brewing. In addition to producing alcohol, each strain of yeast contributes a different flavour to the beer. This is particularly the case in Belgian-style beers, where the yeast contributes to the characteristic sour and funky tastes.

As well as these four basics, brewers sometimes include such ingredients as spices, fruits or fruit extracts, honey, maple syrup, and even spruce needles or juniper berries. Called additives, as distinct from adjuncts, these items do not generally influence the alcohol content of beer but contribute additional flavours to the basic ones created by the interactions of the water, malts, hops, and yeast. When beers are aged in wooden barrels, they often acquire subtle traces of the rums, whiskies, wines, or other alcoholic beverages that had previously been stored in the vessels. The type of wood out of which the barrels are made (usually oak) also influences flavour.

BREWING AND BREWING EQUIPMENT

Brewing begins after the brewer chooses a specific recipe, gathers the appropriate ingredients, and perhaps most importantly, makes sure that the brewing equipment is clean—very, very clean. Without completely sanitized equipment, the possibilities of creating bad, spoiled beer are increased greatly.

The first step is **milling** chunks of malt into grist, which is then deposited in a large metal vessel called a **mash tun**, where it is mixed with water that is heated to around 65 degrees Celsius. In the resulting "porridge" or **mash**, the malt's starches are converted into fermentable sugars. The mash is strained, and the **wort**, the sugar water, placed in a **brew kettle**, to be vigorously boiled for between one and two hours. This process sterilizes the liquid and helps prevent contamination. During the boil, hops are added. The boil completed, the hop residue is separated and the liquid passed through a **heat exchange unit** where it is quickly cooled.

At this point, the liquid is essentially malt-and-hop-flavoured water. However, after it is transferred to a **fermentation tank** and yeast is added, the wort's transformation into beer begins. Within 8 to 10 hours, the process of fermentation is under way. For ales, which are made with top-fermenting yeast, the temperature in the fermentation tank is kept between 16 and 20 degrees Celsius; for lagers, which use bottom-fermenting yeast, the tanks are kept around 9 degrees Celsius. The fermentation period for ales is a week to 10 days; for lagers, between three and four weeks. After fermentation is complete, the now alcoholic beverage is transferred to **conditioning or aging tanks** to mature. Ales are conditioned for up to two weeks, lagers for six weeks or more. At this point, the beer is ready to be delivered from the tanks to taps in a brewpub, or to be packaged in kegs, bottles, or cans.

PACKAGING BEER

For centuries, people took a pitcher or small bucket to the local pub or tavern, where they had it filled with beer to take home. Late in the 19th century, when glass became cheaper to manufacture, beer began to be bottled, and after the Second World War, tin and later aluminum cans became the preferred containers for beer. Before the widespread availability of bottles, most beer was consumed away from the home. After that, consumption shifted to the home. Beer ads in the 1950s showed well-dressed adults enjoying a cool one in their living rooms. When breweries became major sponsors of weekend televised sports, much beer was consumed by armchair athletes sitting in front of the television. And then, as satellite and paid television became available later in the 20th century, sports bars began to spring up, all of them with numerous television sets, each tuned to a different game. The consumption of beer outside the home was making a comeback.

When the craft brewing revolution began in the late 1970s, purists insisted that bottles were the only acceptable containers. Cans, they said, gave beer a funny taste, and perhaps more important to them, they felt that aluminum containers promoted ungenteel connotations of big-bellied men chugging pale-yellow, fizzy, mainstream lagers as they sat on the hoods of their pickup trucks.

Over the past decade, however, attitudes to canned beer have changed. Many microbrewers either have switched from bottles to cans or have begun to package in both bottles and cans. Bottles are expensive to clean and to ship and can easily break or chip. Lightweight cans cool more quickly and, because they are airtight and keep light out, ensure a fresher, unspoiled product. They are popular with hikers and picnickers as they are easy to carry to and from a recreational destination.

At first, the major disadvantage for craft brewers considering switching from bottles to cans was the fact that canning machines were very expensive, and cans, which had to be printed with the label for a specific product, had to be ordered in large quantities. Having made an investment in up to 100,000 cans, a brewer had to commit to making a large volume in the style indicated on the label. Bottles permitted the brewing of smaller quantities and different styles; all that was required was a different label on the bottle. During the last few years, smaller and less expensive canning machines have come on the market, and a method was developed that made it possible to have preprinted labels affixed to cans. In addition, there are now companies that own mobile canning facilities and travel to smaller breweries where they are able to can as much beer as the brewery or brewpub needs.

But if people want beer fresh from the conditioning tanks, just the way their great-great-grandfathers got it, they may be able to head to a nearby microbrewery or brewpub. They won't have to bring a bucket or pitcher; they can just ask for a growler—a 1.89-litre/half-gallon, reusable, screw-top glass bottle—or a crowler, a large can that can be filled at one of the tasting room taps and then sealed.

BEER IS SURROUNDED BY ENEMIES

Beer has many enemies. They aren't legions of keg-smashing temperance zealots; they're light, heat, air, and time. Exposure to light (especially fluorescent light and sunlight) will cause a beer to become light struck and give it a "skunky" flavour. Clear glass bottles are not beer friendly. Brown bottles or, better yet, cans keep the harmful rays away from the liquid. Of course, sun can also warm the beer and make it taste insipid. If it is shelved in non-refrigerated areas at retail outlets or at home, or if it undergoes a series of temperature changes on the way from the store to home, its flavour can be changed for the worse.

Fresh air may be good for people, but it isn't good for beer. When oxygen interacts with it, the result is a stale, cardboard-tasting beverage. If there's too much space between the cap and the liquid level of the bottle, or if the cap isn't fitted tightly, the enemy air may be working on the contents long before you decide to pop the cap.

The final enemy of beer is time. With the exception of some high-alcohol beers such as barley wine, beer has a fairly short lifespan. After three or four months of sitting in the refrigerator or on store shelves, beer should be retired and sent down the sink to its final rest. Check the best-before date if there is one on the label, and if there isn't, check to see that no dust has gathered on the shoulders of the bottle or the top of the can. A dusty beer is probably an old beer.

When you get home, put your beer quickly into the fridge (making sure that the light is out when the door closes), and don't save it for a festive occasion that is too far in the future. Don't be fooled by those ads showing a clear-glassed, open bottle of beer that's been set on a table at the edge of a sunlit tropical sea. The weather may be great, but probably the beer isn't.

ENJOYING YOUR BEER

Many people can remember mowing the lawn in the backyard or chopping firewood at the campground or cabin and opening a can of what has been called "lawnmower beer," the stuff that's priced way below the other beers, and chugging it back. It quenches the thirst, and if it gets warm or is spilt, it doesn't matter, because not only was it really cheap to begin with, but also it probably didn't taste that good. But to enjoy fully a well-brewed lager or ale, it shouldn't be grabbed ice-cold from the refrigerator or the ice chest and gulped from the bottle or can. In the last two decades, aficionados have developed a series of steps for enjoying beer that are as intricate as those obsessed over by wine lovers. Enjoying a glass of good beer is a wonderful sensory—some would say aesthetic— experience involving sight, smell, taste, and tactile sensations.

The first thing to remember is that the beer should be served at the proper temperature. Of course, it would be pretty inconvenient and expensive to have several mini-fridges each set at the appropriate serving temperature for a certain style of beer. In her book *Cheese & Beer*, Janet Fletcher offers a very practical method for making sure that the temperature of the beer you are about to pour is just right. Pale ales, IPAs, kolsches, wheat beers, and pilsners should be served straight from the fridge. Amber and red ales, amber lagers, bocks, Oktoberfests, saisons, and sour ales should stand for 15 minutes. Belgian-style strong golden ales, dubbels, and tripels, as well as stouts and porters, should leave the fridge half an hour before they are opened and poured. And barley wine, extra special bitter, and imperial stouts have the longest waiting time—45 minutes.

When it's at the appropriate temperature, pour the beer carefully into a very clean, non-chilled glass. An improperly washed glass may contain traces of soap or other residue that can alter the taste of your beer. Glasses chilled in the freezer compartment may have attracted condensed moisture and food odours, and when beer is poured into them, the chill may lower the temperature below the intended serving ranges. If you want to make sure the glass doesn't have any dust in it or hasn't become too warm where it has been standing, fill it with cold tap water, swish the water around inside it, pour the water out, shake the glass to remove any drops, then pour. Do not dry the glass. If you're trying more than one style of beer at a single setting, it's recommended that you use a new glass for each different style of beer.

Different shapes of glasses have been developed to enhance the appearance, aroma, and taste of specific styles. For example, the thin, tapered pilsner glass helps to support the delicate head and to release the carbonation of lagers. The goblet, resting on a thick stem and base, maintains the rich head of stronger Belgian ales. The weizenglass, tapered gracefully outward from the base and then slightly inward, captures the aromas of wheat beers. A brandy snifter is just right for swirling, sniffing, and sipping such high-alcohol brews as barley wine.

There are two schools of thought on how to pour a glass of beer. However, both have the same goals: to avoid spillage, to create a head that's about 2.5 centimetres high, to capture the beer's aromas, and to release the appropriate amount of carbonation. One school advocates pouring the beer into the middle of an upright glass, pausing as often as necessary to prevent the foam from overflowing. The other recommends initially pouring the beer into a tilted glass, then gradually raising the glass to a vertical position to complete the pour.

Once the pour is completed, it's time—not to start drinking but to admire the beer in the glass. Notice its colour, the texture of the head, and the bubbles coming from the bottom of the glass. Lift the glass to your nose and enjoyed the subtle malt and hop aromas rising from the foam.

Now it's time for the first taste—the most important one, because the palate loses some of its sensitivity with succeeding sips. Take a hearty, rather than a delicate, sip—not an Adam's apple–wobbling, chugalug, "gee, it's hot today" gulp, but enough so that the beer can slide over and along the sides of your tongue on its way to the back of your mouth. The first impressions may be of the malt flavours, usually sweet and, in the case of beers made with darker malts, having notes of coffee or chocolate. The bitterness of the hops usually comes later, counter-balancing the malt's sweetness and often contributing floral or fruity tastes. Depending on the types of hops, malts, and yeasts used, a range of delicate flavours contrasting and complementing each other can be enjoyed in a sip of beer. And if the beer has additives—fruit, spice, or other things nice—taste them as well. They should be delicate and subtle, not overwhelming.

As your sip is working its way across your mouth, you'll also experience what the beer experts call mouthfeel, the beer's texture. It will range from thin to full-bodied, depending on the style, and may be more or less effervescent, depending on the level of carbonation. Lagers, especially mainstream ones, tend to be thin-bodied and highly carbonated, the darker ales more robust and frequently not so highly carbonated. Important though it is, the first taste won't tell you everything about the beer you are drinking. With later sips, different characteristics will become evident. Some beers become undrinkable as they get warmer, but others "warm well," revealing new and different flavours and aromas.

If you're having a beer-tasting party, it's recommended that no more than five different styles be sampled; after that, palate fatigue may set in. At a tasting party, provide each guest with a separate glass for each beer to be sampled. (Small juice glasses, wineglasses, special beer sampler glasses, or even small plastic glasses can be used.) Each guest should have a bottle of water and either some bread (such as slices from a white baguette) or plain, unsalted crackers. This food, along with a swig of water, will cleanse the palate between samplings.

For decades, much has been said about pairing wines and foods. Recently beer connoisseurs have stated that beer is a more complex beverage than wine and can be paired with a great variety of foods. It's more than just a beer and a hot dog at the ball game or a beer and a burger in the backyard. Some brewpubs and restaurants have beer cicerones trained to assist patrons in choosing the right beer or beers to accompany whatever menu selections they decide on. Restaurants and brewpubs frequently put on special dinners, with a different beer complementing each course. Three excellent books on food-beer pairing are Janet Fletcher's *Cheese & Beer* (Kansas City: Andrews McMeel Publishing, 2013), Garrett Oliver's *The Brewmaster's Table: Discovering the Pleasures of Real Beer with Real Food* (New York: HarperCollins, 2003), and Julia Herz and Gwen Conley's *Beer Pairing: The Essential Guide from the Pairing Pros* (Minneapolis: Voyageur Press, 2015).

Enjoy the full experience of the beer. And when you're finished, don't forget to wash and rinse the glass thoroughly. Remember, cleanliness may or may not be next to godliness, but full enjoyment of your next beer depends on it.

READING ALE ABOUT IT: A TWO-FOUR OF BEER BOOKS

Not only has the number of breweries and brewpubs increased greatly during the first two decades of the 21st century, so too has the number of books about beer. Here is an annotated list of 24 fairly recent books that I've found entertaining, well written, and very informative.

Acitelli, Tom. *The Audacity of Hops: The History of America's Craft Beer Revolution.* Rev. ed. Chicago: Chicago Review Press, 2017.

A very thoughtful, detailed history of the craft beer movement in the United States from the middle of the 1960s to the middle of the second decade of the 21st century. Very interesting stories about nearly all the important American craft breweries and brewers of the last half century.

Alworth, Jeff. *The Beer Bible.* New York: Workman Publishing, 2015.

This is an exhaustive, but by no means exhausting, discussion of beer styles, with examples from around the world, written by one of the United States' most respected beer writers. After I've read the chapter about a specific style, I enjoy going to my favourite liquor store to pick up some examples.

Appleton, Frank. *Brewing Revolution: Pioneering the Craft Beer Movement.* Madeira Park, BC: Harbour Publishing, 2016.

A pioneer in British Columbia's craft beer movement, Appleton provides a lively, well-written account of his role in the establishment of breweries not only in Canada but also in the United States and other countries.

Beaumont, Stephen. *The Great Canadian Beer Guide*. 2nd ed. Toronto: McArthur & Company, 2001.

Stephen Beaumont, the dean of Canadian beer writers, gives accounts of Canadian breweries and brewpubs at the beginning of this century. Although there have been many changes, including the demise of some of the breweries he chronicles and, of course, the founding and flourishing of many new ones, the book is valuable as a portrait of the craft beer scene in Canada at the end of the 20th century.

Brown, Pete. *Man Walks into a Pub: A Sociable History of Beer*. London: Pan Books, 2003.

One of Great Britain's most popular beer writers presents an entertaining history of the social aspects of the consumption of beer and the places in which it is consumed. The tasting room and brewpubs of the craft beer movement are reintroducing the convivial social aspects of the sipping of suds.

Cameron, Steve. *Canadian Book of Beer*. Edmonton: Blue Bike Books, 2009.

A witty compendium of facts about all aspects of beer, especially in Canada. Each of the short sections of the book can be quickly consumed as you wait for someone to bring you your first or next cold one.

Campbell, Robert A. *Demon Rum or Easy Money: Government Control of Liquor in British Columbia from Prohibition to Privatization*. Ottawa: Carleton University Press, 1991.

———. *Sit Down and Drink Your Beer: Regulating Vancouver's Beer Parlours, 1925–1954*. Toronto: University of Toronto Press, 2001.

Reading both of Campbell's thoroughly researched histories has helped me understand why the places I drank beer at during my college years at the University of British Columbia were so dark, dreary, and depressing.

Coutts, Ian. *Brew North: How Canadians Made Beer and Beer Made Canada*. Vancouver: Greystone Books, 2010.

Delightfully written and full of very interesting photographs, beer labels, and ads, this book covers the Canadian beer scene from the birth of Molson Brewery to the "New Guys." The visuals alone make buying the book worthwhile; the written text is great, too. A great "beer table" book.

Fletcher, Janet. *Cheese & Beer*. Kansas City: Andrews McMeel, 2013.

It's not just a matter anymore of munching Cheezies while gulping down a can of lawnmower beer. Fletcher shows how pairing specific styles of craft beer with specific cheeses brings out the nuanced flavours of each. The photographs are enough to make a person both hungry and thirsty.

Herz, Julia, and Gwen Conley. *Beer Pairing: The Essential Guide from the Pairing Pros.* Minneapolis: Voyageur Press, 2015.

> Don't stop with beer-cheese pairings. This book pairs beer styles with a wide variety of foods, including chocolate. There are chapters on organizing beer dinners and on cooking with beer.

Mofford, Glen A. *Aqua Vitae: A History of the Saloons and Hotel Bars of Victoria, 1851–1917.* Victoria: TouchWood Editions, 2016.

> If you thought pre–First World War Victoria was all about elegant high teas served to fashionably dressed ladies and gentlemen, you were only partly right. A lot of whisky and beer and a lot of painted ladies were found in many establishments. Mofford has done very thorough research and presented very interesting anecdotes and social commentary.

Mosher, Randy. *Tasting Beer: An Insider's Guide to the World's Greatest Drink.* North Adams, MA: Storey Publishing, 2009.

> This is a very thorough, frequently quite—but not overwhelmingly—scientific guide. Among the topics covered are "Brewing and the Vocabulary of Beer Flavor," "Sensory Evaluation," beer styles, and beer and food.

Ogle, Maureen. *Ambitious Brew: The Story of American Beer.* Orlando, FL: Harcourt, 2006.

> In this compact survey of brewing in the United States from the colonial era to the early years of the craft beer movement, Ogle offers astute commentary on the social and political trends that influenced the making of beer.

Oliver, Garrett. *The Brewmaster's Table: Discovering the Pleasures of Real Beer with Real Food.* New York: HarperCollins, 2003.

> One of the rock stars of the craft beer movement, Garrett Oliver is a brewmaster (Brooklyn Brewery), a foodie, and a writer. This is a superbly written book that matches beer styles with complementary food pairings, explaining not only what works, but also why it does.

——, ed. *The Oxford Companion to Beer.* New York: Oxford University Press, 2011.

> When I was a graduate student in English, the Oxford literary companions were essential reference books. Now, this one about beer is always close at hand. Hundreds of entries, written by 165 experts, include such topics as breweries, brewing, brewers, ingredients, history, biography, and countries.

Pashley, Nicholas. *Cheers! An Intemperate History of Beer in Canada.* Toronto: Collins, 2009.

> The blurry photograph of a Mountie on the cover sets the tone for this humorous and informative book that includes sections on "Beer in Canadian History," "Beer in Canadian Life," "Becoming a Connoisseur," and "Looking for Canada's Beer" (travels).

Rabin, Dan, and Carl Forget. *Dictionary of Beer and Brewing.* 2nd ed. Boulder, CO: Brewers Publications, 1998.

> Over 2,500 terms from *a-acid* (an abbreviation for alpha acid) to *zythum* (an ancient Egyptian name for barley wine).

Sherk, Lawrence C. *150 Years of Canadian Beer Labels.* Victoria: TouchWood Editions, 2016.

> Published during the 150th anniversary of Canadian Confederation, this book contains an amazing array of labels from the 19th century into the second decade of the 21st. The descriptors on some of the labels reveal changing attitudes about the importance of beer over the last century and a half.

Smith, Gregg. *Beer: A History of Suds and Civilization from Mesopotamia to Microbreweries.* New York: Avon Books, 1995.

> Although the focus in its 250 pages is on the United States, there are some chapters about what happened elsewhere and earlier.

Sneath, Allen Winn. *Brewed in Canada: The Untold Story of Canada's 350-Year-Old Brewing Industry.* Toronto: Dundurn, 2001.

> A ground-breaking history. The "Chronological History of Brewing in Canada" is a very useful appendix. An index would have made this book even more useful.

Stern, Brett. *99 Ways to Open a Beer Bottle Without a Bottle Opener.* San Francisco: Chronicle Books, 2014.

> Just in case you need to know.

Wiebe, Joe. *Craft Beer Revolution: The Insider's Guide to B.C. Breweries.* 2nd ed. Madeira Park, BC: Douglas & McIntyre, 2015.

> An excellent handbook, not only for its essays on the craft breweries operating as of 2015, but for its information about changing laws, beer festivals, notable people, and other significant facts.

Wilson, Bill. *Beer Barons of B.C.* Lantzville, BC: Tamahi Publications, 2011.

> An alphabetical listing by city of every brewery known to have operated (and some that didn't) in British Columbia, complete with dates, addresses, and where known, owners and brewery personnel. The 16 coloured pages of beer labels are a real treat!

ACKNOWLEDGEMENTS

No book is written alone, even if only one author's name is on the title page. That is certainly true in the case of *Island Craft*. The people at TouchWood Editions, brewery owners and brewers, friends, and family members have contributed in so many ways to help me bring this project to conclusion and to make the book a better one than it would otherwise have been.

Thank you to Taryn Boyd, Tori Elliott, Renée Layberry, Warren Layberry, Colin Parks, and Meg Yamamoto of TouchWood Editions for your support and all the time you've given to this project. To all the brewery owners and brewers who took time to be interviewed, showed me around their breweries and brewpubs, and so generously supplied me with "research materials" (i.e., beer) goes my sincere appreciation. I hope that I've done your breweries and your beers justice in my accounts.

Thank you to my friend John Rowling for writing the foreword and for having done so much over so many years to enhance the craft beer scene in British Columbia. To my sister Sheri, who made her home a "home base" during my research trips to the Island and always had a glowing fireplace and a hot supper waiting when I returned from my researches, you have provided wonderful endings to the long but rewarding days. The travels would have been much lonelier without a welcome homecoming at the end of them. And as usual, to my daughter Clare: know that your constant support is always appreciated.

To all of you: you have made *Island Craft* a better book. Thank you!

INDEX